ACHIEVE
FINANCIAL
FREEDOM–
BIG
TIME!

ACHIEVE FINANCIAL FREEDOM—

BIG TIME!

Wealth-Building Secrets from Everyday Millionaires

Sandy Botkin, CPA, Esq.
Matthew Botkin, CPA

New York Chicago San Francisco Lisbon London
Madrid Mexico City Milan New Delhi San Juan
Seoul Singapore Sydney Toronto

1 2 3 4 5 6 7 8 9 0   QFR/QFR   1 8 7 6 5 4 3 2

ISBN 978-0-07-179850-1
MHID 0-07-179850-1

e-ISBN 978-0-07-179851-8
e-MHID 0-07-179851-X

This publication is designed to provide accurate and authoritative information in regard to the subject matter covered. It is sold with the understanding that neither the author nor the publisher is engaged in rendering legal, accounting, securities trading, or other professional services. If legal advice or other expert assistance is required, the services of a competent professional person should be sought.

> —*From a Declaration of Principles Jointly Adopted by a Committee of the American Bar Association and a Committee of Publishers and Associations*

Note: This publication is based on the expertise of the authors and experts who have been interviewed and have reviewed the chapters. Since everyone's situation is different and since laws change over time, nothing in this book should be construed as an accounting or legal opinion. You should check with a financial professional before implementing the strategies noted in this publication.

McGraw-Hill books are available at special quantity discounts to use as premiums and sales promotions or for use in corporate training programs. To contact a representative, please e-mail us at bulksales@mcgraw-hill.com.

This book is printed on acid-free paper.

6573

To my wife, Lori, for her endless patience and for her great feedback

Contents

Acknowledgments

We would like to dedicate this work to all the wonderfully talented people who participated in this book, including the financial writers and multimillionaires who gave their time and shared their knowledge with me, many of whom didn't want to be specifically identified.

We especially want to thank Keith Cunningham for his significant contribution to Chapter 6, "Getting Out of Debt Forever." He is allegedly the "Rich Dad" in Robert Kiyosaki's book *Rich Dad Poor Dad*. Cunningham is the author of the *Keys to the Vault: Lessons from the Pros on Raising Money and Igniting Your Business*.

We also want to thank Jeff Sella, CPA, CFP, and the owner of SPC Financial, for his numerous contributions, suggestions, and edits made in Chapters 1 through 10 of this book.

We also want to thank Alan Williams and Peter Jepson from Money Mastery for providing some great suggestions regarding savings and retirement planning.

We also wish to thank Jennifer Ashkenazy, our editor at McGraw-Hill, for her input and timely suggestions as well as Jane Palmieri for her editorial input.

We also want to thank you, our wonderful readers, for your desire to improve your life when you bought this book. We won't let you down!

Introduction

When a person of money meets a person with experience, the person with the experience will get some money, and the person of money will get some experience.

—Harvey Mackay, *Swim with the Sharks Without Being Eaten Alive*

The Beginning of the Beginning

This book is about money—namely, your money, or the possible lack of it. My goal is to make you the person of experience so you can become both the person of money and the person of experience.

The idea for it started innocently enough with a complaint from my legal book sales representative. We were having some "small conversation about life" when he also noted that his father had some form of dementia. When he tried to find some information about how to obtain support for evaluations for his father's condition and how to evaluate various types of nursing and independent-living facilities, most of it was in legalese. And he had numerous other financial issues about insurance, mortgages, investment alternatives, and college funding strategies for which he also couldn't find any clear answers.

His main complaint was that almost all of the financial books written were by people who had a bias such as wanting to sell more insurance or wanting to attract more clients or even simply wanting to sell other books that they had previously written. Even worse, some of the information was just outright wrong in his opinion. He cited a guy who had a bestselling book on forming foreign trusts in order to avoid taxes. That same guy had been recently indicted for fraud! He also felt that there were few financial books that were clearly written, comprehensive, and practical for baby boomers and generation Xers.

At first, I thought he didn't research the topics enough. However, when I started conducting my own research, I realized that he was right! Many books clearly had biased or wrong information. Some books were just too elementary or were too complicated. One scam artist was a writer who promoted whole life insurance for everything and anything. Another famous bestselling author had written books whose main goal was to simply sell other books that he had written. Essentially, each book was simply a marketing piece for his other books. The content found in most of his works was either outright wrong or just plainly nonexistent.

Even worse, there are thousands of seminars conducted by so-called experts, who speak on wealth creation. Yet, when I listened to many of these speakers, I was stunned at the bad information they presented and the huge seminar fees that they charged in order to give participants the "right information." Almost every financial presentation was a giant sales presentation for their upcoming seminars and materials. There was almost no content! In fact, the next time you attend a seminar, ask yourself at the end of the speaker's presentation, "What two ideas can I use right now that will make me money?" I would bet that for many presentations, you won't be able to find even two immediate, practical ideas that will either change your life or make you money.

I especially focused on speakers who lectured on debt reduction. Many of them were very good, and they usually noted which debts should be avoided or prepaid first. However, not *one* speaker ever mentioned where the money could come from in order to start prepaying these debts!

In fact, due to the vast ignorance of the general public, the IRS has warned of a plethora of financial scams that can easily be avoided with the right knowledge, many of which will be found in this book or in the appendixes of this book.

Here is another real-life but sadly common problem that affects families who are financially naïve. One of my friend's sisters ended up taking care of her grandmother. In order to facilitate the care, the sister cosigned on the bank accounts of the grandmother in order to pay her grandmother's necessary bills. All went according to plan until the grandmother died. Despite having a clause in the grandmother's will that all of her assets were to go to her only daughter, all of her bank accounts were transferred to the cosigner on the accounts, which was the granddaughter. The reason was that joint ownership overrides a will. The granddaughter felt that she had earned the money. This conflict caused an irrevocable rift in the family between that granddaughter and everyone else! The sad part of this story is that this could have easily been avoided with proper advice to the grandmother.

My problem, however, in trying to address the information gap I had discovered in my research was that I was just an ordinary guy. Although I was a "product of my products" and I had done fairly well in life by eliminating all my debt and I had undertaken other important financial steps, I wasn't a financial planner. My wife, Lori, came to the rescue. I guess behind every great man is a greater woman. She suggested that with the tremendous contacts I had made in the seminar business being a tax lecturer, I could interview multimillionaires that I knew to be successful and get their opinions on a variety of practical, financial concerns. Moreover, my son Matthew, who has a master's in financial planning and just recently passed the Certified Financial Planners exam, could oversee the technical accuracy of the material and add a lot of content that might be omitted in the interviews. This is how this book got started.

What's in It for You!

As a result of many years as a CPA and tax lecturer, I have received numerous financial questions. Accordingly, here are some of the financial questions that I will be covering in this book:

- Do you have the right mortgage and the right amortization period?
- What is the best life insurance to have, and how much should you really have?
- How much do you need for retirement, and most important, how can you save this amount of money?
- What are the best retirement investments for most people?
- Why do so many people fail financially? Why should people formulate a financial plan?
- How can people set realistic goals? How can people set the "right goals"?
- How can you pay for your children's college education?
- How can you get in-state tuition for an out-of-state student?
- Is that dream school worth incurring substantial indebtedness? Moreover, what amount of debt constitutes "too much debt" for undergraduate studies?

- What techniques work about 80 percent of the time to eliminate damaging credit information on your record?
- What is the best way to get out of debt? How can you find the money to accomplish this?
- What is the maximum amount of debt you should have?
- Is renting a home better than buying? Under what circumstances is renting better?
- Should you take a 15- or 30-year mortgage on your home or investment property?
- How can you eliminate mortgage insurance forever, and why is it important to do so?
- What is the best type of mortgage on a home?
- What are reverse mortgages, and how can you evaluate them?
- How can you evaluate which type of bond or CD is better for you?
- How can you know for sure whether you want tax-exempt bonds or taxable bonds or CDs?
- Who should buy annuities, and are they good deals?
- What are the best mutual funds to buy? How much of your portfolio should you have exposed in the stock market?
- When should you take social security? Age 62, 66, or 70? If you took it at the wrong time, how can you correct your mistake?
- Should you have disability insurance? How do you know which type of disability insurance is right for you?
- How do you evaluate homeowners insurance?
- Should you have long-term care insurance? How do you evaluate long-term care policies?
- How much money should you have for emergency reserves, and where should the reserves be invested?
- Should you buy or lease a car? What should you look for in a car lease if you do lease a vehicle?
- What types of legal estate documents should you have?
- Can you really avoid probate forever?
- Why should you never, ever draw up your own will? Why should you not be cheap when it comes to estate planning and wills?
- How can you avoid most capital gains taxes for the rest of your life in the United States?
- How can you plan for your own incapacity and for the incapacity of relatives?
- How can you evaluate nursing homes and other alternative living communities for the elderly?

- How can you plan your estate for blended families with children from previous marriages?
- How can you plan your estate for your live-in partner?
- How can you plan your estate for your pets?
- How can you plan your estate for children with special needs?
- If you are expecting either a recession or significant inflation, how can you plan for these to maximize your profits?
- What steps can you take to reduce your tax burden considerably?
- With the passing of the Affordable Care Act, what one thing should you implement in addition to having health insurance?
- How can you evaluate and check out a financial planner?
- How can you limit the possibility of having someone like Bernard Madoff steal your hard-earned money? How can you limit the damage you might be exposed to from scamsters?
- And many, many more questions!

Although I think I wrote this book in an interesting and clear manner, it is a very content-driven book, and it still will take some work in terms of note-taking for you to implement the information contained in it.

If you don't want to become a multimillionaire or if you don't want to expand your wealth from its present state, don't get this book. If you want lots of jokes or lots of fluff, don't get this book.

However, if you do get this book and you let me and the other successful people interviewed in this book mentor you and you take action on its content, I will make a promise to you: *This book will change your life! It will get you out of all debt including your mortgage. It will provide you with the tools you need to have the fulfilling retirement that you could only dream about, and it will probably make you a multimillionaire.*

However, the book's content must be taken holistically. You shouldn't follow the advice in just one chapter at the expense of ignoring the advice in the other chapters. For example, it would be absurd for you to save money using the concepts in Chapters 4 and 5 if you have to incur debt in order to get the savings accomplished. There is an interplay among all the chapters.

I have had hundreds of people keep in touch with me over the years about how much my programs have changed their lives. If you like what you read, which I know will be the case, you can get more great financial information at my website www.sandybotkin.com and also at the website www.taxbot.com. And there's even more great financial information in my other book *Lower Your Taxes—Big Time!*

Sandy Botkin

ACHIEVE FINANCIAL FREEDOM—

BIG TIME!

1

The Beginning: We've Got to Start Somewhere

The first step towards getting somewhere is to decide that you are not going to stay where you are.

—John Pierpont Morgan

> **What You Will Learn**
> - The problem: Why so many people are failing financially
> - Sixteen reasons people fail financially at retirement

The Problem: Why So Many People Are Failing Financially

It was a great day to see my friend Jeff, although the gray clouds were creating an ominous haze in the background. What would one of the top financial planners in both our state and in the country say to my wife, Lori, and me?

I have known Jeff for many years. He is one of the top CPAs and financial planners in the country. He manages a lot of money for a large base of clients. What I like most about Jeff is that he is straightforward. There is no "beating around the bush" for him. He will tell me the truth even if it goes against his own self-interest.

When I reached Jeff's home, I was surprised at a number of things. First, his house was smaller than I remembered. I had figured that someone as successful as Jeff would be living in a McMansion. Second, the house was all white! Basically, it was a scaled down replica of the White House!

Jeff greeted us warmly as Lori and I entered his well-furnished home and he ushered us into his private home office for our interview.

"Well, Jeff," I asked, "how's business?" He chuckled a bit and said, "Other than my clients, folks are in worse shape than ever. With all the seminars being given and books being written, you would think that people would be taking the right financial steps. Sadly, they are no better off than their parents were 30 years ago, and maybe they are a bit worse off."

Shocked, I asked dumbfoundedly, "What are you talking about?"

Jeff bristled at the thought of the problem that he was going to cover and responded, "Sandy, let me share some sobering statistics."

"First, total consumer debt is about $2.4 trillion.[1] If you count mortgages it is over $13 trillion. Average Americans, until recently, saved an average of only $397 a year,[2] and for many years, there were negative savings. This means that they borrowed more than they saved!"

Lori and I were both shocked. "Are you kidding, Jeff?"

He answered with a drawn look. "No, I am serious. I wish I were wrong. Moreover, about 60 percent of those who reach age 50 have a net worth of under $60,000."

Lori started at Jeff's last comment. I turned to her and said, "Don't worry, honey. I have plenty of insurance. You will be a rich widow." She rolled her eyes, which made me chuckle a bit.

Jeff further noted, "Over 22 percent of all those who reach age 65 live in poverty, of which the majority are women!

"In fact, many years ago a study was conducted that determined that only 4 percent of those who reached age 65 retired with the same standard of living that they had before retirement. The rest had to continue working, live on some form of charity from the kids, or substantially reduce their standard of living. From what I can see today, most Americans are going to be in that same boat when they retire. In fact, generation Xers, those born between 1960 and roughly 1981, will have it much worse than the baby boomers. Many of them won't get a pension, and the date for receiving their full social security will be age 67 and thereafter, which is a year later than it is for the baby boomers."

16 Reasons People Fail Financially at Retirement

I then asked Jeff, "With all these depressing statistics, what do you think were the reasons that many people failed financially?"

"Sandy, there are a lot of relatively new developments that have caused some of these problems as well as some old, recurring problems."

Scowling, I said, "I know two changes: the economy and the attitudes of people in our country. When my parents were growing up and when they were raising kids, most people worked for the same firm all of their lives. They were well taken care of with medical insurance, a great pension, and other benefits. I keep remembering the old TV shows such as *Ozzie and Harriet* (for us old coots who remember these shows) and *My Three Sons* and *Leave It to Beaver.* The couples stayed married all of their lives and worked at the same job in the same occupation forever. Besides attitudes, what else has changed?"

"You are right, Sandy. Attitudes and circumstances have changed in this country. However, there are many other factors that are causing folks to fail financially. I will outline the major factors that cause people to not be rich, and I'll also outline those risks that can not only keep you from getting rich but actually wipe you out."

1. People's Longer Lifespan

"First, people are living longer than ever," said Jeff.

Chuckling, I noted, "I have no intention of dying in order to save money. That isn't one of my favorite planning techniques."

Jeff laughed, but he continued: "During the time of the ancient Greeks, the average life expectancy was around 20 years old. As little as 200 years ago, the average life expectancy was under age 35. In 1900, it was about 47. In 1930, it rose to about age 60, and today it is about 78.[3] This has caused numerous problems. For example, people have multiple families (due to increased divorce rates) and multiple careers. And, of course, they have more costs for the longer periods of time they are sustaining their lives. Living longer also increases the chances that people will be sued. In addition, people incur more medical and dental costs by living longer. It is no wonder that people have more month than money these days."

"Jeff, don't forget that living longer might increase the chances of having disabling health problems, either physical or mental, which could create the need for a variety of services such as independent-living assistance and/or nursing care. There really are a lot of issues here."

Jeff agreed, "Yes, Sandy, you are quite right. Moreover, costs for everything have skyrocketed over the past 20 to 30 years." As an example, Jeff showed us some budgeted estimates for his son's friend's wedding:

- Flowers: $2,500
- Invitations: $600
- Photography and video: $2,000
- Music: $2,500

- Clergy and church (or synagogue) rental: $1,000
- Limousines: $450
- Engagement ring: $2,500
- Wedding ring: $700
- Groom's tuxedo: $175
- Reception, including food: $22,000

Jeff continued, "Think about prices today for many items such as cars ($25,000 to $30,000). The average price of homes in our area is $350,000. People will also need enough funds to have a successful retirement for 365 days a year for at least 20 years. But nursing home costs can easily be $55,000 per year and more."

Scowling, I said, "Okay, Jeff, stop. I get the point. You are depressing me."

"So, living longer is one problem," concluded Jeff.

2. The Huge Amount of Information People Must Process

"The second problem is that we require much more knowledge to deal with the burgeoning amount of available information. The Internet has geometrically accelerated the growth of information available to people."

I didn't initially understand the problem. But Jeff explained: "The problem is that folks just can't keep up with everything."

Caustically, I noted, "You're telling me. You know how fast our tax laws are changing?"

"Yes, that is exactly one of the situations I was referring to," said Jeff.

3. Inflation

"The third reason is inflation. Most people don't worry as much about inflation or taxes as they should because of what is referred to as the 'lobster phenomenon.' Imagine placing a lobster in boiling hot water. What do you think he will do? The answer is that he will squeal and try to get out. However, if you place the same lobster in lukewarm water, he will stay there even if you slowly raise the temperature till he cooks to death!

"Most people are accustomed to inflation and having taxes withheld from their earnings. Thus, they don't really feel the ever increasing bite that both of these problems have on their life."

4. People's Lack of Understanding of Compound Interest

"Okay, let's get on to the fourth reason people fail financially: they don't understand exactly how compound interest works. Einstein is credited with saying that compound interest is the eighth wonder of the world. It can work for you or against you. You really need to know how this works and fully understand its ramifications."

Lori, looking puzzled, asked, "Isn't compound interest merely making money on your money and on your interest earned?"

Jeff wryly noted, "Yes, Lori, that is true. However, there is a **lot** more to it that everyone should understand and that I think Sandy will devote some time to in Chapter 3."

A bit chagrined, I noted, "Jeff, I will be interviewing one of your clients about this. He is Sam, who owned the bank that was bought out. If a banker doesn't know all about compounding, then who will?"

Chuckling, Jeff said, "Yes, Sam would be a great interview. I can't wait to see what he says."

5. People's Failure to Diversify Their Investments

"The fifth reason people fail financially is that they fail to diversify. Diversification is the key to reducing your risk while getting good returns in the future."

I noted, "Yes, and diversification means more than just buying a bunch of different types of mutual funds. It also means diversifying money managers and planners. All those folks who lost their life savings with Bernie Madoff would have been much better off if they had put only 10 percent of their total investable assets with him."

Jeff responded, "Yes, you are absolutely right. The government will protect only up to $500,000 of assets from fraud. Ideally, my clients should leave only 10 percent of their investable wealth or $500,000, whichever is greater, with only one custodian or firm. This way, if a Madoff situation occurred, they would never lose more than 10 percent. This is one reason why diversification is crucial."

6. People's Failure to Plan for Retirement

"The sixth reason people fail is that they don't plan for retirement. This is a special type of planning that everyone should do. It is astounding how poorly people plan for this. Instead of managing their money, they let their money manage their lives. It is sad."

I noted, "Jeff, I remember reading in the *Miami Herald* about some elderly people who were forced to live on dog food because they couldn't afford to live otherwise. Yuck!"

Scowling, Jeff said, "There are an estimated 70 million baby boomers headed into retirement. Among older workers aged 55 to 64, a whopping 20+ percent have no personal savings. Nada. Zilch. Even more startling is that only 15 percent of those considered to be 'elite households'—that is, people who are in the upper middle income or higher earnings brackets—have saved only four times their yearly earnings. In fact, even at four times your earnings, you don't have enough for retirement. I know a couple whose combined earnings are $120,000 per year. If they saved only $480,000 for retirement and earn and spend only 3 percent of their earnings each year, they will earn only $13,400 in interest *before taxes, which is 3 percent of $480,000.*"

"Jeff," I noted, "I have a great website with a number of savings and retirement calculators that everyone should check out. It can be found at www.sandybotkin.com."

"Yes, Sandy, I agree. You did a nice job with the tools on your website," noted Jeff.

Jeff continued: "Anyway, I would estimate that folks who do not have a good pension should have at least $2 million to $3 million worth of *investable* assets (not counting the value of their home) to have a reasonable standard of living at full retirement."

7. People's Failure to Save for Large Future Expenses

"This leads us to the seventh reason people fail financially, which is that they fail to save for other large future expenses. We all have some need for this. Folks should be saving for things like cars, education for kids, and houses. Instead, they overspend and use credit unwisely because of it, which is usually a recipe for financial disaster and is one of the six Horsemen of Financial Death. Here is a startling statistic: a college that costs $50,000 a year today will probably cost about $96,500 a year in 2020!"[4]

There are many issues involved in large expense planning including the following:

- What is the best way to save for college costs?
- With cars, should you pay cash, accept dealer financing, use home equity loans, or even use the IRS versus actual method of deducting a car for business use?

I noted, "Yes, I intend to spend a lot of time in this book on how to save money, how much to save, and where to find the money in order to save it, not to mention how to get out of debt. This means that accumulating savings is quite doable for many people. They just need to learn new habits."

8. People's Failure to Create Short- and Long-Term Financial Goals

"The eighth reason people fail financially is that they do not set both short-term and long-term financial goals. Setting these goals is crucial. In order to meet some predetermined future goal, you need to set goals and have a path for meeting your projections. Simply saying 'I want out of debt' or 'I want to become a multimillionaire' won't help you achieve these goals. You must also take some well-thought-out steps to achieve them. Do you know what the definition of *insanity* is, Sandy?"

"No, Jeff, but I bet you are going to tell me," I said chuckling.

Smiling, Jeff said, "Insanity is doing the same thing year after year but expecting different results. If people don't change what they are doing with their lives, nothing will change in their lives."

9. People's Failure to Plan for Divorce and Multiple Families

Jeff continued: "The ninth reason people fail financially is that they fail to plan for divorce and multiple families. With a 67 percent divorce rate for first marriages,[5] you would think that folks would learn their lesson, unless their names are Donald Trump and Larry King and they can easily afford divorce. For everyone else, planning is essential. Sadly, many people not only pay alimony and child support but also support a whole new family. I call this 'going broke loudly.' This change in family makeup and permanency certainly necessitates at least a whole new review of your planning documents. Moreover, there are some important tax planning issues, as you know, Sandy, that deal with divorce that everyone should know."

10. People's Procrastination in Confronting Reality

"The final reason people fail financially is procrastination. Do you remember when we met with a client who thought her broker got her invested in Jiffy Lube stock, which is a good stock, when it was in fact a Jiffy Lube limited partnership, which wasn't sellable?"

"Yes, it was horrible. I also remember her reaction when we told her about it, and she said, 'But the certificates were so gorgeous.'"

"Yes, Sandy, that is exactly what I am talking about. Folks don't want to confront reality, and many times they ignore my advice, and they ignore advice from other professionals too.

"Here is an interesting tidbit of little-known information. If you revisit the stories about all the people who lost a fortune when Enron crashed, many indicated that some professional advisor (financial planner, attorney, or accountant) had recommended diversification and that they had ignored that advice. They were waiting for Enron to hit some higher and more magical price.

"Most people's motto seems to be, 'Why do today what we can put off till tomorrow.'"

Wrinkling her nose, Lori noted, "Yes, Jeff, we have a son who had that philosophy."

"I do understand that, Lori. I must have a similar son. The problem is that there is a high cost for procrastination. An example will illustrate this:

"I have a client named John who is 25 years old and decided, as I advised him, to put away the full $5,000 each year into his Roth IRA for 40 years till he retires at age 65. If he earns a long-term rate of 6 percent on his money, which is a very likely long-term return on the stock market, he will have at retirement $820,238. However, if he puts away the money for only 30 years, which is only 10 years less, he will have only $419,018. If he were to get a long-term rate of 9 percent, a rate that is 50 percent higher, he would get an even more astounding $1,841,459 for 40 years of savings versus $742,876 for 30 years of savings."

"The next six reasons are because people have not dealt with the major unexpected risks of life, which I call the Six Horsemen of Financial Death."

"I have heard of the Four Horsemen of the Apocalypse, Jeff, but you seem to have added a couple more horsemen. What are the *six* horsemen?"

"Sandy, these are the six factors that can totally kill people financially and quickly but that most people are ill prepared for. Unlike the other factors noted here, these six factors could totally wipe you out very quickly or make a huge dent in your family's finances. What is also interesting about these six factors is that with proper planning (usually with the right kind of insurance) most of the negative effects arising from them can be either avoided or severely reduced." These are the factors Jeff described for us.

11. Disability

"Disability, the first horseman, was the most common cause of mortgage foreclosures until unemployment took over the top spot. Disability during one's life may also be the cause of a lot of unemployment. Believe it or not, approximately 3 in 10 people will face some kind of disability before retirement. Moreover, 1 in 7 people will be disabled for five years or more. This is a situation for which far too many people are ill prepared and grossly underinsured. This is an area that you should discuss in later sections of your book."

"Yes, Jeff, I agree, and we will be discussing this in the insurance section of the book."

12. Premature Death

"This isn't my favorite topic, but since the mortality rate for human beings is 100 percent, it is a crucial topic and it is the second horseman. Sadly, most people have never written a will, or if they have a will, they haven't updated it to reflect changing circumstances. In fact, many people have the wrong type of will. In addition, there are many sources and references about death planning that recommend the best type of life insurance, but that makes up only part of the solution. In addition to life insurance, there are certain legal documents that everyone should run out and get immediately. In addition, estate planning is crucial, as noted below."

13. Lawsuits

"Did you know that you have a 1 in 200 chance of being sued during your lifetime and that those odds go up if you have a business? Lawsuits are the third horseman."

"Is it really that high, Jeff?"

"Yes, it is. In fact, if you have a business, the chances of your being sued increases dramatically. It is estimated that there are about 15 million lawsuits filed each year. That turns out to be about one every two seconds! What is even more astonishing is that most people can significantly reduce their liability exposure and the ability for lawyers to collect money. It just takes a few simple steps, which most people haven't done!"

I noted, "Yes, we will be presenting a chapter on asset protection, and we have a great person to interview for it."

Jeff grinned and said, "Good. Folks will really need that."

14. Estate Taxes and Probate

"The fourth horseman is the estate tax and probate. As you know, starting in 2011, the estate tax is applied to those estates over $5 million at a flat 35 percent rate."

Lori, looking a bit confused, asked, "That is a huge percent to tax people, but do a lot of people, Jeff, have estates of over $5 million?"

Jeff noted, "Good question, Lori. Actually the estate tax is not only on everything you own but on things that you wouldn't normally think of such as the face amount—not the cash value—of the life insurance that you own. It also includes the value of your pension, IRA, 401(k), jewelry, the fair value of your house, and the value of your business. It is very possible for many people to exceed the $5 million exemption especially when life insurance is factored in. Moreover, if this isn't enough, many states have state inheritance and/or estate taxes in addition.

"Finally, there are probate costs charged by the lawyer, and these amount to about 3 percent of your probate estate, which can apply to everyone. All of these costs can really add up."

Jeff then noted, "What is most interesting, Lori, is that with a little bit of estate planning, most of the estate taxes and probate costs can be completely eliminated or at least significantly reduced. It just takes some simple planning. I should also note that this $5 million exemption is scheduled to expire after 2012 and become $1 million, and the federal estate tax rate is scheduled to increase to a whopping 55 percent unless Congress changes the law. This could be a big problem if nothing is done."

15. Overspending and Unwise Use of Credit

"This brings us to the fifth horseman of financial death, which is the average person's overspending. Did you know that most people in the United States have three or more credit cards? Did you ever ask yourself, 'Where did the money go?'"

Lori answered, "Yes, Sandy asks this all the time."

Jeff continued, "The reason that you ask this of yourself is that you are probably piddling it away with such things as Starbucks coffee [I shot a look at Lori at this point], a breakfast pastry, eating out too often, cigarettes, and so on. There is a company called Money Mastery, out of Bountiful, Utah, that has seen folks who make over $200,000 per year with a lifestyle deficit. When this is combined with inflation, the effect is financial death, which means bankruptcy.

"In 2011, a typical household averaged $15,956 of credit card debt. Even worse, the average interest rate that these people were paying on that credit card debt was a whopping 12.78 percent. Today, in total, Americans alone have over $13 trillion in consumer and mortgage debt. So, people need an answer, which I know you will provide them here in this book.

"Americans and those in many foreign countries are not saving enough money. In fact, the majority of people both inside and outside the United States are spending more than they take in, and they literally are not saving for that longer life we talked about."

Being concerned, I said, "Yes, I am aware of this. This is one of the reasons for this book and why I am here."

Jeff said, "If people will listen to everything you say here, we will change a lot of lives, which is why I agreed to help you with this book."

16. Income Taxes

"The sixth horseman is, as you would say, . . ."

Smiling, I said, "Ah, taxes, yes, they are a killer."

"Yes, Sandy, taxes drain you of your wealth every day, every minute. There is a day that is known as Tax Freedom Day, which is the day that all of your federal and local and state taxes are paid so that the rest of the year, you are working for yourself. Do you know what day that is, Sandy?"

Chuckling, I noted, "I can tell you that many people in my audiences have thought it would be December 28. However, although it does depend on your resident state and the amount of your income, for many people it is deemed April 17 in 2012 according to the Tax Foundation.

"This means that most people are working about 107 days a year to pay their taxes, which is about 30 percent of their gross income. If you combine this with the fact that most people spend 20 to 30 percent or more of their income on debt or committed money such as mortgage debt or rent, car loans, education loans, and consumer debt, the average person must spend 50 percent or more on just taxes and debts alone! This leaves little room for everything else including insurance, gas, repairs, food, clothing, education for kids, retirement, gifts, or medical and dental expenses. No wonder most people are underwater financially.

"Moreover, according to the Tax Foundation, if we raised taxes in order to cover our federal government's annual deficit, Tax Freedom Day would be May 17."

Being a bit startled, Jeff noted, "That would be disastrous."

"I don't know what the government is going to do about the deficits. We are mortgaging our kids' lives and grandkids' lives. However, one thing I do know is that if we want to get the deficits under control, the government needs to not only curtail spending but to raise taxes."

"Sandy," said Jeff, "I don't want to get too far off course, but the reason that the government has such huge deficits is the same reason most people are in dire financial condition. They refuse to deal with the reality that is driving many European countries as well as the United States into the toilet. This is true for the government, corporations, and individuals. No one wants to deal with the reality of what wars cost in both human and financial terms. No one wants to deal with the fact that previous politicians promised benefits that are no longer paid for. No one wants to deal with the reality that home prices don't always go up or the reality that few people have retirement accounts that are even close to what they will need. They don't want to deal with the reality of what recent college graduates earn or deal with the reality of the massive debt that many people incur by going to their 'dream school.' Until we all start dealing with these realities, we will never be on the track to financial health."

Grinning, I said, "Jeff, I absolutely agree with you. If you ever want to run for president, count me in as a voter."

Jeff then said, "Folks need to take action now and start implementing good planning in order to avoid problems."

> **A Review of What You Have Learned**
>
> "Well, Sandy, that summarizes what I wanted to say today about the problems. Let's see how well you learned our lesson. What are the 16 reasons people fail financially and the six horsemen of financial death?"
>
> Smiling thoughtfully, as well as scouring my notes, I listed the following:
> - Longer lifespan
> - The huge amount of information people must process
> - Inflation
> - Lack of understanding of compound interest
> - Failure to diversify their investments
> - Failure to plan for retirement
> - Failure to save for large future expenses
> - Failure to create short- and long-term financial goals
> - Failure to plan for divorce and multiple families
> - Procrastination in confronting reality
> - And the six horsemen of financial death
>   1. Disability
>   2. Premature death
>   3. Lawsuits
>   4. Estate taxation and probate
>   5. Overspending and unwise use of credit
>   6. Taxes

"So how did we do, Jeff?"

"Sandy, you and Lori are great students. You are going to like Sam. He will give you some real insight in compound interest and savings."

Notes

1. http://www.money-zine.com/Financial-Planning/Debt-Consolidation/Consumer-Debt-Statistics/.
2. http://www.doctorhousingbubble.com/american-savings-americans-save-an-average-of-392-per-year-total-consumer-debt-is-over-25-trillion-the-dark-knight-of-debt/.
3. http://www.efmoody.com/estate/lifeexpectancy.html; see also http://wiki.answers.com/Q/Life_expectancy_of_ancient_egyptians and http://wiki.answers.com/Q/What_was_the_average_life_expectancy_in_1700's.
4. This assumes that tuition will increase at 6 percent per annum, which is what it has done over the last decade.
5. http://divorcerate2011.com/divorce-statistics.

2

Reserves

By failing to prepare, you are preparing to fail.

—Ben Franklin

S am was not what I expected from a banker. Yes, he did meet some of my stereotypical views of bankers in that he was over age 60, balding, and overweight. However, he was pleasantly gregarious and even humorous. Imagine: a humorous banker! He was also undeniably one of the most successful people I have met, having owned a bank and then having sold it before we had this recession.

"Sam, I have to ask you: How did you ever think of starting a bank?" His answer took me back a bit.

"Sandy, I was a builder. I always had those financial ups and downs. However, no matter what happened in the economy, the bankers were the only ones smiling. I figured that it was something that I should do too."

I growled, "Yes, I should have done what you did. If I made money, I could keep the profits. If I lost money, I would get bailed out. What other business could get this benefit?"

Sam chuckled at that.

Why Reserves Are Absolutely Necessary

We brought up the subject of why reserves are not only essential but are also the first consideration in any sound financial plan.

"Sandy, I know that both you and Lori are here to talk about saving money. However, I want to suggest another more pertinent topic that we need to discuss. This will be illustrated by a lady client of my prior bank. This lady was about 45 years of age and was a real estate agent who earned about $65,000 per year. She wanted to know where she should invest her savings of $3,000. Sound familiar?"

Chuckling, I said, "Sam, I get that question or variations on that question a lot, which is why I wanted to talk about saving money."

Sam went on to say, "I asked her a very important question: 'How much do you have for a reserve for emergencies and for tough economic times?' Sadly, her answer was, 'Other than the $3,000, I don't need any emergency funds since I have an IRA and some life insurance cash value!'

"Frankly, the answer just astonished me since IRA money can be taken out without penalty only when you are at least 59½. Even at that age, you also have to pay income tax on the money. In addition, borrowing money out of a life insurance contract shouldn't occur since there is interest on the loan. Even worse, the interest is not deductible, and excessive loans may eventually lead to a cancellation of the policy. This could completely undermine a sound financial plan in the event of death." Sam further noted, "When I started researching what planners recommended about emergency reserves, I found that the answers given were quite varied. There really was no one good place where folks could get unbiased, good information on this question."

"So, Sam, you think we should discuss emergency reserve requirements first?"

Sam, nodding his head said, "Absolutely, for without reserves, people are at the mercy of the economy. Getting great returns won't help them if they don't prepare for unexpected financial setbacks."

"Okay, Sam, so let's get started. Why do we need reserves?"

Giving me a pensive look, Sam said, "If all goes well in life, we generally won't need reserves. The problem is that life has its constant ups and downs. Unanticipated calamities and unanticipated large expenses constantly keep occurring with ever increasing frequency. Thus, it is vital for everyone to have some sort of reserve fund for emergencies and for big unexpected expenses. In fact, one big reason for indebtedness for many people is their lack of planning for the big expenses that crop up in life."

Sam then gave us his definition of a reserve:

A reserve is a risk-free and penalty-free fund of money that will be immediately available for use upon the occurrence of a major expense or a big unanticipated expense.

Lori perked up by noting, "Sandy, remember when two of our real estate investments needed over $20,000 worth of repairs? If we hadn't had the reserve money, we would have been desperate. We would have had to borrow the money on our credit cards, assuming we could even get that much money."

I responded, "Lori, having a reserve was something that you were always big on. Your emphasis on that really did come in handy."

Smiling, Sam then noted, "Yes, women tend to be more security conscious overall than guys. They like having reserves. Their problem is that they want all of their money to be in reserves."

Lori rolled her eyes at Sam's statement.

I then asked Sam, "What types of calamities and expenses should people keep reserves for?"

Sam listed the following circumstances:

- Job losses: If you lose your job, you will need cash to live and pay your ongoing debts.
- Start-up living expenses: If you start up a business, you may not see any income from that business for at least one or two years. Thus, you need to cover your living expenses and business overhead expenses for at least two years.
- Braces for kids that will be needed within the next three years.
- Big upcoming medical and dental expenses that won't be covered by insurance such as dental implants.
- Wedding costs that will be incurred within three years.
- College costs that will be incurred within three years.
- Other unanticipated and unexpected expenses such as car repairs or home repairs.

Being a bit surprised, I asked, "So reserves are not just for unexpected expenses? They are for big, upcoming expenses within the next two to three years?"

Sam quickly answered, "Yes, reserves are for both unexpected expenses and for big upcoming expenses that will be incurred within the next few years. Thus, if you have a large wedding or college tuition coming up within the next few years, money should be put away in a risk-free account for these obligations. Sadly, many folks left much of their college funding in the stock market when they knew they would absolutely need those funds within the next few years. Thus, when the market dropped precipitously, they lost most of their funding. It was a very dumb move."

How Much People Should Have in Reserve

I then asked Sam, "How much should I have in reserve?"

Sam wisely noted, "That is the $64,000 question.[1] If you were to ask 12 financial planners, I would bet you would get 12 different answers. Most will say at least 6 to 12 times your monthly living expenses and debt payments. However, this isn't totally accurate. Let me give you a banker's view on this."

Factors for Computing Needed Reserves

"The amount of reserve should vary based on the following several factors."

Income Stability. "Let's face it. If both you and your spouse have very stable jobs (such as government jobs), the chance that both of you will lose your income is much slimmer than it is for folks who don't have stable jobs. Generally, those with stable jobs might only need two times their monthly living expenses (plus a reserve for imminent big upcoming expenses) while those with unstable incomes or jobs might need 12 times their monthly living expenses plus a reserve for the imminent big upcoming expenses."

Living Expenses. "Generally, the greater your monthly living expenses, the greater the amount you will need for reserves. When I consider someone's living expenses, I am talking about everything that that person spends such as mortgage payments, insurance, gifts, food, clothing, debt payments, negative cash flows from real estate, utilities, allowance for repairs on cars and homes, college payments for kids, support for kids, phone service, and Internet. Everything!"

I then asked Sam, "How would someone know how much this is?"

Sam quickly answered, "You would need to track what you spend in a month. You can do this by going to your check register and your credit card bills for a three-month period and taking the average. It is really important that you know what you are spending each month so you will be able to have an adequate reserve. You also want to track expenses for at least three months in order to pick up nonrecurring items such as insurance premium payments."

"Sam," I said. "We have a new product called Taxbot that I want to call to all of my readers' attention. It works on iPhones and Droids and on the iPad 2 or later version and most Droid Tablets. What it does is exactly what you wanted. It tracks all expenses including automatically giving the questions that IRS requires for entertainment, travel, and automobile. It also has an integrated mileage tracker with a GPS system. We will even soon have an integrated credit card service that will input charges from the credit card into Taxbot. Thus, people can track all of their expenses for budgeting and for tax purposes. It is available on Taxbot.com."

Sam chuckled at my obvious plug but responded, "Yes, I did see what you did on Taxbot. It is a **very** interesting and needed application that will help many people save a bundle."

Unanticipated Expenses. Moving on, Sam added "Another factor in determining the amount of reserves would be big possible expenses such as those for house repairs, car repairs, or medical expenses. Certainly, you should have at least $3,000 and preferably $5,000 for these possible upcoming calamities."

Being a bit grouchy about this, I noted, "Yes, my wife had to spend over $2,000 on these run-flat tires and other car repairs due to leaks. I am glad I had a reserve fund."

Big Anticipated Expenses Occurring Within Three Years. "In addition to the above, Sandy and Lori, you should have a reserve for big anticipated events that you expect to occur within the next three years. Examples of this would be college tuition, weddings, and braces."

Formula for Computing Needed Reserves

"Okay, Sam. I see that there are many factors. For our readers, can you put this into a formula that they can use immediately?"

Sam chuckled at that request and answered, "Sure, here is a conservative formula that assumes that you and your spouse don't have very secure jobs."

1. 12 months of living expenses, plus
2. $5,000 to $10,000 for unanticipated big expenses, plus
3. Large expenses expected to be incurred within the next three years, plus
4. If you start up a business, two years of business and personal overhead expenses

"The sum of all this will equal your total required reserve."

"Sam, can you give an example of how this formula works?"

"Sure, I know someone who works for General Motors. I think you will agree that working for most private companies won't provide a lot of job security. If his family's monthly expenses are $5,000 and they expect to pay $30,000 for an upcoming wedding in less than two years for their engaged daughter, their reserve should be computed as follows."

Monthly expenses × 12 =	$60,000
Reserve for unanticipated big expenses	$ 5,000
Upcoming big anticipated expense (wedding)	$30,000
Total reserve required	$95,000

"Sam, I would imagine that if you are single, such as a single mom taking care of kids, unless you have a **very** secure job, you should have at least 12 times your monthly living expenses?"

Sam quickly replied, "Yes you are right. Single people are completely dependent on their own earnings. Accordingly, they should probably have **at least** 12 months of living expenses in most cases and probably even more. I might even advise single people to have two years' worth of living expenses as a reserve."

Where People Should Invest Their Reserve Funds

"Okay, Sam, now that we know how much to have in reserve, the next question becomes: Where should our reserve money be placed, and what kind of investment return should we seek for this money?"

"That's a good question, Sandy. Interestingly, your return on investment for reserve money is irrelevant. Say that five times!"

"Okay, investment return is irrelevant, investment return is irrelevant, investment return is irrelevant."

"Okay, Sandy, that's enough. You get the point."

Sam added, "What is **key** is that your money must be safe, safe, safe! Did I say it has to be safe? Thus, it can't be subject to stock market fluctuations or interest rate fluctuations, and it can't be subject to penalties for withdrawals, and it must be very liquid! This means that you can get it with a few days' notice."

Sam listed the following possible places for reserve funds:

- Safe, hidden trap doors or mattresses (just kidding)
- Checking accounts
- Savings accounts
- Money market accounts
- Treasury bills whose duration is less than or equal to 30 days **if** you have other funds to tide you over for the 30-day wait

"What are **not** good places for reserve funds are in anything that is risky, involves penalties on withdrawal, or is illiquid. Thus, investments in the stock market, bonds, annuities, life insurance cash value, qualified pension funds, or real estate should **not** count in figuring reserves."

I probed Sam with the following question: "How about using Series EE government bonds? They are very safe."

Sam snorted and said, "Yes, they are safe, and at first glance they may seem like good places for reserve money. However, they have a six-month waiting period. In addition, you are taxed on all accrued interest when you cash in the bonds. Thus, I don't recommend putting your reserve money into Series EE bonds **unless** you have other funds in reserve to accommodate the six-month waiting period."

While I was pondering Sam's answer, Lori chirped up and asked, "Sam, what is the best way to save sufficient funds for reserves, especially if we are not making a significant return on the money in reserve?"

The Best Ways for People to Save Money for Reserves

"Good question, Lori. Sandy, you have a smart wife," noted Sam. "I get this question a lot. Let's face it, we Americans (and not just us but people everywhere in the world) are horrible savers. I meet folks all the time who tell me that they can't save a dime. Here is what I would recommend to everyone who wants to know how to save money. It might be a bit premature since it will be covered in Chapters 4 and 5 on savings, but it is a tried-and-true method, and it is worth repeating. However, it will take some discipline." Sam gave us the following secret:

> **Have a fixed amount of each paycheck taken out for savings. Learn to live on what is left over!**

Interrupting Sam, I said, "The government has been doing this for years. It is called withholding on taxes. Folks have had to learn to live on what was left over." I then teasingly added, "However, unlike the rest of us, the government can't seem to live on what is being paid them through withholding."

Sam roared about that when he added, "Yes, you are quite right. If you have a fixed amount taken out of each paycheck, you will eventually learn to live on what is left over. You may have to track your expenses and see where you can cut back on spending such as that daily Starbucks latte."

Lori interrupted, "Er, maybe not that one."

Both Sam and I laughed at that statement. "Well, there might be some expenses that you can cut back that can be found only by tracking the expenses. Moreover, don't ever touch the reserve fund unless it is used for one of the items noted above."

Lori, with a quizzical look, asked Sam one final question: "Sam, how much should people have taken out of each paycheck in order to save enough of a reserve?"

With a glint in Sam's eyes, he answered, "Lori, the answer is that they should put away as much as they can. I would recommend 10 to 15 percent of their take-home pay or even more if they can afford it. However, if due to other commitments they can't seem to meet their obligations taking out that much, then they should put away only 5 percent. The point is that something will be better than nothing! Moreover, the reserve comes first, even before retirement savings."

When we talk about savings in Chapters 4 and 5, we will give specific strategies on how to find the money and be able to reach a higher savings limit than most people realize.

A Review of What You Have Learned

"Okay, Sandy and Lori, let's see what good students you were. Here is a test. First, why do we need reserves?"

Lori quickly responded with, "We need them for unanticipated expenses such as repairs, for 12 months of living expenses in case of a job loss (assuming a not-so-stable job), and for current upcoming big expenses, such as weddings or college costs, that are expected to be incurred within three years. How did I do?"

Sam smiled and said, "Great, so far. Second, how much reserve should we have?"

I answered, "It is the following formula."

1. 12 months of living expenses, plus
2. $5,000 to $10,000 for unanticipated big expenses, plus
3. Large expenses expected to be incurred within the next three years, plus
4. If you start up a business, two years of business and personal overhead expenses

Lori also added, "Single people might have to add even more for their reserves since they are totally dependent on their own income."

Sam said, "You two are great students. Now for the third question: Where should reserve money be placed?"

I smiled and noted, "In safe, liquid accounts that do not have any withdrawal penalties or risk of losing money."

Lori added, "The investment return is irrelevant."

Sam smiled, and said, "Almost done. Okay, here is the final question: How do we save the money for the reserve?"

Knowing that answer like the back of my hand . . . or should I say . . . like knowing the withholding tables, I answered, "Have a fixed amount taken out of each paycheck for the reserve funds and learn to live on the rest."

"You both get *A*'s. I can't wait for tomorrow when we will start making people as rich as . . . well . . . rich bankers."

I smiled at that.

Notes

1. The reference to the "$64,000 question" was based on an old quiz show by that name. I guess knowing this dates me.

3

Compound Interest: The Eighth Wonder of the World

The most powerful force in the universe is compound interest. It is the eighth wonder of the world.

—Attributed to Albert Einstein

What Bankers Know About Compounding That the Average Person Doesn't Know and Should Absolutely Know

What You Will Learn
- What bankers know about compounding that the average person doesn't know and should **absolutely** know
- How compounding works and why it is so powerful for all investors
- How time correlates with the results of compounding
- Why slight increases in interest can magnify results
- Two great formulas that everyone in the world should know about
- The myths and drawbacks inherent in the formulas and calculators

"It is fabulous seeing you again, Sandy, and your lovely wife Lori," which caused Lori to blush a bit. "I guess you weren't overwhelmed with all of the information from yesterday," said Sam.

"Actually, we really enjoyed our conversation yesterday and came back for more. I guess I am a glutton for knowledge. Or is it a glutton for punishment? Anyway, can we talk about savings now?" I replied.

Sam looked at Lori and me thoughtfully and said, "We need to discuss one topic before we have any discussion about the concept of savings. This one topic permeates everything that will be discussed in your book, and the topic is *compounding*. Every banker knows about this implicitly, and everyone in the world needs to understand this topic. It is the reason I became a banker. It is the reason I started a bank, and it is a primary reason I became rich."

My only reaction after that was to say, "Well, after that, I can't wait to see what you have to say."

Sam excitedly leaned forward and said, "I never cease to be amazed at the power of compounding in an investment program. In fact, seeing pocket change become literally millions over time is truly breathtaking, even today after all these years.

"There was a story that I found searching the Internet about an ancient Athenian merchant entrusted with a large sum of money to establish a trust that was supposed to run 2,000 years. Supposedly the Athenian pocketed all of the money except for a single drachma, which he invested in Athenian bonds paying a measly 3 percent interest, compounded annually.

"Supposedly, the money disappeared over time, and he certainly didn't live long enough to have seen the results, but after 2,000 years that single drachma would have wound up being worth more than all the assets on the Earth!"

I wryly added, "It's too bad Greece didn't invest this money for that length of time. The country wouldn't be in the horrible economic situation that they are in now."

"What is most interesting, which I understand will be covered in a later chapter, is that most multimillionaires didn't make a huge amount of money from their jobs or businesses. They were, for the most part, average folks who were savers for retirement and never touched their retirement savings until retirement. Compound interest did it for them. Interestingly, folks who took out too many loans or financed a bigger home than they could afford or who overpaid their taxes due to ignorance had the power of compound interest work *against* them, which is why a thorough knowledge of compound interest is so profoundly important for everyone."

Interrupting Sam, I said, "Okay, would you explain how compounding works from a banker's perspective?"

How Compounding Works and Why It Is So Powerful for All Investors

Sam replied, "The concept of compound interest is fairly simple; however, its application can be a bit tricky to understand. Compounding means that you earn interest or dividends on not only your original investment but also on the money that you reinvest. You continue to earn interest and dividends on both your original investment and on the additional interest and dividends that you earned in prior years assuming these additional earnings get invested at the same rate of return."

Sam continued, "Let me give you an example. If you were to invest $10,000 today and earn 4 percent interest, you would have $10,400 by the end of the year (ignoring any potential tax issues). If you continued to earn the 4 percent during your second year, you would earn the 4 percent on both the original $10,000 and on the interest of $400 that you reinvested."

Lori interrupted with, "But Sam, we don't always earn the same rate of return on our reinvestments as we did with the original investments, right?"

Sam responded, "Yes, you are right. This is a drawback of the compound interest formula, which might require a different interest assumption on your earnings versus that of your original investment. However, the interest rates are often the same. For example, if you invest in a company that pays dividends and reinvests those dividends, you will be earning the same amount of money each year on all of the money, even the reinvested dividends. The same can be said for savings accounts too."

Smoothly, Sam continued with, "In general, you would need to know several facts in order to figure out what your money would be worth."

You would need the following information:

- The amount of money that you will be investing initially. This is called the *present value* or *initial investment*.
- The amount of money you will be investing or adding each year, if any.
- The interest rate that you expect to make.
- The number of years for the compounding to take effect.
- The result (also known as *future value*) that you wish to accumulate over your projected number of years.

"There is a complicated formula for all this, but the **much** easier way is simply to go to a savings or *future value calculator* found on the Internet."

"Sam," I interjected, "as you know, I have some terrific savings and retirement calculators in the Tools section of my website at www.sandy botkin.com. The calculators are free and very simple to use."

While smiling, Sam said, "Yes, I have sent people to your site. It is very well done. What I particularly like is that if the investor knows any four of the above five factors, the calculator can compute the missing factor.

Thus, if the investor wants $1 million at retirement and has only $10,000 today but can invest a certain amount such as $5,000 for 30 years, your calculator will tell that investor what interest rate he or she will have to earn. If the investor assumes an existing interest rate and future value and wants that future value in a set number of years, the calculator will tell that investor how much money needs to be invested over each period in order to have that desired amount of money. The calculators are very valuable tools indeed.

"Sandy, I was playing around with your calculators, and I want to share some of my important observations. Here are some of my results. If my son, Tom, were to invest $5,000 annually, at the end of each year, into his retirement plan for 30 years, he will have, at 6 percent interest, $419,008 in his retirement plan such as a Roth 401(k), which is nontaxable in the United States. Many other countries such as Canada have similar types of tax-free retirement savings plans."

How Time Correlates with the Results from Compounding

Without pausing for a break, Sam continued: "This result assumes that Tom deposited his $5,000 yearly contribution at the end of each year, which is what most people do. *However*, if he had the foresight to make these same yearly contributions at the same interest rate for the same number of years, but he invested the money at the beginning of each year rather than at the end of each year, his total at retirement would be $449,319. Thus, by taking one simple step of changing his investment timing to the beginning of each year instead of the end of each year, he would have a whopping extra retirement amount of $30,311! So here is the important point of all this."

> **The earlier in the year you make your contributions, especially for all retirement plans, the more you will have at retirement. This point cannot be overstated.**

Sam was on a roll when he excitedly added, "In addition, if you were to invest the same $5,000 per year for 5 more years, which would be 35 years, and you did so at the beginning of each year, your principal amount at retirement would be $631,341, which is about an extra $180,000 more for the extra 5 years."

Getting even more excited, while gesticulating like crazy, Sam enthusiastically added, "If you were to invest the same $5,000 per year for 40 years instead of the original 30 years and you did so at the beginning of each year, you would have at retirement $874,753. This is almost double what you would have had after 30 years. And it is more than double what you would have had after 30 years if you had invested this money at the end of each year rather than at the beginning of the year!"

Sam's point was this:

As the number of years that you make deposits without taking withdrawals increases, the amount of your savings increases—significantly. In fact, this amount grows geometrically over the years. Adding a few extra years of deposits can literally double or even triple your accumulation.

"Sam, I really didn't realize that it made that much of a difference adding a few years of savings," said Lori dumbfounded.

"Yes, Lori, even a few extra years of savings really does make a huge difference. Also a few extra years of payments on loans also makes a huge difference except that the compounding goes against you. This is why we bankers are very happy giving you a 30-year loan or even a 40-year loan instead of a 15-year loan. It drops the borrower's monthly payments each month, but it increases the cash that borrower pays to the bank over the lifetime of the loan."

Why Slight Increases in Interest Can Magnify Results

Still excited, Sam went on to say: "Moreover, even slight yearly increases in the interest rate *dramatically* increase your savings and your potential retirement fund. Let me give you an example. Suppose you were to deposit the same $5,000 per year in a retirement plan, at the beginning of each year, for either 30 or 40 years, but instead of the 6 percent that we originally assumed, you get a compounded rate of return of 9 percent on your investment, which is an extra 3 percent return over what you were originally getting. The results are:"

	6%	9%
30 years at $5,000 per year	$449,319	$815,185
40 years at $5,000 per year	$874,753	$2,012,641

Note: All results assume that the deposits are made at the beginning of each year.

Without seeming to take a breath, Sam said, "A great illustration that really shows the interrelationship between time and investment returns would be to use what we paid for Manhattan in 1626, which was a measly $24. If the Native Americans had invested this amount at a paltry 3 percent until today, the amount would have accumulated to $2,101,565. If, however, they were able to get a long-term rate of 6 percent, which would be double the assumed original rate of return, the amount would now be worth (drum roll) $132,730,083,818.24. This would be 63,157 **times** what they would have gotten at 3 percent. This example dramatically shows the following point."

> **Even slight increases in your investment's rate of return geometrically magnifies your return.**

Lori and I looked at each other in complete disbelief. It was just astounding how slight increases in interest rates can so magnify the results.

Sam waited for all this to sink in. After getting us some tea, he went on by saying, "The result of what I said above has a lot of profound implications, and I want to make this very clear: **compound interest can work for you, but it can also work against you.**

"Here is an example. If you were to start off with $1 and you doubled your money every year without paying taxes (which I know is an exaggerated example), you would have about $1,042,000 at the end of a 20-year period. Now if you were to pay 35 percent of that in taxes (considering income taxes, local taxes such as state and provincial taxes, sales taxes, Internet taxes, gas taxes, value-added taxes [VATs], and excise taxes), over the same 20-year period, the balance would be about $23,000."

Being a bit shocked, I said to Sam, "That is a huge difference! Is it really that much of a difference?"

Sam smiled with an alligator smile and said, "Yes. The reason is that you are losing both the tax money that you give the government and all the compound interest that you would have made on that money."

I interrupted Sam by saying, "This is why I keep telling folks that it will be very difficult to get rich unless they get their taxes down to the legal minimum, which is why most multimillionaires get as much tax planning as they can."

"I agree, Sandy, which is why I have always been a fan of your work from afar. I bet you didn't know that. In fact, after Jeff showed me your book *Lower Your Taxes—Big Time!*, I wanted to meet you. I have been recommending that book to everyone I have met.

"Anyway to get back on point, banks understand the concept of compounding very well. What is it that banks want you to do? Answer: They want you to take out as long a loan as possible and to pay the highest interest rate possible, which is why banks love adjustable rate mortgages."

(More will be discussed later in Chapter 8 of this book about the benefits and detriments of different types of loans.)

Sam continued, "Here is an example that I ran for my son, Tom. Let's say that you are offered three alternative mortgages at 5.5 percent for an initial loan for $400,000. One is for 15 years, one is for 30 years, and one is for 40 years (some banks in California were offering 40-year loans when Tom was looking at mortgages). The table below shows what you will pay by the end of the loan term, not counting loan costs such as mortgage insurance or taxes."

Loan Term	Monthly Payment	Total Amount Paid to the Bank at End of Term
15-year loan	$3,268	$588,300 paid by end of 15 years
30-year loan	$2,271	$817,614 paid by end of 30 years
40-year loan	$2,063	$990,279 paid by end of 40 years

Sam quickly added, "I also want to note that generally longer-term loans usually garner higher interest rates and costs due to greater risk by the bank of interest rate fluctuations. I assumed in my example that the interest rate was the same for all lengths of loans."

Lori, looking perplexed, said, "Sam, are you saying that folks would always be better off with a 15-year loan since they would be paying a lot less in interest?"

Sam diplomatically said, "Not necessarily so, because you have to evaluate how much you can make on your money. If you honestly feel that you can do better than what the bank is charging you, you might want the use of the bank's money for a much longer time. However, since market conditions vary greatly during most people's lifetime and since our sanity and stress seem to follow market conditions, many people might prefer (and might be better off with) the lower-term loans. I have almost no loan balance, which in today's environment, now seems like a smart idea in contrast to having more money exposed to risk in the stock market. It is also interesting that you can pay off a 30-year loan in 15 years by simply adding about 50 percent more to each monthly payment, not counting what is paid each month for taxes.

"I should note that some bankers feel that having a longer-term loan allows for more flexibility. They reason that if you want, you can make additional payments in order to shorten the loan period. Moreover, if you want the use of the money, you can keep making your normal monthly payment, which does ensure greater flexibility. In fact, once you decide on a 15-year loan, you have less flexibility unless you want to pay it off even quicker or you are able to refinance your loan."

Lori then asked, "So what is your personal belief?"

Sam said, "Frankly, people have a hard time saving money. There is just something comforting about not having a mortgage payment at retirement. In addition, if the market goes against you or if the economy incurs a recession, having no mortgage will of course help you avoid mortgage foreclosure. Thus, I personally believe in making additional payments in order to shorten the loan term. However, I will admit that there are other bankers who don't agree with me for the reasons that I gave above."

Lori looked very composed in thought as she considered Sam's answer.

Two Great Formulas That Everyone in the World Should Know About

Sam then switched topics and said, "Ever wonder if there was an easy way to calculate how long it would take for your money to double or even triple?"

I quickly responded, "Yes, I do know the formula for calculating how long it will take to double my money, but I never knew there was a formula for calculating how long it will take to triple my money."

"Well, Sandy, I am glad you wondered about all that because there is an answer. That smart Einstein even figured this out for us." The rules are as follows:

1. **For doubling your money:** Take the number 72, and divide it by the interest rate that you want or will get. This will give you the number of years it will take to double your savings.
2. **For tripling your money:** Take the number 115, and divide it by your interest rate. This will give you the number of years it will take to triple your savings.

"Let's take an example," said Sam. "Let's say that a stock pays a 6 percent dividend on all shares. If you invest $50,000 today, your investment will double (assuming the money is reinvested in the stock at the same rate of return) in 12 years (72/6 = 12 years).

"If you wanted to see how long it would take to triple your money, it would take a bit over 19 years (115/6 = 19.17 years).

"In fact, using basic algebra, if you have two of the unknowns, you can figure out the third figure. Thus, if you wanted $100,000 in 10 years from now and had $50,000 invested today, you would need to earn 7.2 percent interest in order to double your money in 10 years, which is computed as follows: 72/10 years = interest rate needed = 7.2 percent)."

"Sam, I consider myself a pretty smart CPA, and I never knew about the rule of 115. That really is ingenious. However, what are the drawbacks to both of these rules?"

The Myths and Drawbacks Inherent in the Formulas and Calculators

Sam was obviously gathering his thoughts together when he then said, "There are some obvious drawbacks to both of these rules as well as using the savings calculators.

"First, the biggest drawback is that all these rules and calculators assume that you will make the same rate of return each year on your investment and on your reinvested money, which many times isn't the case regarding reinvested income.

"Second, interest rates and dividend rates might vary from year to year unless you get a bond or flat rate certificate of deposit (CD). Thus, you may earn more or less than the projected rate.

"I guess the bottom line," noted Sam, "is that all of these rules are very valuable and should be studied. However, there are drawbacks that you should always take into account.

"Okay, Sandy and Lori, now for the test. What did you learn from our discussion. Feel free to use your notes."

A Review of What You Have Learned

- Compound interest is indeed miraculous and can make everyone rich. However, it can work against us too. I guess we should listen to Einstein and understand how compounding works because its implications are vitally important to everyone.
- If you know four of the five factors, you can figure out the fifth factor. Thus, if you know all the factors except for the interest rate needed, you can calculate for this, or if you know all the factors including the interest rate but not the projected savings at the end, you can calculate this too. The five factors are these:
  1. Amount of money you will be initially investing or depositing
  2. Amount of annual or monthly investment or reinvestments
  3. Amount of interest that you can earn overall
  4. Number of years you want for compounding
  5. Total amount that you want at the end of the projected term of years

- Folks should go to my website at www.sandybotkin.com and use the financial calculators in the Tools section. "I had to give my site a plug, Sam," to which he chuckled.
- The earlier in the year that you make your savings contributions, especially for retirement plans, the more you will have at retirement. Even a few years of extra contributions can make huge differences in retirement savings.
- Slight increases in your return on investment, even a few points, will greatly magnify your overall return at retirement.
- If you can slightly increase both your rate of return and your years of contribution, you geometrically magnify your savings.
- Compounding can work for you with investments or work against you with loans and tax payments. Thus, you will find it difficult to get rich unless you get your taxes down to the legal minimum and manage your debt to affordable limits.
- Reducing your mortgage length from 30 years to 15 years reduces the total amount paid to the bank in interest by *over* 50 percent and is a form of savings. In addition, it takes only a few hundred dollars more per month in payments, which is generally about 50 percent more than the normal monthly amortization payment.
- If you want to know how long it will take to double your money, take the number 72 and divide it by your long-term interest rate earned.
- If you want to know how long it will take to triple your money, take the number 115 and divide it by your long-term interest rate earned.

"I think that is everything," I quipped.

Sam then said, "Sandy, you did very well, but you forgot one thing."

- Start saving now. Don't procrastinate. There is a high cost for procrastination.

"Well, Sam," I said, "there was a lot of information here."

"Sandy, I said at the beginning that although the concept of compounding seems easy enough, there is a lot to know. I wasn't kidding."

Lori smiled and said, "I can see why you are so excited about this, Sam. It really is exciting."

4

Saving Money, Part I: The Real Secret of Wealth

*I am not overspending. You are
underdepositing.*

—Anonymous

What You Will Learn
- Why so many people have a poor retirement and how to avoid this problem
- Why saving is crucial for wealth creation and a good retirement
- How much money people should be saving for retirement
- Rich banker secrets to saving for retirement and finding the money for your three savings goals

I LOVE UTAH! Did I say that with enough emphasis? The people are so friendly that I suspect they take smile pills. The landscape is gorgeous, dotted with breathtaking mountains and lush greenery. Moreover, the streets of the main cities, such as Salt Lake City, are pristinely clean. I really do suspect that they have gremlins cleaning the streets each evening.

What brings me here, however, is not the innate beauty of Utah or its friendly people or even its great skiing. I have friends, Alan and Peter, who own a financial literacy company that has been immensely successful in getting people to stop overspending, get out of debt, and retire wealthy. Peter's background is particularly compelling since he was powerfully impacted by a serious car accident at age 19, and he knows firsthand what crushing financial debt can do to a person. He incurred hundreds of thousands of dollars in medical debt as he struggled to recover. Using the principles he now teaches, Peter was able to get out from underneath that financial burden in just five years. I therefore felt that there could be no better person who could give advice for saving money and getting out of debt than Peter. In addition, I was looking forward to seeing him. I just felt that Peter would be the better choice for this interview than most anyone else, even Sam the banker.

Greeting Lori and me at his office door, he warmly said, "How are you doing, fella." You really have to like Peter with his great warm smile, big bear hugs, and puppy dog demeanor. If it weren't for his slightly fire-scarred face, I would never have thought that this big bear of a guy had suffered through such a calamity.

Ushering us into his office, Peter calmly asked, "So you want information on saving money and getting out of debt, right?"

"Yup," I said with as deadpan a look as possible.

Peter then went on with, "Well, the best way to handle this is to break up the topic into three topics: saving in general, saving for college, and reducing debts."

I nodded in agreement because they were all topics that I wanted to discuss. I guess great minds think alike since I was going to have one chapter on each of his suggested topics, and this book reflects that goal: this chapter covers saving in general, Chapter 5 covers saving for college, and Chapter 6 covers reducing debts.

Why So Many People Have a Poor Retirement and How to Avoid This Problem

Peter looked steadfastly at me and then Lori and asked, "Do you want the good news first or the bad news?"

Lori swallowed hard and said, "Give us the good news first."

"Okay. The good news is that for the first time in many years, Americans are saving more than they are spending. Typically Americans are now saving about 3 to 6 percent of their income depending on the study performed, which is also becoming true for others around the world. Loans are harder to get, and cash is being used more than ever." Peter then growled about the bad news. "The bad news is that this is the first time in many, many years that Americans have been savers. Traditionally, as late as 2007, most people didn't save money. In fact, for most Americans, we had negative savings, which meant that they spent more than they took in. In fact, in 2008, which was a banner year for saving money, the average American saved a paltry $397 for the year!"[1]

Lori looked at me with disbelief.

Peter then smoothly went on to say, "I would bet that when credit gets a bit easier, which the government is trying to accomplish, most Americans will go back to their old habits of borrow and spend. This will also be true for businesses. Here are some other statistics from the Employee Benefit Research Institute (EBRI, www.ebri.org): Fewer than 12 percent of all Americans have a net worth, not counting their primary home, of under $25,000. And a whopping 50 percent of Americans have a net worth of under $100,000. Around the world, this situation is much worse.

"The table below gives Americans' average net worth (which includes their pension and home) broken down by age. The table comes from the article 'The Average Net Worth of Americans: Where Do You Stand?,' on the Money Relationship website."[2]

Under 25	$1,475
Ages 25–34	$8,525
Ages 35–44	$51,575
Ages 45–54	$180,125
Ages 55–64	$232,000

Peter continued, "Here are some other sobering statistics that I gleaned from an Internet search:"[3]

- The average American family has $3,800 in the bank.
- 50 percent of American households don't have a retirement account.
- The 50 percent of households with retirement accounts only have $35,000 saved up (per family).
- The average family owns a house worth $160,000, $95,000 of which is mortgaged.
- 40 percent of working Americans are not saving for retirement.
- $117,951 is the average American household's debt, which includes the mortgage.
- 25 percent of households have no savings whatsoever.
- 24 percent have postponed retirement.
- Only 18 percent are very confident about their retirement situation.

"Moreover," Peter continued, "things are much worse than they seem. These numbers include the average net worth of Americans' homes, which isn't generally spendable for living expenses. In addition, these statistics are a bit skewed by people such as Bill Gates and Warren Buffett who have an enormous net worth. In fact, if you take out the top people like Bill Gates, you would have an average net worth at age 55+ of about $55,000!" With a dour expression, Peter added, "Even worse, these statistics were based on the last census before the big stock market crash. This means that most people are in very bad shape for retirement. I should note that this 3 to 6 percent savings rate is endemic in the United States as a whole. In a few other countries such as Japan, France, Canada, and China, savings rates can be from 11 to 15 percent."

After hearing all of this negative information, Lori asked, "Peter, what does this mean for the country?"

He gave a great answer. "Lori, you are asking an important question. Just as, without adequate savings, your individual standard of living will decline in retirement, future generations of Americans will see their standard of living decline if the U.S. economy loses ground against global competition."

After being a bit dejected, I asked, "Is there good news?"

Peter chuckled and said, "Yes, the good news is that we can turn most people around. It will take some time, but it is doable," which made me smile a bit.

Why Saving Is Crucial for Wealth Creation and a Good Retirement

"Okay, Peter," I said. "Let's start with an easy question. How much should people save for retirement?"

Looking at me rather thoughtfully and with a glint in his eye, he responded, "What you really want to know is not how much should you save. That is the second question. The first issue should be, 'What do we want to save for?'"

I was a bit taken aback by this. I responded, "For retirement, of course."

Peter diplomatically corrected me by saying, "Sandy, people **should** have at least three types of savings in addition to the reserve account. The first that you mentioned is for retirement. The second, however, should be for consumer goods, which also includes some funds for emotional spending (which we all are guilty of doing), and the third is for big ticket items. There are several secrets known to us planners that most people never find out, unless they use the services of companies like Money Mastery." I chuckled at his obvious attempt at marketing his company.

"The first secret is the following one."

Secret 1. Never borrow for a consumer good.

After seeing the puzzled look on both Lori's and my face, Peter elaborated by saying, "Thus, don't borrow to buy a TV, furniture, refrigerator, dishwasher, vacation, or similar goods unless it is an absolute emergency. Everyone should put away a *rainy day fund* for such future purchases and for breakdowns of equipment. The only expensive items for which I can see the need for incurring debt would be a house purchase, college tuition (if reasonable in amount), and maybe a car. Moreover, if you can save for a car, I would pay cash for that too. In addition, there should be a third savings account for big ticket items such as future wedding costs and education for kids."

I interjected, "That is a lot of savings."

Peter nodded in agreement. Peter then went on: "In addition, everyone should save for retirement. Remember the ant and grasshopper fable by Aesop. If you spend what you have each year the way the ant did, you will have nothing left for retirement. The key is to save enough."

How Much Money People Should Be Saving for Retirement

"Peter," I asked, "let's start with the retirement. How much is enough?"

He answered, "Generally, we have recommended to all of our clients that they save at least 10 percent of what they earn solely for retirement. It should never be touched for anything such as education for kids, big ticket items, or vacations. It is strictly for retirement. This is in addition to the savings for an adequate reserve and for future expected big ticket items, such as a wedding and college costs."

Offering what I considered to be a smart response, I said, "Is the 10 percent figure on their net income after taxes or before taxes?"

Peter rolled his eyes and said, "It should be on the gross before taxes. If you can afford only 10 percent of your net income after withholding, then just start by saving 10 percent of that."

I then asked Peter, "What if people have great retirement programs such as the programs for federal and state government workers?"

Peter grimaced and said, "With the way retirement funds are going, they may well get very little of their promised benefits. Moreover, most new government retirement plans are shifting to employee savings programs that resemble 401(k) accounts. **Putting money into a 401(k) or an IRA is part of that 10 percent.**"

"Okay, Peter, that covers the retirement, but what about education and wedding savings?"

Peter responded with, "I think that we should address the college saving issue in another session since there is some information specific to college education savings that we want to cover as a separate topic. As for weddings, I would assume a cost of at least $20,000 if I had a daughter and $10,000 if I had a son. Thus, I would put away about $50 to $100 per month in a special account for each child beginning from when he or she was born."

"Okay, Peter. Let's get into the topic of savings."

Peter's eyes widened with that infectious glint and said, "Okay, Sandy. Here is the second secret that we planners know that most people don't realize. You don't need to budget in your life. I do know that many people are told to budget for their expenses. But the real secret is the following one."

Secret 2. You can have anything that you want. You just can't have everything that you want.

Being a bit puzzled, Lori inquired, "Can you explain what you mean here, Peter?"

"Okay. If you ever go on a diet, you can eat anything, but you need to make choices. If you exercise, you can eat more than if you don't exercise. If you eat a big steak dinner, you probably can't have dessert. Diets are about choices. The same is true for saving and spending money. If you choose to have a big house, you might have to give up on an education fund. If you want to eat out every day, you might not have enough money to go on vacation. Again, it is all about choices. This is why we say that you can have anything you want but not everything you want."

I decided to interject my comments here by saying, "Peter, I think we need to clarify your statement. With enough saving and planning, many people probably can have almost anything they want. It just can't happen instantaneously."

"Yes, Sandy, you are right, which is why savers are planners. Those who plan for their retirement and big expenses, with proper saving, can have a much better lifestyle as they get older."

"Okay, Peter, I get it," I said. "However, how do people save 10 percent of what they earn to put toward retirement and still find the money to save for things like education and weddings? Heck, many people are having a hard enough time just making their current financial ends meet."

Rich Banker Secrets to Saving for Retirement and Finding the Money for Your Three Savings Goals

"Sandy, that is the $64,000 question," Peter said with a deadpan facial expression. "There are three additional secrets that are needed to accomplish these goals. To maximize your benefits, you should implement all of the secrets or you probably won't meet your savings goals.

"The third secret is the following one."

Secret 3. Pay yourself first.

"The government has learned this secret, and so it requires that taxes be withheld on each paycheck. It knows that without withholding, people will spend the tax money. The same concept applies to saving money. You have to have your 10 percent savings plus any other money needed for the future taken out of your paycheck before you pay any bills! You must, in effect, pay yourself first. This is crucial. If you don't see the money because it is taken out, you won't miss it. What is that old saying? Out of sight, out of mind.

"I know that you have questions about this, which will be answered by the fourth secret. The fourth secret is simple to understand but less simple to apply. Here it is."

Secret 4. Learn the difference between a need and a want.

Looking a bit astonished, Lori notes, "Peter, my needs are my wants."

Peter and I both laughed. Peter then said, "Lori, do you really need dozens of pairs of shoes, or are they things that you want? Do you really need a new car, or can an older, cheaper car do the same thing? Do you really need a new 55-inch TV, or will a cheaper model do? Do you really need designer clothes, or will Target clothes do? These are the difficult choices that I am talking about. If you do want a lot of shoes, maybe you can cut back in other areas such as eating out less or eating at cheaper restaurants. In a few minutes, I will give you some great ideas that we share with our clients at Money Mastery.

"The final secret, which is very important to implement, is the following one."

Secret 5. You *really, really* need to track your spending for at least three consecutive months.

"Did I say that with enough emphasis?

"The reason for the tracking is that you can't control what you don't know about. Every client that we have had has been able to find hundreds per month in expenses that they could easily cut back and, in many cases, were duplicated elsewhere. Tracking allows people to really control their overspending."

I interrupted this with, "Yes, Peter, my friend Jeff mentioned that overspending is one of the six horsemen of financial death. He really made a big deal about this in another discussion (Chapter 1)."

"Yes, Sandy, people are greatly overspending due to buying things that they don't necessarily need. The sad part is that we are besieged with ads encouraging us to buy . . . buy . . . buy. Did you notice that there are more advertisements on TV than ever? Soon, we will have no content at all . . .

just ads. Everywhere we go, we are bombarded with messages to buy goods and to spend money. It is sickening. Folks really need to resist these messages that have been skillfully designed to affect people both consciously and subliminally.

"In fact, here's a list of some great ideas that could help you substantially cut your expenses while not affecting your lifestyle greatly."

- Put all change in a piggy bank. This can add up to about $20 to $30 each month.
- Have your doctor subscribe pills that are double dose and buy a pill splitter. I have been doing this for my cholesterol medication for years. Essentially it gives me 180 days of pills for the 90-day price.
- Do some work around your home, such as mowing the lawn and cleaning the house, rather than hiring someone to do it.

Lori looked at me and said to Peter, "You don't know Sandy's abilities. He can't even hammer a nail into a wall without hurting himself and the wall," which caused Peter and me to chuckle.

- Shop at used-clothing and consignment stores. This can save 60 to 80 percent off of the regular price of new clothing. No kidding.
- Turn down the hot water thermostat to 100 degrees and save about $20 to $35 a month. Even better, consider getting solar panels and a solar hot water heater. You will get a whopping 30 percent tax credit and reduce your electricity usage a lot. Solar panels have about a 12-year breakeven based on my calculations.
- Consider installing a tankless hot water heater. This appliance heats water only when you need it. You are not paying to keep stored water hot. This can save a lot more money than most people realize.
- Consider installing a geothermal heating and cooling system for your house. In most areas of the country, the difference in cost is offset by the tax credit, and the operating cost is significantly lower than it is for conventional heating and cooling systems.
- Use bathroom fans in the summer to vent the steam and water vapor from your bath or shower. Make sure that your exhaust fan works. Most installed fans are too weak to draw out moisture. Replace the fan, if needed. This step will save you money in removing mildew and mold.
- Add insulation to your attic.
- Insulate your hot water heater and pipes.
- Install a solar powered attic fan in the summer to cool your attic. This will greatly help with your cooling bill, and it will increase the life of your roof.

- Also, consider solar panels for your electricity usage for your home. The cost is about $21,000 to $30,000; however, you will not only get a whopping 30 percent tax credit from the government but you will also get subsidies from both the state and from your utility company. When you run the numbers, solar panels will give you about a 10 percent rate of return on their net cost (after the federal tax credit).
- Raise the thermostat to 73 or 74 in the summer, and lower it to 68 in the winter.
- Shop at eBay and Amazon.com. The vacuum cleaner dealer I bought my vacuum from quoted a price of $279 for a vacuum hose. I found the same hose, brand new, for $179 on the Internet.
- Share the cost of little used equipment such as snowblowers and lawn mowers with your neighbor.
- Cook many items at one time. This eliminates the need to eat out and reduces cooking time. This step could easily save hundreds a week over eating out.
- Get a vacuum sealer to store items. The leftover food will last much longer, and less food will be wasted.
- Always seek out frequent eater plans at restaurants.
- *Never* impulse buy. Wait a day, or wait till you get to the store again.
- Mute your commercials. I like to exercise on my treadmill while commercials are going on.
- Track your expenses as I noted before.
- Ditch your gym for a community center. This could save you $500 a year and provide enough savings for your daughter's wedding alone.
- Consider car pooling. You can find ride shares at www.erideshare.com or at www.carpoolconnect.com or by checking the local bulletin board at your company.
- If you use your cell phone less than 200 minutes per month, consider a prepaid wireless plan.
- Use the library to rent videos and books instead of buying them or even renting them. This could save you $30 per month.
- If you travel, bypass Travelocity.com, Expedia.com, and Orbitz.com. Use KAYAK.com, which searches not only those three sites but many other sites such as priceline.com as well.
- Brown bag it to work instead of eating out. This could easily save you $60 per month.
- Kick your smoking habit. This could save you $50 per week or more.
- Always get credit cards with rewards. I get a 5 percent cash rebate.

- Generally avoid charge cards with fees *unless* you are using them for business charges or the credit card company gives you special benefits such as access to airline clubs.
- Whenever possible, pay off the charge cards each month: 18 percent is a lot of interest to pay if you don't pay off the cards each month.
- Avoid cash advances on charge cards. I was reading that some cards charge a whopping 25 percent on cash advances.
- For your health insurance, use your flexible spending account (FSA) at work, or establish a health savings account (HSA) with a high deductible. These accounts are available to all Americans.
- Bake your own bread.
- Shop at garage sales and Goodwill stores.
- Save gas by running all your errands in one day.
- Make sure that your tires are properly inflated.
- Consider buying compact fluorescent bulbs for your whole home. They reduce energy consumption by as much as 75 percent, and they run much cooler than do incandescent bulbs. In addition, they last longer.
- Here is a big secret: Get at least a dental discount card and maybe even a medical discount card too. Many medical insurance plans and dental insurance plans don't cover big ticket items. For example, medical insurance doesn't ordinarily cover orthotics and cosmetic surgery. Dental insurance is even more limited. This type of insurance usually covers only big ticket items at 50 percent, and it doesn't cover some big ticket items such as dental implants. Moreover, the dental plans usually have a limit of $1,500 per person each year. Dental and medical discount cards can help in ways conventional insurance plans can't. The key is to make sure that your providers are participating members under the dental or medical discount card plan that you get. These plans cost about $80 for individuals and about $129 for families. I saved over $550 on an implant and root canal. I got the card immediately upon finding out from my dentist about needing these procedures. There are no preexisting conditions; however, there might be a 30-day wait before you can use the plan.

"Peter, I do discuss the benefits of getting a health savings account (HSA) in both my home study course *Tax Strategies for Business Professionals* and in my book *Lower Your Taxes—Big Time!*, which can be obtained via my website at www.sandybotkin.com. I just thought I would mention that."

Peter laughed at that obvious plug for my site.

"Yes, Sandy, I do like your material, and I have been recommending it to my clients for years. Anyway, here are more ideas for cutting spending."

- Bundling up your phone, Internet, and TV saves about $50 per month.
- Get a digital thermostat. This will save about 10 percent on your bills. Even better would be a programmable digital thermostat.
- Definitely pay off all credit cards each month and save on huge interest rates that can be as high as 18 percent or, in some cases, even more.
- Raise your car deductible for collision from the usual $250 deductible to $1,000. This will significantly lower the premium.
- Always max out your 401(k) at work *especially* if there is a matching contribution.
- It is almost always cheaper to repair a car than to buy a new one. If you do need to buy a new car, buy one that is used that has an existing warranty left over in case of problems. Always buy a used car instead of a new one. You avoid the major depreciation hit that occurs within the first three years of buying a new car.
- Beware of scams, and especially no-interest deals. It might be that there is no interest charged for only a certain period of time, or it might be that you don't pay any interest for a period of time but the interest will still be accruing, and you'll have to pay it eventually. There is a big difference between being charged no interest at all and being charged interest that accrues but that you don't pay for a while.

"Peter, that was a huge number of very practical tips. This is even better than I anticipated. WOW! I would bet that if my readers implement even half of these tips, they would save as much as they need for any major expenditure."

"Sandy, I can tell you that if people would track their expenses and do what we tell them with Money Mastery or with your Taxbot product, which I like, we could easily show people how to save literally hundreds each month. I have seen some folks save thousands each month by following these tips."

Peter then added, "By the way, Sandy, one thing that we didn't discuss and that I know you talk about a lot in your book *Lower Your Taxes—Big Time!* is tax savings."

I really perked up, which is my custom when talking about taxes. "Yes, taxes are the biggest expense that most people have. Taxes consume about 28 to 35 percent of their monthly income. If they can save some money in taxes, it is better than a raise since it is tax free. Saving a few thousand in taxes with legal tax planning can make an enormous difference in people's lives."

"Yup, you are right, Sandy. As you note, the best way to save taxes is to start a legitimate home-based business and use the tremendous tax benefits that accrue to being in business to your advantage. Being able to write off part of your house, your spouse (by making your spouse your employee), and the equivalent of your kid's education and wedding, while being able to set up a pension that makes any government pension seem small by comparison, is *huge*."

Grimacing, I noted, "Yes, but I never tell people to start a business just for losses or just for tax breaks. That has never made sense to me. People have to try to make money in order to get the great business tax benefits accruing to them. As long as they are running their business with an honest expectation of profit, they will be able to get many of the same tax breaks that companies like General Motors can get."

Peter chuckled and said, "Yes, but they won't get the same government bailout that General Motors or the banks got."

We both chuckled at that, but I added, "Yes, in a way, they will. They can get their own personal bailouts with tax breaks. It may not be equal to that of the banks, but it certainly will help a lot."

Peter agreed and noted, "In tomorrow's session, we will expand on this and show everyone the best way to save for college. Then, in the session after that [Chapter 6], we will discuss how most people can get out of debt in less than 12 years, including their mortgage debt."

Lori perked up and said, "Wow, that will be exciting and will change a lot of lives."

Peter smiled and noted, "Yes, we could change many lives throughout the world if people would simply listen to us. Sadly, more people will read Harry Potter than a book like this."

Peter then said, "Okay, guys, what did you learn from our conversation?"

A Review of What You Have Learned

Looking at our notes, I answered as follows:
- The average savings rate is abysmal for most people. This has to change if they want a successful retirement.
- You should have three types of savings plans.
- The first savings plan is for retirement. You should save at least 10 percent of your paychecks.
- The second savings plan is for unexpected large expenses such as repairs, and these savings can be part of your reserve accounts.
- The third savings plan is for expected large ticket items such as homes, education for kids, weddings, and cars.
- There are two essential and pervasive rules for saving money.

> - ₒ The first is that you should never borrow for consumer goods including vacations.
> - ₒ The second rule is that you can have anything you want, but you can't have everything you want. Tough choices need to be made.
> - There are five secrets to finding the money you need to meet your savings goals.
>   1. Never borrow for a consumer good.
>   2. You can have anything that you want. You just can't have everything that you want.
>   3. Pay yourself first. If you don't see the money, you won't spend it.
>   4. Learn the difference between a need and a want.
>   5. You *really, really* need to track your spending for at least three consecutive months.
> - Take tax planning very seriously.

Use the tips in this chapter to find ways to save additional money for your goals. Even using a few of the tips can result in hundreds of dollars of extra money that you didn't know you could save.

Notes

1. See http://www.doctorhousingbubble.com/american-savings-americans-save-an-average-of-392-per-year-total-consumer-debt-is-over-25-trillion-the-dark-knight-of-debt/.
2. See http://www.moneyrelationship.com/retirement/the-average-net-worth-of-americans-where-do-you-stand/.
3. See http://www.freemoneyfinance.com/2011/02/finances-of-the-average-american.html.

5

Saving Money, Part II: How to Pay for College

Successful colleges will start laying plans for a new stadium; unsuccessful ones will start hunting [for] a new coach.

—Will Rogers

What You Will Learn
- The four best ways to save for college costs
- The cons of incurring substantial debt for a dream school's undergraduate education
- Three ways to get in-state tuition for an out-of-state student

I couldn't meet with Peter on the next day due to commitments, so he had his partner, Alan, meet with me. Alan is an interesting guy. He is almost as friendly as Peter and certainly as knowledgeable. Alan, however, is more business driven than Peter. He tends to be more of a no-nonsense kind of guy.

I also brought my son, Matt, who will be coauthoring this book. Matt is an interesting guy to say the least. He was only 23 when he achieved a master's in financial planning, got his CPA, and passed the Certified Financial Planners exam, and he is now attending law school. He would, therefore, be a great help to me.

When we got to their offices, Alan certainly lived up to my perception of him when, with very little small talk, and after introducing him to my son, Matt, and my wife, Lori, he stated, "Okay, we want to discuss saving for college tuition, right?"

I responded, "Yes. Peter suggested that this be the next topic."

"Sandy, I am going to discuss the four best ways to save for college and graduate school tuition that everyone in the United States should know. For those that live outside of the United States, there might be similar programs available in their country. Moreover, some of the information that will be discussed about indebtedness for that dream school will also be valuable to your readers."

The Four Best Ways to Save for College Costs

"There are four principal ways to save for college assuming that you don't want to take on any indebtedness upon graduation. The first two, and the best two, are known as *qualified tuition plans*. They consist of two different types of plans: *prepaid tuition plans* and *qualified savings plans*."

Prepaid Tuition Plans

"The first type, *prepaid tuition plans*, covers four years of college tuition, as well as required fees, regardless of the rate of inflation. Generally for a flat charge, which can be paid over time, parents can ensure that all tuition and required fees will be paid to the college. It essentially locks in future tuition at today's rates, which can be a steal considering how much college tuition has risen over the years. The prepaid tuition plans are generally run by the states specifically for their state universities. Moreover, any monies used for the tuition and required fees are tax free! In addition, you can change beneficiaries. Thus, if your kids don't want or need the money for college, it can be used for your grandkids or nephews, and so on.

"I should note that a number of top private schools have set up a consortium that will accept prepaid tuition for future tuition costs, inflation increases, and required fees, which is called the *independent 529 plan*. This is a form of prepaid tuition that will be accepted by hundreds of private schools and lets you lock in the future tuition at today's rates. You can find out about this private plan by going to https://www.private college529.com/OFI529/.

"Although I really like the state prepaid tuition plans, one problem with these prepayment plans is that they are woefully underfunded in many cases. I do wonder whether they will be able to fulfill their obligations."

I asked, "So, Alan, I just want to make sure that all of the readers understand this point. If I pay into the Maryland or Utah or some other state prepaid tuition plan, I am guaranteed to have my tuition and required fees covered for my grandchild in 18 years if he or she goes to a home state school where I have contributed to his or her prepaid tuition?"

"Yes, Sandy. That is exactly what the prepaid tuition plan will do. You will essentially be charged today's tuition rates that will lock in these rates forever for each beneficiary that you fund with this plan. Considering that college tuition has risen faster than almost any other cost, this could be a great deal. I suggested this to one of my clients, and she has been sending me thank you notes each year that her daughter is in college. Again, all this assumes that the states have the money to meet these guarantees. Since they are basically unfunded obligations by the states, this could be a real problem in the future."

I was still a bit puzzled when I asked, "Alan, what happens in most states if a student doesn't want to go to a state university to which the state prepayment is made?"

"Good question, Sandy. First, these prepaid tuition plans apply to any state school in that state. However, if the beneficiary of the plan goes out of state, then the rules depend on the plan. Some plans simply give you back your money with some nominal interest, which is a bad deal. Many states, like your home state, Maryland, will pay what they would have paid in tuition to their own state universities. Thus, you are ensuring some degree of guarantee even in terms of inflation."

I said, "Alan, we did this with my daughter, who attends an out-of-state university in Ohio. Maryland paid to the University of Cincinnati the amount of tuition the state would have paid to the University of Maryland. It was fabulous! I have a lot of jealous friends.

"Alan, I have one further question. Should the prepaid tuition account be owned by the child or the parent?"

Alan smiled and noted, "Prepaid tuition funds are counted as assets when financial aid is calculated. If the parent owns the fund, only 5 percent of that money is deemed usable for tuition each year for financial need calculations. However, 35 percent of the money in the kid's name is deemed usable for tuition for financial need calculations. This is because the financial aid folks feel that parents will need some assets for retirement sooner than their kids will need assets. Thus, having the prepaid tuition plan in the name of the parent might be better if you will be filing for financial need aid. However, there is one situation, which you personally utilized, in which having the prepaid tuition plan in the kid's name will be beneficial: when you want to get in-state tuition for an out-of-state student, which we will discuss later on in our meeting."

Lori smiled at that and said, "Yes, that worked very well."

Qualified Savings Plans

Alan then continued with his normally focused attitude by saying, "The second method, and in my opinion the preferred approach, is to use the normal qualified tuition plans known as *qualified savings plans*. These are akin to investing money in a mutual fund in that investments are made in a wide variety of stocks and bonds and consist of funds by many participants. They come with no guarantees, and they do not lock in the future cost of tuition. However, unlike prepaid tuition plans that are available only for qualified tuition and mandatory fees, these plans can be used for any school's tuition plus room, board, supplies, Internet, and even required computer purchases as long as you are attending school at least half-time."

Alan enthusiastically continued: "I really like these Section 529 plans because they offer great flexibility regardless of the school that your kid wants to attend. In addition, the monies can be used for professional and graduate programs." He then noted the following:

> **Probably the best approach is to fully fund your state's prepaid tuition plan and add some extra money to a qualified savings plan in case your kid doesn't go to your state university.**

I was eager to add the following to Alan's comments: "Alan, in addition, many states give a deduction or credit for contributions to qualified in-state tuition plans, particularly for prepaid tuition plans. Thus, if you make any contributions to these, you should check with your accountant about your state's treatment of these contributions.

"Also, you are generally limited each year to the annual gift tax limitations (assuming you don't want to incur a gift tax) of $13,000 per kid if you are single and $26,000 if you are married, although you do get a lifetime gift tax exemption of $5 million in addition to these yearly exemption amounts.

"Finally, there is an interesting gift tax rule that allows you to contribute up to five years of the annual gift limit in one year and elect to amortize the gifts over the five years for gift tax purposes. This simply means that a single taxpayer could gift $65,000 and a married taxpayer could gift up to $130,000 in the first year without having to use any part of their lifetime exemption."

Alan grinned and said, "I figured you would add some tax tips, and you are absolutely right about that."

Setting Up a Roth IRA for the Child's Earned Income

Chuckling, I said, "I bet I know the third method to finance a college education, which is to set up a Roth IRA for any of the child's earned income."

Alan quickly responded with, "Yes, you are right. The government allows people to put 100 percent of their earned income up to $5,000 each year into a Roth IRA for either retirement or for qualified tuition provided that their total income is below certain limits. Withdrawals are tax free if taken after age 59½ **or** for qualified higher education expenses. Moreover, these expenses include tuition at an 'eligible educational institution (which means accredited and eligible for federal student loans)' and room and board if the student is enrolled at least half-time. Qualified higher education expenses also include fees and the cost of books, supplies, and equipment required for enrollment or attendance. This is a great addition to the qualified tuition plans; however, the student has to have earned income in order to qualify for the Roth IRA. Thus, we have the two types of qualified tuition plans and the Roth IRA. There is also an educational IRA, but it is a lot more limited, and thus, I don't mention it."

"Okay, Alan, so what is the fourth method of paying for college costs other than by assuming debt?" I asked.

Having a Rich Relative Pay Tuition and Other College Expenses Directly to the College

"The fourth method is to have a rich parent or grandparent make the full tuition payments right to the university or college."

I roared over that while saying, "Yes, but that requires rich relatives."

Alan responded, "Yes, but by paying funds right to the college, there is no yearly gift tax limits that you would find in funding qualified saving plans, and the money is not included in the estate of the relative in case he or she dies."

The Cons of Incurring Substantial Debt for a Dream School's Undergraduate Education

Lori then inquired, "Alan, I see a lot of parents and/or kids incurring substantial debt for what they consider their dream school. There is a lot of debate about this on various college forums such as 'College Confidential.' What is your take on this?"

Alan looked at us grimly and composed his thoughts for a few seconds before answering. "Let me say at the outset that college should be about fit. If you have a kid that has learning disabilities, you may not have a lot of choices. In fact, there is a great book, *Peterson's Colleges with Programs for Students with Learning Disabilities or Attention Deficit Disorders*, that I recommend. Likewise, if you have a kid who wants a major that isn't offered by your local state universities, he or she may have to go to an expensive school. If you have a kid who gets a great scholarship, attending an out-of-state school might actually be less expensive than the in-state alternative. However, I will tell you that I have never met anyone, in my 30-plus years of financial coaching, who was happy with incurring substantial debt for his or her undergraduate school or even graduate school. Most people that I meet who have significant debt incurred from undergraduate studies are really in financial trouble. In fact, there was a recent article in the Money section of *Time* magazine online titled, 'Sixty and Still Not Out of Student Loan Debt' (see http://moneyland.time.com/2012/04/03/60-and-still-not-out-of-student-loan-debt-seniors-facing-36-billion-in-college-loans/). It is a very sobering article about student loan debt."

Alan excitedly continued with, "The problem is that both the students and parents don't want to understand financial reality. First, most schools in my experience pay only about 50 percent of the real financial need for college costs. There are exceptions, but I have found that 50 percent is the general rule, and parents should be aware of this. Moreover, if the kid has a high student debt of $150,000 as an example, this could cost a whopping $1,819 a month for 10 years! Even at $100,000 of debt, the cost would be about $1,212 per month for 10 years. This monthly debt burden has to be compared to the starting salary for most kids, which is between $3,200 and $4,500 per month. In addition, at least one-third of their salary goes out in taxes. This leaves about $2,100 to $3,000 left (after taxes) on a monthly basis to pay not only the debt payment but also rent, food, clothing, automobile, gas, insurances, gifts, repairs, entertainment, travel, utilities, Internet, and so on. It would be almost impossible for a new college graduate to pay even $1,200 per month, let alone $1,800 per month in addition to their living expenses.

"Even $50,000 of total debt would require payments of $607 per month, which would be very difficult to do. Thus, incurring substantial debt of over $50,000 for undergraduate education would, in my opinion, be very foolhardy."

"Alan, I completely agree. Even worse, the IRS allows you to deduct only up to $2,500 a year in student loan interest. This means that you can't deduct interest on student loan debt above approximately $33,000. Thus, I would go so far as to say that kids should limit student loan debt to no more than $33,000 if they can."

"Absolutely, Sandy. In addition, most students need to understand that there are two types of student loans."

Lori looked puzzled at this. "Alan, I thought a loan was a loan."

Alan chuckled and said, "No, there are two types of loans. One is a *subsidized loan*, which is lent by the government and provides that no interest be charged or accrued nor payments be made until the kid gets out of school. The second type, which I consider to be a dangerous scam, is the *unsubsidized loan*, which also provides that no payments be made until the student gets out of school. However, it differs from the subsidized loan in that interest does accumulate while the kid is in school. Thus, a measly $30,000 in total debt might actually be $42,000 or more in debt by the time the kid graduates. An $80,000 unsubsidized loan can be $110,000 or more by the time the student graduates. It is vital to try to get subsidized loans, which are sadly available based only on financial need and are very limited in amounts."

"Alan, one thing that my daughter's best friend did was to work throughout school and in the summer."

Alan grimaced while noting, "Yes, working at a job can reduce your debt. The problem is that generally kids who work part time don't make enough money to really affect the indebtedness situation. It certainly beats a 'stick in the eye,' but it really doesn't help that much financially, and it takes a lot of time away from their studies."

Thinking of what my parents did for me, I asked Alan, "How about having the parents incur the debt for their kids? Certainly, parents can make more money."

Alan pursed his lips and said, "I don't have a problem with parents' paying for their kid's education or even taking out a loan *as long as* they can do so without compromising their retirement. The problem is that most people can't afford to spend $100,000, not to mention incur this amount as additional debt. As Peter noted, the average net worth for people age 40 to 60 isn't much, and it is usually under $100,000. Paying for private school or incurring a large indebtedness could be financial suicide for the parents. I guess if the parents were rich or had very strong earning potential without having a lot of debt themselves, I might think differently.

"Sadly, too many parents give into their kid's desire to attend that dream school without having the financial wherewithal to pay for it and without having a good enough reason for incurring the expense at these expensive schools. Also, Sandy, here is the real kicker. Most studies have shown that top students who attend state universities do just as well financially over their lifetime as those who go to top private schools or Ivy League schools."

I wryly noted, "Alan, you would never know that from the promotional literature these expensive schools provide. You would think that they provide an instant ticket to financial heaven if you graduate from there."

Alan snorted and said, "Yes, these schools do tend to exaggerate the benefits of being a student there. They have that fancy marketing literature with pictures of ivy-covered buildings and smiling, good-looking students, and pictures of successful alumni, which helps fuel that false dream. Many kids soon learn at graduation that their dream school has become a nightmare. It is very sad."

Alan then added, "Interestingly, some schools have some form of debt counseling upon graduation, but none that I know of have any debt counseling during the admission process.

"One further point that I want to make is that if after graduation the kids are unemployed or can't afford the repayments, they might be eligible to participate in the federal income-based repayment program whereby federal loan payments on college debt are limited to only 10 percent of their income. Moreover, the whole remaining debt is wiped clean after 25 years. However, this only applies to federal student loans and *not* to private loans. Moreover, to get this income repayment protection, you have to authorize the IRS to provide last year's tax return to the Department of Education."

Alan then added, "Sadly, federal loans are not plentiful, and they are severely limited in amount. Thus, most loans that students incur are not subject to this income repayment law."

Three Ways to Get In-State Tuition for an Out-of-State Student

"Alan, I want to share one other idea that I wrote about that may help your clients and that helped us with my daughter's college costs. The report that I wrote was *Getting In-State Tuition Rates for Out-of-State Students.*"

The Student Applies Through an Academic Common Market

"Among the techniques mentioned, I do want to focus on three of them. The first is that many schools belong to a form of *academic common market*, which quietly offers in-state tuition rates for out-of-state students if the major that the student wants is not available in his or her home state. Thus, a student who wants to pursue a major, such as animation or digital arts or Jewish or Islamic studies, that isn't offered in his or her home state can go to a school in the regional consortium to which the student's home state belongs and attend that out-of-state school at in-state tuition rates. This is a form of reciprocity among the states within defined regions. Right now the following four regional programs have been set up for this type of reciprocity."

- **New England Board of Higher Education (NEBHE):** This includes Connecticut, Maine, Massachusetts, New Hampshire, Rhode Island, and Vermont. The board can be reached by calling 617-357-9620.

- **Midwestern Higher Education Compact (MHEC):** This includes Kansas, Michigan, Minnesota, Missouri, Nebraska, and North Dakota. The compact can be reached by calling 612-626-1602.
- **Western Interstate Commission for Higher Education (WICHE):** This includes most of the western states: Alaska, Arizona, California, Colorado, Idaho, Montana, Nevada, New Mexico, North Dakota, Oregon, South Dakota, Utah, Washington, and Wyoming. (Yes, North Dakota belongs to two associations, and it is the only state that does.) It also includes Hawaii. The commission can be reached by calling 303-541-0200.
- **Southern Regional Education Board (SREB) Academic Common Market:** This includes Alabama, Arkansas, Delaware, Florida, Georgia, Kentucky, Louisiana, Maryland, Mississippi, North Carolina, Oklahoma, South Carolina, Tennessee, Texas, Virginia, and West Virginia. The board can be reached by calling 404-875-9211.

The Student and/or the Parents Move to the State the Year Before the Student Applies as an In-State Resident

"The second method of getting in-state tuition is to simply switch to become a resident in year 1 and claim this in-state status starting in year 2. Thus, you would immediately obtain, for example, a new driver's license and voter registration, and you would file tax returns for the new state. The catch is that this works easily only in Florida, California, Colorado, Kentucky, Missouri, New Jersey, and Utah. States in which students will find this change fairly hard to accomplish without a lot of prior planning are Alabama, Georgia, Iowa, and Minnesota. States that make it very hard to change residency absent one of the other methods noted here are Arizona, Illinois, Indiana, Maryland, North Carolina, Ohio, Tennessee, Texas, Virginia, Washington, and Wisconsin."

The Student Establishes Independent Status and In-State Residency

"If your kid is not in a state where it is easy to change residence status, there is still a way to obtain in-state tuition, and that is for the student to establish independent status, which is a method that worked for my daughter. Once kids have attended a college for a year, they can usually apply for a change in resident status. This is a little secret that many schools tend to hide."

Alan interrupted me and said, "Yes, I didn't know this myself until you pointed it out to me."

"Well, obtaining this status takes planning. Kids will need to show that they are financially independent of the parents and have truly established state residency. Thus, they will need to change their driver's license and voter registration to their new state of residence as soon as possible in their freshman year. In addition, they will need to file tax returns in their new state and *not* be claimed as a dependent of the parents, which is the only drawback. The real kicker though is that they need to demonstrate that all expenses for tuition, room, and board are being paid by the student out of the student's own funds! This can be accomplished either by working or, with proper planning, by having sufficient assets in the kid's name such as with qualified tuition plans.

"We did this for my daughter, Allison. For years, we were putting money in her name in order to save up for college. This included a prepaid tuition plan and a qualified savings plan. We stopped claiming her as a dependent in her freshman year. She paid all of her own expenses including tuition, rent, and utilities. She was granted in-state status for tuition purposes in her third year, which saved us over $10,000 per year! It is doable, but it takes advance planning."

Alan smiled and noted, "I really like that technique. However, I want to note that putting money in a kid's name has some possible undesirable consequences for some people. First, for financial aid purposes, any funds or investments in the kid's name (other than assets located in Roth IRAs, insurance policies, or annuities) are counted more heavily against the student for financial aid than if the same funds were in the parent's name. Thus, if you are considering a private school for your kid's college education, keeping assets in the parent's name would be the better choice. However, if it is possible or probable that a kid will attend a public university out of state, this technique of establishing independent status can work very well, as it did for your daughter."

Alan quickly added, "The other major potential risk to this strategy is that by putting funds in your child's name, it is the child's money. Thus, the child can use the funds for any purpose and is not obligated to use the funds for college costs."

Matt looked at me and said, "Don't worry, Dad, I only have two more years of law school," which made all of us laugh.

I said, "Also, Alan, not every state offers the ability to switch status from being a nonresident to that of being a resident. Indiana, in particular, didn't offer this benefit. Ohio, on the other hand, does offer this benefit with some proper planning. Thus, parents *really* need to read over the website for the out-of-state school to see if this technique is available. If not, parents may have to use one of the other techniques that I have noted in Appendix B."

"Okay, folks, let's see what you learned here."

A Review of What You Have Learned

Looking at my notes, I responded as follows:

- There are two types of qualified tuition plans: prepaid tuition plans and qualified savings plans.
  1. A prepaid tuition plan generally applies to your in-state public universities; however, a number of private schools now offer independent 529 plans. A prepaid plan covers solely tuition and required fees. It locks in the tuition at today's rates forever. It is fully transferable too. All payments made for tuition and fees at accredited universities are tax free. However, the worry is that the states won't have the funds to honor their guarantees.
  2. A qualified savings plan resembles a mutual fund in some respects and is strictly a savings plan. There are no tuition guarantees. However, the funds can be used for any school, and they can be used for tuition, fees, room and board, required supplies and equipment such as computers, and even Internet charges. Distributions are tax free when used for the qualified educational expenses at accredited colleges.
- A Roth IRA can also be used for qualified educational expenses including tuition, fees, room and board (if the housing is owned by the institution), and required supplies and equipment. You can fund the Roth IRA with 100 percent of earned income each year up to $5,000 per year.
- Parents or grandparents can pay the tuition and fees directly to the college without being subject to any annual gift tax limits.
- Incurring substantial debt for undergraduate education is not advisable since most kids won't make enough to pay back the loans. Substantial debt is generally around $50,000 or more, but some commentators feel that anything over $33,000 is too much because the interest paid on loans above that amount is generally not deductible due to the $2,500 annual deduction limit for student loan interest.[1]
- Parents should also *not* incur substantial debt for their kid's education if it would severely compromise their retirement; however, this is a choice that parents have to make in consideration of their particular circumstances.
- If your child attends an out-of-state public school, he or she might be able to get in-state tuition if the school is a member of a consortium that your state belongs to and if the child wants a major that isn't offered by your home state schools.
- The parent and/or the child can move to the state in which the child wants to attend college before the child applies to that state's university. Thus, the family would meet the residency requirement of having lived in the state at least one year before the application so that the child can be deemed an in-state resident.
- Finally, your child might be able to change his or her status to that of being an in-state resident by relocating into the state and changing his or her voting registration and driver's license to reflect that. Students who do this would also have to show that they are truly paying their bills with their own funds. This could be established even if those funds might have initially come from the parents or grandparents. This does take some advance planning. Moreover, not every

state allows for this type of residency change. People really need to check the proposed college's website to see if the student will be able to switch to in-state status.

"So, how did we do?"

Alan smirked, "You guys are my best students. Tomorrow will be the conclusion of our three-part discussion. It will deal with debt reduction. We will change a lot of lives with this."

Lori perked up, "I can't wait to hear what you have to say. I know a number of people who are in debt up to their ears."

Notes

1. This all assumes that the student loan rate will remain at the current 8 percent rate.

6

Getting Out of Debt Forever

Some debts are fun when you are acquiring them, but none are fun when you set about retiring them.

—Ogden Nash

What You Will Learn
- The magnitude of the debt problem
- Ten reasons people overspend and have too much debt
- What factors show that you have a potentially serious debt problem
- How much debt is too much
- The seven steps people need to take to get out of debt
- FICO scores and dealing with credit bureaus

As we were driving to our appointment with Peter, I couldn't help thinking about my friend who felt that his wife was constantly overspending. He politely asked her, "Honey, do you know the opposite of spend?" She thought about this for a few seconds and said, "Charging, of course?" He knew he was in trouble.

Seeing Peter at the door was always refreshing. His warm "How are you doing, fella," always brought a smile to both Lori and me. We couldn't wait to start discussing getting out of debt, which is a huge problem for most people around the world. Peter also remembered meeting my son Matt and greeted him with a warm handshake. After offering us some nice lemonade, Peter began, "I am so glad that we will be discussing this topic. It is a monumental problem to everyone, and it may well be the single biggest killer of wealth."

I couldn't help thinking of my friend's overspending wife.

The Magnitude of the Debt Problem

"Let me give you an indication of how big this debt problem is. The average person can go 17 days without a paycheck."

All of us looked at each other in disbelief.

Peter then said, "One out of five people has over $10,000 in consumer debt alone. In addition, about 41 percent paid nothing on the principal balance of their debts. In fact, according to MSN.com, 43 percent of American families spend more than they earn each year, and personal bankruptcies have doubled during the past decade. In fact, the average person spends 18 percent or more of his or her yearly income on debt, and in many cases, it is significantly more than 20 percent.

"Even worse, young people are not showing any signs of improvement. According to a recent *USA Today* article, the average credit card debt for people between ages 20 and 29 is $1,800, and total debt for twentysomethings averaged $45,000."[1]

Peter then added, "Schools are not doing the job. Only 13 states require students to take a finance class. Moreover, 60 percent of people ages 18 to 34 don't even keep a budget."

Lori, Matt, and I looked at each other in disbelief. Lori broke the tension when she said, "Aren't you glad that I am not high maintenance," which made all of us laugh.

Peter then added, "Finally, most people don't realize that education debt is the fastest growing debt in the United States, which makes sense considering how high tuition is getting at schools these days. In fact average student loan debt for the class of 2010 was $25,000, yet they have an unemployment rate of 12.4 percent.[2]

"The good news is that Americans are shedding debt faster than ever before (which is less than I can say about those unwanted pounds of weight) but usually as a result of defaults and foreclosures."

I just had to ask Peter, "So what is causing this problem?"

Ten Reasons People Overspend and Have Too Much Debt

"Sandy, we aren't born with debt. In fact, we are born with no debt, other than maybe the debt to our parents for bringing us into this world. Sadly, there are many factors that contribute to this disease, and believe me, it is a disease."

1. Denial

Peter then continued, "First, **most folks are in denial**. We get clients only after they have almost hit rock bottom. People are generally unwilling to change their behavior unless they absolutely have no choice. There are a couple of warning signs that clearly indicate that, as was said in the *Music Man* play, 'There is trouble in River City.'

"Here are the following signs of too much debt."

1. You have maxed out your credit limit.
2. You have debt that isn't being reduced. Even worse, your total debt is increasing.
3. Over 27 percent of your total income is being used for payments on your debts.
4. You tend to argue with your spouse or partner a lot about debt.
5. You are constantly taking cash advances from one credit card and using them to pay other cards.
6. You have no idea of exactly how much you owe.

Peter continued, "If folks would realize that these are signs of big trouble, most people would be better off."

2. Instant Gratification

"The second reason for this problem, and it is the widespread root of the problem, is that . . . drum roll . . . **people have high expectations for instant gratification**. Most people are *very* shortsighted. We want our companies to produce profits now, and we do not want to wait for the long term. Folks want things now and are not willing to invest or save for their future. Thus, most people want *premature instant gratification*. This is caused by buying what they want, when they want it, and *not* considering whether they need it, as was discussed in the prior chapters."

"Peter," I said. "Let's remind people of the difference between a need and a want. I know that we discussed this in the savings chapter [Chapter 4], but I think that it could use repeating."

Peter chuckled and said, "Okay. A *need* is something that you must have. A *want* is something that you want to have but don't absolutely need. For example, you might absolutely need a car to get to work, but you don't need a new car or a new luxury car. You might need to eat, but you don't need to eat out every day when eating at home will fill the same need. You might need to have nice clothes for work, but you can satisfy that need by going to Nordstrom's Rack or Target instead of some nice designer boutique. Do people really need a latte or Starbucks coffee every day at $4 per day, or would Maxwell House or Dunkin' Donuts coffee do the trick?"

Lori perked up at that last comment and said, "Sandy, I don't care. I am not giving up my Starbucks morning coffee," which made both Peter and me laugh.

Peter then said, "Lori, you can keep your Starbucks coffee as long as you know that you are trading off something else. We all want some form of instant gratification; however, there is a cost for too much of it," Peter diplomatically noted.

I said, "Yes, I was reading that there are a large number of women who are purchasing dresses that are designer dresses, normally sold for thousands, but sold over the Internet at discounted prices of $1,000 and more. It seems to me that they need designer dresses as much as they need a hole in the head. This is clearly a want and not a need."

Peter completely agreed.

Peter then smoothly continued: "**The key to getting needs over wants is to understand that spending is emotional.** Nothing gets people more emotional than money. You can see it all the time when a will is read and some relatives get less than they wanted. There are *huge* estate fights among beneficiaries because of the money. The key is the following."

> **People need to become much more logical about their money and less emotional.**

Wagging my finger, I said, "Peter, this may be true, but it is easier said than done."

Peter laughed and suggested helpfully, "Yes, but if folks simply focus on what they are spending and why they are buying a particular item, they can become more logical about it. The key is to not be in denial. If you, for example, shop every time you get upset with your spouse, this becomes an emotional buy. Understanding this is the first step to recovery. There is even a name coined for this behavior: *shopaholicism*. People shop in order to feel better about their lives or about themselves. These must be identified as emotional purchases and should stop. One approach that we have recommended at our firm is to have a monthly savings budget for those emotional purchases that we all make intermittently. The key is to not spend more than what is allocated by the monthly savings plan."

3. Unexpected Expenses

"Okay, the third reason that folks get in over their head with debt is that **they have to deal with unexpected large expenses**, which is a phenomenon also known as *crisis spending*. Something breaks down, or there is a leak in the roof, or a tooth breaks, and big unexpected expenses must be incurred.

If people don't have the money, they have to incur some consumer debt. Big, unexpected medical and dental bills are some of the most common culprits for causing this."

When we started working on this book, we anticipated that Peter would cover this topic. I told him, "I absolutely agree, which is why I have discussed the need for a reserve account as the essential first step that people should undertake. That is in my second chapter."

4. The Get-Rich-Quicker Mentality

Peter nodded in agreement and then said, "Okay, since you will have discussed this, I will go on to the fourth reason. This isn't discussed by a lot of financial commentators, but it is an all-too-common problem: **people have a get-rich-quicker mentality.**"

Being very puzzled, I said, "You may be right, but why would a get-rich-quicker mentality cause overspending?"

Peter chuckled and said, "Many companies are now trying to monetize the savings you will receive from buying a product. They note that the product will pay for itself. Thus, if you buy a new hot water heater or furnace, it might save enough in fuel to pay for itself in six years. Solar panels supposedly have a breakeven in 12 years, and so on. Folks reason that by buying these products, they will save money in the long run and get rich quicker. In fact, there might even be coupons promising discounts from the normal pricing. The problem with that thinking is that it often leads to multiple large purchases. People are focused on the savings they hope to make, and they don't take into account their prior spending. Thus, they overspend on too many products."

5. Borrowing for Consumer Goods

"The fifth reason," Peter said, "is that **people borrow money to buy consumer goods**, which is always a bad idea. Remember when I said that we are born without debt? What happens is that we get bombarded with buying messages all day. People want to go on vacation, and they charge on their credit cards all the expenses that they might not be able to afford. They need to buy the latest advertised gadget. They then charge various commitments such as dental bills to their credit cards. They might even charge large expenses such as weddings or big parties to their credit cards. This adds up. If they can't pay these off when due, they are incurring an 18 percent interest charge on consumable items that have no value."

Peter continued excitedly, "I have said it before, and I will say it again: **people should *not* borrow for consumable purchases that they can't pay off immediately. They should save the money beforehand to make those purchases.**"

Being a bit perplexed, which my kids will tell you is my usual state of affairs, I said, "Wait a minute. What exactly is 'borrowing for consumer goods'? Can't anything such as a house or a car be deemed a consumer good?"

Peter chuckled a bit and said, "Yes, Sandy, you raise a good point. To me, consumer goods are purchases that don't generally appreciate in value. Actually, not all debts have equal value. There are both good and bad debts, and people need to understand the difference."

Peter continued, "*Good debts* are those incurred for needs and are usually for things that appreciate in value. And they must, *must* be affordable. Let me elaborate. Debt incurred to purchase a home would normally qualify as a good debt because we all need to live somewhere anyway, and real estate does tend to appreciate in the long term. However, if you are house rich and can't afford anything else, it wouldn't be such a good debt. Debt incurred to buy rental property would normally be considered to be good debt because of the long-term appreciation potential of real estate. However, if it creates a strongly negative cash flow, it might not be a good debt. Cars are needed commodities. Thus, incurring a debt for a car would probably be deemed a good debt, but I personally would advise people to save enough money to enable them to pay cash for the car because cars don't appreciate in value.

"In fact, I would even classify educational debt as good debt because of the long-term benefits of education *as long as* the debt isn't excessive. I personally feel that anything over $33,000 in debt, especially if it is from a private, unsubsidized lender, is too much educational debt. However, that is my personal opinion."

I added, "Peter, I would also imagine that if someone incurred a debt with the Small Business Administration to start a business, it would be a good debt as long as it was possible to pay it back from the business income."

Peter agreed.

6. Equating Self-Worth with Net Worth

"Now for the sixth reason people get in over their head financially: **people equate their self-worth with their net worth**. It is astounding to me that many people view their life by the number of things that they have or their perceived lifestyle as others might view it. This is so extraordinarily stupid, I just can't explain it. However, it is clearly the case for many people. Just consider how most car commercials seem to equate buying a car with sexy girls, thus, giving the clear message that a new car will make a guy a chick magnet."

7. The Inability to Earn Enough Money

"Okay, the seventh reason is simply that **some people are unable to earn enough money.** If you are spending more than you are taking in, you will incur debt. This is why our discussion about savings in the prior two chapters [Chapters 4 and 5] must be read together with this chapter."

Peter grimly added, "Let me give you some statistics for average people on what they spend, from their gross income, in various categories. This will give you an idea of where your money goes."

- 28 to 45 percent in total taxes
- 20 to 25 percent in housing
- 15 to 20 percent for food, clothing, and dry cleaning
- 5 to 10 percent for transportation, which included all vehicle expenses and payments

"This leaves between zero and 32 percent for everything else such as medical and dental needs, education for the kids, retirement, repairs, smoking, gifts, insurance, fun, and other loans.

"Here is a great example of what a little overspending can do. If you were to go to a movie and dinner once a week, it would probably cost you about $120 a month or more."

Lori sarcastically said, "I wish it were only $120 a month. We can spend that much on one Saturday night," to which Matt and I chuckled.

Peter waved Lori off and said, "Yes, we are being very conservative here. Thus, if we were to save the same $120 per month for 12 months, assuming a long-term interest rate for earnings of 6 percent, we would have at retirement an extra $230,036. Thus, cutting this down to once in two weeks would put an extra $115,000 in your pocket at retirement, and this is just one small thing.

"Here is another startling example. If you were to eliminate that $4 daily latte, over your lifetime, it would be worth an extra $214,700 at retirement! Maybe folks should reconsider that daily latte.

"I will promise you, Sandy and Lori and anyone else reading this book, that **saving money is very simple to do, but it does take some planning and motivation.** Giving up that latte, cigarette, or some entertainment might not seem like a big deal, but it can make a *huge* difference for your retirement or for your kid's education."

Peter then noted, "I will say it again: **You can have anything you want. You just can't have everything you want.**"

8. Lying to Your Spouse or Significant Other

"Reason eight," Peter went on, "is that **people lie to their spouse or significant other.** Financial dealings with spouses, partners, and significant others have to be both transparent and honest. If one person is secretly spending money unwisely without good communication among the parties, it can be a financial train wreck. It is crucial that everyone understand and agree to a spending plan and especially so before entering into any big expenditure." Peter then added, "Think of your financial life as a rowboat with two rowers. If one rower is rowing from front to back and the other rower is doing the reverse, the boat won't move much. All involved parties have to be rowing the same way and be on the same communication wavelength."

Lori, Matt, and I all agreed that this was important.

9. Risking Home or Retirement

"Reason nine," Peter added very seriously, "is that **people risk their home or retirement, which they should** *rarely* **do.**"

I decided to quiz Peter on this by stating, "Peter, people usually need a mortgage on their home in order to buy their home. Thus, how can you say this?"

He quickly retorted, "Sandy, I am *not* saying that you shouldn't have a mortgage on your home in order to acquire your home. I am not against that at all, although I do believe in paying off the mortgage as quickly as possible. What I am against is people mortgaging their home or putting a lien on their retirement for obligations incurred during life.

"For example, as you know, home equity loans allow for the deduction of interest on loans up to $100,000 of debt. Many people use these loans to buy a car, or they pledge their home for a loan in order to pay for college or start a business believing that at least they can deduct the interest. I do *not* recommend doing this. **Your home has to be your last bastion of defense, and it must be your safety net.** I do *not* recommend mortgaging it or putting a lien on your retirement for almost any reason except when you absolutely, positively have no other choice. Even then, I would try to find another way around doing this."

Being a bit excited about this, I noted, "Yes, I have seen people lose their homes because they couldn't pay the car loans or make the education loans. I would add one more thing to this discussion. Be *very careful* about cosigning for a loan. If the original obligor defaults, the lender will come to you looking for the money that you cosigned on."

Peter responded, "Yes, I have seen that all too frequently. I would avoid cosigning on a loan for just about anyone including kids' loans unless it was absolutely necessary."

10. Not Managing Debt and Savings Properly

Peter then finished his reasons for overspending with reason 10, which is this: "**People should understand proper debt and savings management in order to maximize the use of their money.**

"People need to understand that lifestyle is the exact opposite of wealth creation. The bigger your lifestyle becomes, the less wealth you will create. There is a great matrix that folks need to understand that relates to either lifestyle or wealth creation. Here is the matrix that I have printed up for you."[3]

Lifestyle	Wealth Creation
Working to pay bills	Need to live
Emotional purchases	Intellectual and logical purchases
Quick fix	Long term, compounding
Short-term goals	Long-term goals
Bad debt	Good debt
Spend and consume	Invest

Source: Adapted with permission from Keith Cunningham's lecture on debt reduction. It is my understanding that Keith Cunningham is the real "Rich Dad" noted by a major author. For more information on Cunningham, go to http://www.keystothevault.com/.

With all this said, my mind was getting a bit foggy. I then said, "Let me get this straight. There are 10 main reasons why people become over-extended in debt."

1. **Denial:** They don't want to admit that they have a problem, which gets worse.
2. **Instant gratification:** They demand instant gratification. And they suffer from *shopaholicism*: they buy for emotional reasons such as trying to feel better about themselves or about their situation.
3. **Unexpected expenses:** Otherwise known as *crisis spending*, people run into problems when something important and expensive breaks down and they do not have enough money to cover it. This is where having a reserve for these types of expenses becomes crucial and is the solution for this problem.

4. **The get-rich-quicker mentality:** They make certain purchases thinking that those purchases will save them money in the long run, but they don't take their previous purchases into account and thus overextend themselves.

5. **Borrowing for consumer goods:** They borrow for consumer goods that don't appreciate in value. However, some debt is considered *good debt* if it is affordable and it is used to purchase items that generally appreciate in value or have long-term value, such as education.

6. **Equating self-worth with net worth:** People equate their perceived self-worth with their net worth.

7. **The inability to earn enough money:** Some people simply do not make enough money to cover their spending, which is why Chapters 4 and 5 on savings are so important.

8. **Lying to a spouse or significant other:** People should never lie to their spouse or significant other. Having honest, transparent dealings about all financial issues will get everyone in the family working in the same direction.

9. **Risking home or retirement:** People should rarely risk their home or retirement on things other than the purchase or improvement of a home.

10. **Not managing debt and savings properly:** Because they lack sufficient knowledge about personal finance, many people mismanage their debts and savings.

"Did I cover all the important reasons for why most people get overextended financially?"

Peter smiled and said, "Yes, you got them all. You guys are great students. If people follow what we have covered here, I think we will change many lives."

How Much Debt Is Too Much

We took a bit of a soda pop break, and then I asked Peter, "Before we get into the steps needed to get out of debt, how much debt should we have, and more importantly, how much debt is too much debt?"

Peter looked at me thoughtfully and answered, "That is a very important question. I can't say how much you should or shouldn't have, but I can give you a matrix that should tell people what financial shape they are in."

Peter continued.

You need to know what your *debt payment percentage* is. It is an important ratio that will tell you what financial shape you are in. This is computed by taking all the monthly debt payments that you have and dividing that number by your monthly take home pay, which is

computed as your net check after the tax, retirement, health insurance, and all other deductions are taken out.

"Thus, if your net monthly check is $3,000 (after all deductions including taxes are taken out) and you have monthly debt payments (which include mortgage, educational loans, car loans, and consumer loan payments) of $600, your debt payment percentage of your income would be, in this case, 20 percent. Here is the result of filling in the matrix so you can evaluate your own financial condition."

1. If your debt payment percentage is less than 16 percent, you are in great shape.
2. If your debt payment percentage is 20 to 28 percent, you are a bit shaky, but you could be fine with some immediate good debt management and planning for savings.
3. If your debt payment percentage is greater than or equal to 30 percent, it isn't hopeless, but you have a potential financial disaster looming and need immediate assistance.

Peter then excitedly licked his lips and said, "Now, we can get to the main course in our discussion, which is exactly how people can get out of debt.

"I am going to give you the strategies that we use with all our clients. I will hold nothing back. If people follow this, we can get just about everyone out of all debt, including their mortgage, in 12 years or less and put them on the track toward financial independence at retirement."

We have to say, we were getting very excited about this for all our readers.

The Seven Steps People Need to Take to Get Out of Debt

Peter then continued, "There are a few preliminary steps that should be undertaken before we actually start paying off our debts."

1. Have Both Short- and Long-Term Goals

"The first step is to **have both short-term and especially long-term written goals.**

"Oscar Hammerstein, the famous playwright, had a great saying in one of his plays, which was: 'If you don't have a dream, how are you going to make your dreams come true?' The same can be said with all goals. If you don't have any, how can you achieve them?

"There was a study conducted by Harvard researchers many years ago that showed that only 3 percent of all students had written financial goals.

However, years after they had graduated, these same people had a higher net worth than the remaining 97 percent who didn't have financial goals. If you want to save money, you need to know exactly what you want to save for and how much you need to save for that goal. Remember what I said before, '**You can have anything you want. You just can't have everything.**'"

2. Prioritize Your Goals

"The second step is to **prioritize these goals by the degree of importance.** Thus, is saving for your kid's education more important than taking fancy vacations or eating out often? You need to prioritize these goals."

3. Track Your Expenses for at Least Three Months

"Step three is crucial, and it is to **track your expenses for at least three months—but preferably six months in order to uncover some semiannual payments such as insurance.**

"Sandy, in order to reduce their debts, people need to either bring in more money or cut their spending."

Being excited myself, I added, "Or reduce their taxes, which is akin to both making money and cutting spending, which I cover in my book *Lower Your Taxes—Big Time!*"

Peter agreed and said, "Yes, cutting taxes is a big deal because people can use the money they save by doing so to get the money to make their debt payments without affecting their standard of living. That is truly a win-win, if done correctly."

I went one step further: "You can't cut any spending if you don't know where you are spending your money! Folks really need to do this. It isn't complicated, but it does take discipline. You can use one of our trackers, or you can download an online tracking software program that you can use on your cell phone to log in the expenses. This service can be found at www.taxbot.com."

4. Make Some Spending Cuts

"Step four is called the *butcher knife approach.* **Once you know what you are spending, you need to take a figurative butcher knife and make some spending cuts.** These can be cutting down on eating out, cutting out your gym, spending less on shoes, spending less for lunch at work, or spending less on consumable purchases. In fact, you can use any of the ideas mentioned in the savings discussion [which is Chapter 4 of this book]. This is why tracking your expenses is so important. You can't cut what you don't know about," said Peter wisely.

5. Create a Matrix of Your Debts

"The fifth step is to **prepare a matrix of all your debts, which shows each creditor's name, the amount of the debt, the interest rate on the debt, the minimum payment needed to amortize the debt, and the years necessary to pay off the debt with that minimum payment.** It might look something like the one that follows."

Creditor	Amount of Debt	Interest Rate	Minimum Monthly Payment	Duration*
Layaway payments	$1,500	9%	$68.53	24 months
Chase MasterCard	$4,000	16%	$88.25	70 months
Visa	$5,000	18%	$113.00	72 months
Educational loan	$40,000	8%	$485.31	120 months
Potomac Bank mortgage	$200,000	6%	$1,199.00	360 months
Total monthly minimum payments			$1,954.09	

*This is the duration in months that your minimum monthly payments will take to pay off the debt.

6. Prioritize the Debts in Your Matrix

"Step six is **prioritize the debts in this matrix by the amount of debt.** This step is important. I have prepared a matrix, like the one above, based on the amount of debt, where the smallest loan comes first and the biggest comes last. The smallest loan incidentally is usually the one with the shortest duration for payments too."

Peter then said, "Many people make the mistake of trying to add payments to the largest loan, which is the one with the longest duration. This would be incorrect. They need to take a different approach."

People should start accelerating their payments on the lowest amount of debt, which is usually the one with the shortest duration.

"Thus, under the matrix above, which debt should I first start applying some extra money to?"

Matt perked up with, "The layaway payments."

Peter smiled and said, "Yes, you are absolutely right. See, it isn't hard to figure out. You would continue to pay your minimum payments, which were $68.53, as shown in the above matrix, *but* you would add some extra money to start paying off the layaway debt. Thus, if you were to add $100 more per month to your $68.53 per month that you are currently paying on the layaway debt, you would be out of that debt in 10 months instead of 24 months. Pretty cool, isn't it? "Moreover, it would only take an extra $100 per month. If you can allocate even more money, say, $150 per month, you would pay off this debt in, say, six months."

Being a bit puzzled, I asked Peter, "Peter, wouldn't it make sense to pay off the debt with the highest interest rate first rather than the one with the smallest duration or smallest debt first?"

Peter smiled and said, "Sandy, you would think that paying off the debt with the highest interest rate would be the smarter thing to do. However, shedding debt is similar to being on a diet. Folks need to see success so they can continue with it. Getting rid of the smallest debt first gives an amazing sense of satisfaction and encourages people to continue with the process. It will also free up more money quicker for other debt payments. Finally, over a 48-month period, the actual difference in payments between an 18 percent debt over that of a 12 percent debt isn't that much. Thus, paying off the smallest debts first should be the priority."

7. Add the Amount of the Payment on Your Expired Debt to Your Next Smallest Debt

"Step seven, which is the real trick, is this: **while making your normal monthly payments, use the payments that you paid on the old expired debt and add this to the minimum amount that you pay monthly on the next smallest debt.**"

Lori looking a bit perplexed asked Peter, "What exactly does this mean?"

Peter quickly responded with, "Take a look at the matrix. You were paying $1,954.09 each month when you had all of these debts before you were making any additional payments. Of this amount, you added an extra $100 per month to your layaway debt, which meant that the total of your monthly payments was $2,054.09—that is, your original payments plus the $100 per month additional payment. Notice that the $68.53 per month that you were paying on the layaway debt was part of the $2,054.09. Now, with no layaway debt left, you have $68.53 a month left to pay other debt. Thus, your total payments will remain the same as you pay off other debts.

"The next lowest debt would be your Chase MasterCard, which has an interest rate of 16 percent and minimum monthly payments of $88.25. You would add the $168.53 per month that you were making on your layaway debt to the $88.25 monthly payment that you are currently making on your Chase MasterCard. This will provide a total monthly payment on the Chase card of $256.78 per month."

Peter added, "It is important to note that your total payments on all debts will be the same throughout the process even as you get to your last debt. You are only adding an extra $100 per month to accomplish all this over what you were paying before you started accelerating your debt payments."

Lori then probed Peter by asking, "So my total debt payments that I was making while paying off the layaway debt will be the same, right? I am just using the saved payments that I was making on the expired debt and applying them to the new debt?"

Peter smiled and said, "Yes, that is exactly what you are doing. You are *not* paying any more than you were when you had the layaway debt and the current payment being made on the MasterCard debt. You are simply using the saved payment that you were making on the layaway debt and applying it to the next debt. This process is called *rolling down your debt*. Your overall payments are not decreasing *as long as* you are not incurring more debt. This all assumes that you stop incurring more debt, which is essential to this process."

Lori smiled and said, "I get it, Peter. Thus, in the above example, once the MasterCard and layaway debts are paid off, I would take the same minimum payments I was making on both debts plus the $100 a month that I added to prepay both debts and add it to the minimum payment currently on the Visa debt in order to pay the Visa debt quicker."

Peter chuckled, "Yes, that is exactly the trick. It is simple to do once you know the steps. The hard part is getting the discipline to make cuts in spending and applying these cuts to the existing debt while not accruing new debt. If you have to, nuke your credit cards and use only debit cards or cash for a while. Overspending must stop.

"In fact, this is what people need to know in order to begin to live a debt-free life, which I know that you and Lori already do."

Peter then added, "I want to add a few more important points to this discussion. Overspending is a disease just like overeating. If people get out of debt but don't curb their emotional buying, impulse shopping, and pursuit of instant gratification, they will be back in the same place. Moreover, all goals need to be evaluated each year. If people find that this is too hard, they can cut the extra payments down to what they can afford. Maybe it is only $50 to $75 per month. Maybe they got a raise and can afford even more additional payments. This will cut their debts even quicker. People need to evaluate their goals and monitor their progress each year.

"Also," Peter noted, "while people are accelerating payment on a debt, they are still making the minimum payments on the rest of their debts. They are *not* stopping payment on any debt or trying to achieve a workout through a credit repair company. Those steps will kill your credit, while my approach will raise your credit rating."

FICO Scores and Dealing with Credit Bureaus

"I want to end our discussion with information about FICO scores and dealing with credit bureaus and other companies because this does impact our credit and thus our life daily."

"**FICO** is an acronym for the name of the company that invented the score in the 1980s: Fair Isaac Corporation. The score varies between 300 and 850; the higher the score, the better your credit rating.

"Did you ever wonder what the FICO scores are based on?" quizzed Peter.

"Now that you mention it, I would like to know about it. Frankly, it seems to be a well-kept secret," I noted.

Peter chuckled and said, "Yes, it has been until today. Here is the makeup of the FICO score."[4]

- Payment history: 35 percent
- Total amounts owed: 30 percent
- Length of credit history: 15 percent
- New credit: 10 percent
- Type of credit in use: 10 percent

Peter went on to say, "You will note that the payment history and total amount owed represent 65 percent of the score. Thus, it is vital to make your payments on time. In addition, every new loan, especially every new credit card, reduces your overall FICO rating, which is why you should use as few credit cards as possible. In fact, the credit rating score decreases a bit immediately after you first apply for a credit card. I bet you didn't know that."

I chuckled and said, "Actually I was aware of that. Most people aren't, however. Credit card companies are great at offering new credit cards and *not one of them* ever warns consumers that their credit rating will drop for each card that they take."

Peter agreed and said, "Moreover, studies have shown that as much as one-half of all credit reports contain errors! These errors usually include loans that have been paid off and loans that might not be your responsibility, which is why I suggest that people get a copy of their credit report every year."

Excitedly Peter added, "Now, an FTC ruling allows everyone to get one free credit report per year![5] You can get a copy of your report by going to annualcreditreport.com or by calling 877-322-8228. Moreover, the ruling doesn't replace the other ways to receive a free credit report. For example, if a company denies you credit, insurance, or a job because of something in your credit report, that company has to tell you which credit bureau provided the information. You are entitled to a free credit report from that bureau within 60 days of being turned down.[6]

"One big source of errors is when the debt isn't removed from the credit report after the statutory period has expired. For most debts, negative items must be removed after seven years from when it was reported to the company; however, there are a number of other factors that can change whether and how long negative items might be on your credit report.

"Bankruptcy, for example, stays on your credit record for 10 years from the filing date! Thus, people should try to avoid bankruptcy unless they have absolutely no choice. Other examples include these: Student loan debts have a 7-year period after default on the student loan debt. Even worse, creditors of student loans have a lot of collection power over that of other loan creditors. These creditors can garnish wages, disability payments, and even social security payments.[7] In fact, student loan debts and certain tax debts are among the only debts that can't be discharged in bankruptcy."

Matt turned to me and said, "I bet that all of the kids who borrowed money for student loans didn't understand that they are subject to tougher collection standards over that of other loans. No one is telling them this type of information."

Agreeing I said, "You are right, Matt. This is why reading this chapter will be crucial for many people."

Peter continued with, "Foreclosures stay on your records for 7 years from the date of filing for foreclosure. Collection actions stay on your record for 7 years from the date of the original delinquency. Finally, tax liens stay on your records for 7 years after the liens are paid and 15 years if unpaid.[8]

"If there is an error, you need to gather your support and write to the alleged creditor and write to each of the three major reporting companies, whose information FICO uses to generate its reports. These agencies are TransUnion, Experian, and Equifax. All correspondence should be sent via Federal Express or any other courier that will provide you with a return receipt, which you need so you will know and have evidence that these companies got your letter. It is important to know that all agencies must respond to your request within 30 days or they must remove the improper item from your credit report. Sometimes, agencies can request an additional 30-day extension so they can obtain additional information. If they do nothing within that initial 30-day period, however, you may have to use a lawyer and sue for damages.

"Finally, you can always provide a statement of up to 100 words explaining any problems that would appear in response to someone's credit inquiry about you."

Peter continued, "The bottom line for good credit is simple: pay on time, get yearly credit reports, write the agencies about any errors you find (and include all supporting materials that prove the error), and reduce the number of your new debts, especially the number of credit cards outstanding.

"One final thing is to **never** agree to settle a bogus claim. Settlement implies that you didn't pay a valid debt, and it will be used against you. If there is a bogus claim, the only action you should take is to insist that it be removed. Period!"

"Peter, I want to thank you for all of this fabulous information that you and your firm provided. I have one more question that I want to get your opinion on. What about all these credit repair companies who promise to get people out of debt or reduce their debts? Should my readers be using these types of companies?" I inquired.

Peter snorted and answered, "Most of these companies are sadly borderline frauds. In contrast, our company Money Mastery does exactly what I have described to you. We have people track their expenses. We look for ways to cut spending and cut taxes and then power down their debts. We will contact credit bureaus **if** we have support that errors have been made.

"Sadly, many of the credit reduction companies try to cut corners. They write the three bureaus claiming mistakes on every negative item without any sort of documentation in the hope that these bureaus will remove the negative items. This usually doesn't work. Then, if the credit reduction companies can't remove the items, they try to negotiate lower payments or waivers of some interest in order to make the debts more palatable to their clients. The problem with these techniques is that the settlement of the debts will kill their clients' credit!

"I can assure you that by following the steps that we have given you in these three chapters, people will get out of debt much quicker than they realize and they will boost their credit rating significantly and improve their retirement situation enormously. If that doesn't change lives, what will?"

"This was great. I want to summarize your points in this chapter in order to make sure that my notes are correct."

A Review of What You Have Learned

- Most people have too much debt. The 10 reasons are as follows:
  1. **Denial.** They are in denial of the warning signs such as more than 27 percent of their income is used to pay debts or that their debt balances are increasing or that they don't know how much debt they have, or they have maxed out their credit limit or argue a lot about finances with their spouse.
  2. **Instant gratification.** They demand instant gratification. And they suffer from *shopaholicism*—they buy to feel better about themselves or their situation.
  3. **Unexpected expenses.** Otherwise known as *crisis spending,* people run into problems when something important and expensive breaks down and they do not have enough money to cover it. This is why having a reserve for these items is so important.
  4. **The get-rich-quicker mentality.** They make certain purchases thinking that those purchases will save them money in the long run, but they don't take their previous purchases into account and thus overextend themselves.
  5. **Borrowing for consumer goods.** They borrow to buy consumer goods that don't appreciate in value. They don't realize that, although there is *good debt*, it should be used only for things that appreciate in value and when the debt is affordable.
  6. **Equating self-worth with net worth.** People equate their perceived self-worth with their financial net worth.
  7. **The inability to earn enough money.** Some people simply do not make enough money to cover their spending.
  8. **Lying to a spouse or significant other.** People should never lie to their spouse or significant other. Having honest, transparent dealings about all financial issues will get everyone in the family working in the same direction.
  9. **Risking home or retirement.** People should rarely risk their home or retirement on things other than the purchase or improvement of a home.
  10. **Not managing debt and savings properly.** Because they lack sufficient knowledge of personal finance, many people mismanage their debts and savings.
- Knowing your debt payment percentage (DPP) formula is crucial. This is the total of your debt payments divided by your net income—that is, your income after all taxes and other deductions are taken out. The following will tell you if you are in good shape:
  - If your DPP is less than 16 percent of your income, you are in good shape
  - If your DPP is between 20 and 28 percent, you could be financially shaky.
  - If your DPP is 30 percent or more, you are in a big financial hole and need remediation quickly.
- The seven steps needed to get out of debt:
  1. **Have both short- and long-term goals.** Develop both short-term and long-term goals, and write them down. If you don't have a dream, how can you make your dreams come true?
  2. **Prioritize your goals.**
  3. **Track your expenses for three months.** Keep track of your expenditures for

at least three months—but preferably six months in order to uncover some semiannual payments such as insurance.

4. **Make some spending cuts.** Use the butcher knife approach. Once you know what you are spending, you will need to take a figurative butcher knife and make some spending cuts. Really focus on the strategies in Chapter 4 on savings to find ways to cut your spending.

5. **Create a matrix of your debts.** This chart will show the creditor's name, the amount of the debt, the interest rate on the debt, the minimum payment needed to amortize the debt, and the years necessary to pay off the debt with that minimum payment

6. **Prioritize the debts in your matrix.** Use the amounts of the debts to put them in order from smallest amount to the largest amount. Thus the debt with the smallest loan comes first, and the debt with the biggest loan comes last.

7. **Add the amount of the payment on your expired debt to your next smallest debt.** In other words, while making your normal monthly payments, use the payments that you paid on the old expired debt and add them to the minimum amount that you pay monthly on the next smallest debt. This is called *powering down* your debt.

- FICO scores, which are ratings of people's creditworthiness, range from 300 to 850.
- The biggest components of the FICO score are payment history and total amount owed. Thus, you should always pay your debts on time.
- Don't ever settle bogus debts. Instead, have them eliminated if they are in fact untrue or not your debts.
- New debt and new credit cards decrease your FICO score. Don't get new credit cards unless you have a great reason to do so.
- Get your credit report every year. Studies have shown that half of credit reports contain errors.
- If you find an error, write the creditor and all three credit reporting agencies (TransUnion, Experian, and Equifax), and enclose your supporting documents. Send all correspondence with a return receipt requested or use Federal Express for tracking purposes.
- Companies generally have 30 days to respond or to remove the negative credit item from your reports.
- Generally, negative items on credit reports must be withdrawn after 7 years; bankruptcies must be withdrawn after 10 years. However, there are some exceptions.
- Don't use a credit repair agency that simply tries to get lower rates for you from your creditors or reduced payments. Those actions could destroy your credit.

"So, Peter, how did we do?" I taunted. Lori and Matt laughed at that.

Peter laughed and said, "You are my best students. If everyone listens to your advice presented here, we could change the world."

I smiled and said, "That is exactly my goal for this book."

Notes

1. *USA Today*, "The Cost of Financial Illiteracy," April 24, 2012, p. 1. The total debt figure includes credit card debt, student loan debt, car loan debt, and mortgage debt.
2. Ibid.
3. This was derived from a lecture given by Keith Cunningham.
4. http://www.myfico.com/crediteducation/whatsinyourscore.aspx.
5. http://www.bankrate.com/brm/news/cc/20010223c.asp.
6. Ibid.
7. https://www.alltuition.com/library/financial-aid/loans/how-student-loans-affect-credit-reports-and-scores/.
8. http://www.experian.com/ask-experian/20090121-tax-liens-and-your-credit-report.html.

Some of the information in this chapter came from Keith Cunningham, who provides wonderful information for business owners on how to improve their business. If you ever get a chance to see Cunningham at a seminar, don't pass it up. He also runs a website called Keys to the Vault (www.keystothevault.com).

7

How to Avoid Scams, Slams, and Shams

No one ever lost money underestimating the intelligence of the Average American.
—Henry Louis Mencken

When a person of money meets a person with experience, the person with the experience will get some money and the person of money will get some experience.
—Harvey Mackay, *Swim With the Sharks Without Being Eaten Alive*

> **What You Will Learn**
> - The top 12 tax scams
> - Two common investment scams
> - Seminar schemes
> - Inheritance scams
> - Pyramid scams
> - Advertised products and services
> - Other scams such as book scams
> - Identity theft

As we flew home from Utah, I couldn't help thinking about all the ways to save money. Of course, as I was reading my local newspaper, I saw an interesting article about how scams and other shoddy deals are bilking people out of literally tens of billions annually. No wonder people have a hard time saving money. Even the IRS acknowledges that fraud seems to be rampant.

We wanted to deal with this issue as soon as possible in order to make you "the person with the experience" that Harvey Mackay mentioned, and there probably is no better person for that task than Mike! For the record, we are using a pseudonym for him since he didn't want his real name disclosed due to his prior government connections as both an IRS attorney and Department of Justice prosecutor.

I met Mike while I worked for the IRS. He is a great guy but very driven and very no-nonsense. This should be a great interview and *very* helpful to you, our readers.

When Mike greeted me at the door, there was none of the warm fuzzies that I got from Peter, although he was cordial to Matt when I introduced him to my son. Mike was, however, all business. In fact, Matt and I had no sooner sat down when he said, "Okay, let's get down to business.

"Sadly, scams are a *huge* problem. They can literally wipe out some-one's savings. The scammers also seem to come up with more scams faster than the government can shut them down. Even worse, they usually are in countries that are fairly inaccessible to the U.S. government. Thus, shut-ting them down is a real problem," Mike ended ominously.

"The key is knowledge. If readers are forearmed with education about them, they can more readily avoid being scammed even from skilled scam-mers like Bernie Madoff. This is why I was willing to help you, Sandy. By the time we are finished, your readers will really know how to avoid most of these. I hope we can help your readers preserve their life savings and save lives in the process."

We have to admit, we were getting very excited about all this.

The Top 12 Tax Scams

With steely eyes, Mike said, "We will start with tax scams. These are the top 12 scams that the IRS publishes each year as their most noticed scams of the year. I will also be adding a few others that the IRS has mentioned often as well."

1. Phishing Letters or E-mails

"The first are known as *phishing scams* where folks are receiving letters or e-mails with the IRS or Treasury Department logo informing them that they may be owed a refund or informing them that they may owe taxes unless they clear up a possible error in identity. In order to obtain this refund or to clear up the error, they have to prove that they are the right people by confirming certain personal information such as social security number, mother's maiden name, or home address. Other examples include phony census takers who ask for personal information.

"Recently one phishing scam involved notices by someone posing as a clerk for the district court who was notifying people that there was an arrest warrant out for them but that the warrant might concern an imposter. Thus, the phishers ask for social security numbers and other identifying information in order to clear up the discrepancy."

Mike's favorite phishing scam, which had just come in the mail, involved a supposed PayPal letter noting that his $1,600 computer that he supposedly had ordered was being delivered. If, however, he hadn't ordered it (which, of course, he hadn't), he only had to click on a special link, which asked for his PayPal account number and password for verification. Again, this was a hoax that seemed so real. In fact, Mike showed us the letter, which certainly seemed authentic.

Mike ominously noted, "To date, the IRS has identified at least 1,500 phishing scams."

"So, what are people to do when they get these types of scams?" I inquired.

Mike answered, "Neither the IRS nor any governmental organization will ever call you or write you asking for this type of personal information. You should never provide it to anyone by phone, letter, or by e-mail. If you get an e-mail requesting this type of information, allegedly from a reputable source such as the IRS, forward the letter to the IRS or send them an e-mail at phishing@IRS.gov."

Matt then jokingly added, "When I hear the word 'phishing,' it sure does give a different meaning than I used to think about when I was on my dad's boat catching trout"—to which Mike and I both chuckled. I looked at Matt, "Matt, I think you're exaggerating. You never did catch much trout if I remember. You usually caught either shoes or crabs," which we all chuckled about.

2. Economic Stimulus Payments

"A second top scam is the Economic Stimulus scam. Some scammers try to trick people into revealing personal financial information that can be used to access their financial accounts by making promises relating to the Economic Stimulus payments, often described as a *rebate*. To obtain these payments, supposedly eligible individuals in most cases will be told they do not have to do anything more than file a federal income tax return. However, these criminals posing as IRS representatives try to trick taxpayers into revealing their personal information by falsely telling them they must provide certain personal information in order to get any payment. Sometimes these criminals ask for bank account information for the IRS to directly deposit the rebates, which then results in the thieves cleaning out the bank accounts." Mike went on to say, "The IRS will **never** ask for this type of information regarding your social security number or bank account information by telephone or e-mail."

3. Frivolous Tax Arguments

"Frivolous tax arguments still are a major thorn to the IRS. In fact, there are a host of these arguments made by promoters of scams that purport to reduce or even eliminate most tax liability. Some of these fallacious arguments are these." Mike listed the following:

- Taxes are unconstitutional or not properly codified by Congress.
- People are promised a nonexistent mariner's tax deduction or slavery tax credit.
- Tax filings are voluntary, and thus, people don't need to pay anything.
- Taxes are required only for federal employees.
- There is no statute that properly codifies the tax code.
- Wages, tips, and other service income isn't taxable.
- And many more.

Mike went on and noted, "None of these frivolous arguments, or others like them, have won in court. In fact, judges are so tired of hearing them that they are assessing the government's legal fees against those that make these arguments in court and assess a civil and criminal fraud penalty against those that use these arguments. These penalties can run $5,000 or more. A more complete list of these bogus arguments that promoters use can be found in IRS Notice 2007-61, which can be found on the IRS website at www.irs.gov.

4. Fuel Credits

Mike noted that a fourth prominent scam was the fuel credit scam. Mike said, "Sometimes there is some truth behind the scam. Farmers and some others are allowed a fuel credit for the use of vehicles for off-highway business purposes. However, some individuals, and even some fraudulent accountants, are claiming the credit for nontaxable uses of fuel when the taxpayers' occupations or income levels make the claim unreasonable."

5. Hiding Income Offshore

"To my knowledge this scam has been around for years, but it is now being aggressively investigated by the IRS. Promoters are promising that by placing assets offshore in foreign banks or tax havens, taxpayers will avoid all taxes and, at the least, not have their incomes discoverable by the IRS in these offshore accounts. Interestingly, some Swiss banks helped promote this scam to the detriment of those involved.

"As an offshoot of this, some promoters set up foreign credit cards for the payment of compensation on these credit cards in the hope that the IRS will not discover this type of disguised compensation."

I disdainfully said, "Yes, U.S. citizens are taxed on their worldwide income. Setting up foreign bank accounts will *not* shield them from taxation. Even worse, on the federal tax return, there is a question about the existence of foreign bank accounts that must be answered truthfully under penalty of perjury."

Mike agreed and noted, "Yes, taxpayers can have foreign bank accounts for many legitimate reasons, but they must at least disclose them on their tax returns or face possible criminal penalties. The IRS has aggressively investigated these accounts, and it has negotiated information sharing agreements with most foreign jurisdictions."

6. Abusing Retirement Account Arrangements

Mike went on to cite the sixth scam that the IRS has listed in its Dirty Dozen Tax Scams: "The IRS continues to uncover abuses in retirement plan arrangements, especially among Roth IRAs (which are normally nontaxable IRAs). The IRS is focusing on transactions that try to avoid income limitations for Roth contributions. People should be very wary of advisors who encourage them to shift appreciated assets into Roth IRAs."

I added, "Yes, the key here is that contributions must be made in cash and *not* with any other assets including appreciated property. Also there are income limitations that preclude some taxpayers from contributing to Roth IRAs."

"I should also note," added Mike, "that there is not an income limitation on who can convert funds from a traditional IRA to a Roth IRA. Therefore, anyone can convert a traditional IRA to a Roth IRA, but the conversion may be subject to income taxes."

7. Claiming Zero Wages

Mike then went on: "Some taxpayers try to file phony wage- or income-related information such as IRS Form 4852, which is a substituted W-2, or they try to file amended Form 1099s (for income, dividends, and royalties) in order to improperly reduce their taxes to zero. Don't get fooled into thinking that this scam works."

8. Filing False Claims for Refunds

Going on, Mike added: "Closely related to the zero wage claims are false claims for tax refunds in which taxpayers file Form 843 to abate previously assessed taxes giving some form of fictitious arguments. Even worse, many individuals who have tried this haven't even previously filed a federal tax return."

9. Return Preparer Fraud

Mike continued: "Sadly, there is a lot of fraud being perpetrated by tax preparers. Many of these folks try to seem as if they can get deductions and credits that more honest tax preparers can't get.

"There is a dramatic increase in enforcement by the IRS against fraudulent tax preparers. It was rare 30 years ago for the IRS to bar more than 2 or 3 tax preparers per week from preparing taxes or representing taxpayers. Today, I have seen, as I am sure you have, Sandy, as many as 30 tax preparers per week barred from preparing taxes.

"Moreover, the range of fraud that these accountants are committing is quite varied. Some simply inflate their credentials claiming that they are CPAs or lawyers, when they haven't earned these credentials. Some claim the fuel tax credits improperly, as noted above. One egregious example involved an accountant who claimed for his clients thousands more in charitable deductions than the clients ever paid!"

I decided to prod Mike: "Why would accountants commit this type of fraud? They would get no benefit from the money saved."

Mike thoughtfully responded, "Well, some accountants do get a percentage of what they can 'save' clients, which is quite unethical, not to mention illegal. Moreover, I think some accountants commit these actions in order to look better than their competition. They probably reason that if they get more deductions for the clients than anyone else, they will attract more clients. It really turns out to be a long-term disaster for everyone. The accountants normally are both fined and jailed, and usually every client that used the accountants' services is audited intensively."

Mike quickly added, "Don't get me wrong. Both you and I advise people to get aggressive accountants who will work on tax planning for them, but these accountants must be honest too. You certainly can be aggressive and honest at the same time."

10. Disguising Corporate Ownership

Mike then ominously added, "Some folks are forming entities in some states in order to hide the owners' identities where these owners are conducting a wide array of illegal activities such as hiding income or laundering money. The IRS is working with all state authorities to investigate these activities.

"Let me assure you that no entity can guarantee complete shielding from the IRS. If the IRS wants to investigate an entity in any state, it can get the names of the owners, names of the officers, and any other pertinent information. There are some states that do promise increased privacy such as Nevada. However, even a Nevada corporation can be investigated easily by the IRS or any other governmental agency. Don't be fooled into thinking that any entity can be used to hide income from the IRS."

11. Misusing Trusts

"A number of promoters promise taxpayers that certain trusts can be used to minimize taxes by deducting a wide array of personal expenses or avoiding estate taxes. While there is a kernel of truth to this, especially regarding estate taxes, these trusts must be set up and administered correctly. Moreover, and this is important, these trusts usually will not save income taxes and will not usually allow for the deduction of personal expenses.

"It is vital to seek a good, qualified tax attorney to verify that these trusts do accomplish what was promised and to be sure that they are set up properly. Moreover, the key point is that if you place property in trust such that you can control the assets or receive distributions, you may be taxed on all of the trust income!"

12. Abusing Deduction Allowances for Contributions to Charitable and Nonprofit Organizations

Mike said, "This is the final scam as part of the IRS's recent Dirty Dozen. Many promoters promise people that they can maintain control over donated property and benefit from this property while taking a deduction. Again, there is a kernel of truth to this with remainders given on your home after you die or with foundations and legitimate charitable trusts. However, the promoters go beyond what is legal. For example, they might recommend taking a charitable deduction for tuition payments made to colleges and claiming these as disguised charitable deductions."

I said, "Mike, when I was at the IRS, we noticed some of these scams years ago. There were promoters who set up scams with paintings and antiques. They would sell these items to taxpayers with a promise to obtain an appraisal that the items would be worth much more in one year. They alleged that the items could be donated to a charity at the high inflated appraised value, which was many times higher than the cost of the item. I guess these overvaluation scams are still rampant."

Mike added, "Yes, each year the IRS publishes a new list of their top Dirty Dozen Tax Scams, although some of these seem perennial. People need to understand that participating in these scams can cost them large penalties and may even subject them to criminal prosecution."

One More Tax-Related Scam

Before we moved on, Mike wanted to discuss another tax scam: "I want to add one more to the list, although it is not specifically on the IRS's Dirty Dozen Tax Scams list. This scam is using companies that promise to reduce the taxes you owe for pennies on the dollar or even to eliminate the taxes you owe. There are a number of these companies such as Tax Masters and J. K. Harris who filed for bankruptcy.[1]

"Interestingly, there is a kernel of truth as to potentially being able to reduce taxes owed the IRS to a lesser amount. This is accomplished by an 'Offer in Compromise.' Here you make an offer to the IRS. You list your assets and income, and you use their rulings to reduce your net income by certain limited living expenses, which the IRS allows. If you do not have the assets to pay the tax bill and your net income, based on the IRS's limited formula, shows that you won't be able to pay them off over time, the IRS will accept something less than what you may owe. The catch is that this is *very* hard to accomplish. You literally have to have no assets. Very few individuals really qualify for this limited benefit. The scam by some of the 'tax settlement companies,' due to several factors, runs in the following way."

- First, the settlement company usually gets a high up-front fee without knowing if it really can help the customer based on the IRS formulas.
- Second, some settlement companies imply or even state directly that they can accomplish this magical tax reduction for the vast majority of their customers, which is patently not true.

"*ABC News* did a show on one of these companies named Tax Masters. You should definitely download it from the Internet. It was quite a wake-up call and a potential warning about using companies such as these. I highly recommend that you don't use companies that advertise that they can get you pennies on the dollar for taxes owed. Use a reputable accountant or tax lawyer who really understands the Offer in Compromise process."

Two Common Investment Scams

Next on Mike's list were common investment scams: Ponzi schemes and stocks and commodities trading software scams.

1. Ponzi Schemes

Mike noted, "Many of us are aware of the Ponzi types of scams like the one perpetrated by Bernie Madoff. In these scams, new investors' money is used to pay other investors. There is very little profit or even an investment made. However, this type of scam not only has been around for a long time, but it seems to be sadly very pervasive."

I then asked, "Mike, how do people avoid being a victim of these Ponzi schemes?"

Mike responded, "Many folks have asked this. The answer involves several commonsense steps. First, always check out the money manager or promoter of the investment. This includes going to the Better Business Bureau (BBB). You may also want to check out the money manager or promoter on www.finra.org to see if there have been any complaints against them. In addition, you should carefully read over the prospectus the company provides on its investments and see if there are any glaring problems. For example, if there is a significant down market, you probably won't be making money absent some very unusual conditions. Don't assume that the managers are necessarily more brilliant than everyone else. Remember, if the offer seems too good to be true, it probably is.

"Moreover, and this is important, you should *never* have most of your money with any one money custodial firm. You should diversify the management of your money. This includes not putting all of your money in one hedge fund or one mutual fund.

"Finally, always use a firm that advertises that it is a member of the Securities Investor Protection Corporation (SIPC). The SIPC will insure loss due to the theft of funds or theft of securities for up to 10 percent of your investable assets up to $500,000 with any one firm or person. (Obviously, if you are worth hundreds of millions, this can be unwieldy.) This means that you should consider putting no more than $500,000 with any one custodial firm. What is important is that the SIPC does not insure investors who are sold worthless stock or other worthless securities."

> **As a rule of thumb, you might want to limit your investment with any one firm to whichever is greater: 10 percent of your investable assets or $500,000.**

Being a bit puzzled, I asked: "Let me see if I have this down. If I am worth about $2 million of investable assets, I should place up to $500,000 with each of four firms. If I were, however, worth about $10 million, I should place no more than $1 million with any one firm. Is this correct?"

Mike smiled and said, "Yes, this is exactly the way to minimize your potential damage from theft. You can and probably should have one planner overseeing this, but there should be several *independent* custodians for the funds. In fact, investors will probably get reports from both the planner and the custodial firms that are investing your assets. Investors should always compare these reports to see if the earnings and any withdrawals are reported similarly on all reports."

2. Stocks and Commodities Trading Software Scams

"Mike," I said. "I was just at a seminar where they didn't charge much to attend, which was my first clue that they wanted to sell me some products or services. There was a lot of excitement in the room with loud motivational music, famous speakers, high energy, and lots of comments about avoiding procrastination and taking action. Suddenly a good-looking, well-dressed speaker started promoting the wonderful value of his various trading software that is used for stocks or commodities trading. The speaker cited the huge profit potential that the software could create. He showed actual profitable trades made by people who had used the software.

"He then showed us pictures of big fancy cars and houses. He even guaranteed a refund of the participants' $2,000 fee if we don't like the training at the end of the first day. The speaker noted that the training classes had limited seats. After he made this point, I saw literally hundreds of people running to the back of the room to register for the company's programs in order to take advantage of this 'wonderful' offer. What do you know about these companies and the effectiveness of their software?"

Mike started to grimace and said, "Sandy, first of all, how do you know that the profitable trades were made using this company's software? Second, how do you know if that big house and car were earned by selling the software or by using the software?"

"Here is the important point," said Mike. "Ask yourself a question: If you had a gold mine that simply needed a shovel to scoop up the gold, would you tell anyone about it, let alone sell entry to the mine? The answer, if you are smart, is *No way!* Look at Warren Buffett as an example. He has made billions investing in companies. Despite this, you don't see him publishing his formulas or his secrets for evaluating companies.

"Moreover, even if you had developed some fabulous software that continually made money by finding bargains or uncovering market trends, couldn't you simply sell it to a major investment house for billions? Not only could you sell it for billions but you would also be taxed at the more favorable capital gains rate on the sale, which would cut your taxes by about one-third over what you would pay on the licensing of the software. This means that you would pay much less in taxes. In fact, the interest alone on the cash sale to the investment company would provide more money than you would make hawking the software at seminars.

"In addition, there is a dirty secret that goes along with most of these big seminars. The promoter of the seminar gets a huge piece of the sale price for getting you in the room, and the salespeople get paid very well too. Thus, why are companies selling this stuff at these seminars?

"The answer, if it hasn't already occurred to you, is that the software either doesn't really work or it doesn't work better than other less expensive software on the market."

Excitedly, Mike went on to add, "Even worse, when you get to the company's 'training' program, usually on the second day of training, which is after your refund period has run out, some of these organizations notify you that you really can't use the best of the software or website or training materials unless you upgrade for a whopping extra $3,000 to $25,000 or more! Hey, you were a sucker once; why not try another pitch on you?"

I interrupted Mike by saying, "If this isn't alarming enough to my readers, I have been told that studies have shown that traders rarely make money over the long term anyway even with good trading software. I can honestly say that I know a number of traders, and very, very few have made money over the long term. So why do people buy into this crap?"

Mike smiled and said, "Because many people are plainly gullible or greedy. PT Barnum was wrong when he said, 'There is a sucker born every minute.' A sucker is born every second."

"Okay, Mike," I interjected. "What overall rules or tips should my readers get about buying a stock or commodities trading program?"

Mike, who looked as if he were in deep thought, said, "Here are my rules for investing in any stock or commodities trading software, which can also be applied to the training programs in general."

Rule 1. *Never* buy software programs at seminars that cost more than $900.

Rule 2. *Never* buy training programs at seminars that cost more than $2,000 *unless* you really know what will be presented at these programs and are reasonably sure the program will pay for itself.

Rule 3. If you are considering ignoring rules 1 or 2, at least wait till the seminar is over and research what others have said about the products or services on the Internet. You can *always* order the same products online and usually for less money. Check out the Better Business Bureau for the company that provides the products or training. See if there are complaints.

Seminar Schemes

"Wait a minute, Mike," I said. "I see nothing wrong with offering additional products and services or more advanced seminars for people to get better training. Seminars can cover only so much in a limited time frame. I myself offer a newsletter, consulting service, and my tax tracker in my seminars. Moreover, putting on a seminar is an expensive proposition due to high hotel, catering, and travel costs. Remember, speakers don't speak for free."

Mike then replied, "Sandy, you are primarily a content provider. You give out lots of moneymaking and money-saving information, and you sell products that are related to your program. I have no problem with people selling products or other training at seminars. In fact, I think that offering more intensive training in an area of interest can be a very good thing.

"*However*, I do have a *big* problem paying $1,000 or more for a seminar that has very little content. I have attended seminars that turned out to be one giant sales pitch after another, which I call a *pitchathon*. If that happens to me, I always try to get a refund. Again, I don't mind some selling as long as the total time spent on sales is less than 10 percent of the total time of the seminar. If it is substantially more than that, it is a scam to my mind. Thus, if it is an eight-hour seminar, I will allow as much as 30 minutes for a sales presentation. Anything substantially more than that not only annoys me but also becomes a real scam in my opinion.

"Now I will admit that I have seen sales presentations that also give out a lot of content. It isn't the rule, but it does happen. In that case, I do not object to the sales presentation by that speaker. However, if I don't get a *lot* of content from speakers and if almost all of the presentations are sales presentations, I find that very objectionable."

"I have to say, Mike, that I do agree with you about checking out the speaker and seminar on the Internet when participants get home, before they buy whatever was being sold at a seminar. This is particularly true for people who are given the opportunity at one seminar to purchase an expensive seminar at yet another event. People could save themselves a lot of aggravation, not to mention a lot of money, by checking out these seminars before they sign up to attend them."

Mike went on to add, "There was an old joke that noted the most expensive thing in the world was a lady who was free for the evening. Today, this has changed to, 'The most expensive thing in the world can be a free or almost free seminar.'"

Mike emphasized, "*No one offers seminars for free or at a very low cost without trying hard to sell you something!* I hope folks will remember this. In fact, I had a case involving some retirees who attended an investment seminar run by an accountant who promised at least 8 percent return on their investment by buying land in Costa Rica. Needless to say, it was a Ponzi scheme, and they lost all of their money. Sadly, most folks trust people, and this is exactly what they should not be doing. The key is to *never* let anyone push you into making an immediate decision."

Mike added, "The easiest way to avoid these types of frauds is to ignore the pitches, hang up on telemarketers, and reject invitations to free seminars, especially free lunch and dinner seminars, and to toss out mail promising free travel and surefire investments."

I reinforced this by saying, "Yes, I have seen folks buy land in Costa Rica for $60,000 after a one-hour pitch at a seminar. I couldn't believe my eyes. Folks really have to use some common sense. Paying for an expensive investment such as land because some pitchmen say it's a good deal is just plainly stupid. I also agree with you about the seminars that promise free dinners. I attended one that promised information on scholarships. The speakers first noted that few scholarships were available to most of the affluent audience and then proceeded to recommend a special savings plan for college, which turned out to be simply whole life insurance."

Inheritance Scams

Without missing a beat, Mike smoothly went on and noted, "There seems to be a number of inheritance scams, otherwise known as *Nigerian scams* because they usually involve some Nigerian who wants you to provide a few dollars in order to get a clearance certificate from the United States. The scam notes that the Nigerian has over $15 million awaiting him, but he can't get the money into this country due to legal hassles and IRS clearance. The Nigerian usually cites some famous folks who can vouch for him in case you have questions. The Nigerian notes that if you can provide an American bank account, he will transfer the full $15 million to you in return for your paying him or her 90 percent of the funds while keeping 10 percent for your effort."

"Mike," I interjected. "Lori and I actually got one of these letters and laughed at its obvious fraudulent content. However, it seems that there are many suckers . . . er . . . victims who have fallen prey to this pitch and have had their bank accounts cleaned out by the scammers."

"Yes, the bottom line is to **never, ever** give out your bank account information and bank routing number. Remember, if it sounds too good to be true, it probably is, which is why people need to be much more circumspect when dealing with strangers."

Matt suddenly asked, "Dad, why would anyone fall for these obvious scams? You have to be really dumb to fall for this."

I gave Matt my usual steely, thoughtful look when I responded, "Matt, sadly many people are both trusting and just plain stupid and greedy. They dream of getting a lot for almost nothing, which is why so many people bet on the lottery. They don't rely on their instincts to run in the opposite direction when they receive these types of letters."

Pyramid Scams

Bristling at the thought of pyramid scams, Mike noted, "These really fall into two categories. The first involves chain letters, which are clearly illegal. This scam perpetrates itself by sending folks a letter with a list of names. The instructions are to duplicate the letter and send each person on the list a copy of the letter with a check, but first you are supposed to add your name to the bottom of the list. If each letter recipient does the same, you will supposedly make a lot of money. The catch is that this rarely happens that way, and it is plainly illegal to participate in this type of endeavor for money. Don't do it.

"The second type of scam concerns illegal marketing pyramids that are structured as multilevel marketing companies."

Having lectured to network marketing companies, I interrupted Mike and said, "Wait a minute, Mike. There are a number of quite legal network marketing companies that offer very viable business opportunities and are clearly *not* illegal. In fact, you can check out an article that I wrote, 'How to Evaluate Any Network Marketing Opportunity,' found in the Articles section of my website at www.taxreductioninstitute.com."

Mike sat back in his seat and said, "Yes, you are right. However, folks need to know the difference between a legal network marketing company and an illegal one. A legal network marketing company should encourage retailing of products in addition to recruiting. If the only way you can make money is to recruit other people and if no one would buy the product without becoming a distributor, it is probably an illegal pyramid. Most court cases require a certain amount of retailing of the company's products to nondistributors for the network marketing company to be considered a legal operation."

Advertised Products and Services

I decided to be a bit aggressive here and noted, "Mike, one thing that personally galls me is the use of celebrities to promote advertised products. I do know that these commercials or infomercials are legal as long as the company lives up to its promises. However, I keep thinking: Who pays for these expensive ads and even more expensive endorsements? Obviously, the answer is the buyers. People who buy a product as a result of expensive television ads pays a lot more for that product than if they bought the product from a company that doesn't advertise as much. This is particularly true if a well-known celebrity is pitching the product, which geometrically increases the cost of the advertisement.

"In fact, I tried to do something about this and learned the hard way about how ingrained advertising is to the media. I had a financial talk radio show for which we had advertisers. On my show I thought I was doing a service to my listeners by mentioning companies that provided the most competitive rates for their industry. Thus, I mentioned companies who had the lowest mortgage rates, brokers that had the lowest commissions for stock purchases and sales, and so on. I even noted those insurance companies that had the best life insurance cash values.

"I then compared them to the companies that had the highest rates or highest prices for the same essential products or services. Little did I realize until I made the actual product and service comparisons for my listeners that the firms that were giving the best deals weren't those that advertised. It was those that gave the worst deals or had the highest interest rates or prices that did the most advertising. Interestingly, over time my advertising base slowly disappeared, and I was eventually removed from the show."

Mike snorted and said, "Yes, there is little that anyone can do about this situation other than ensure that all promises made in the advertisement are kept, and no misleading or deceptive advertising is distributed. People should always carefully evaluate their potential purchases of any products. More often than not, I have personally found some of the more heavily advertised products to be of inferior quality, especially those promoted on television. In fact, I personally avoid all products promoted by celebrities especially for the reason that you gave, Sandy.

"The bottom line is that before people buy into that highly promoted toothpaste, razor, shaving cream, gold buying service, or wonderful new promoted gadget on an infomercial or perfume, they should shop around for a better deal."

Other Scams Such as Book Scams

Without stopping for breath, Mike went on: "Sadly, the number and types of scams are proliferating faster than we humans can shut them down. I have seen many other types of scams such as various types of religious scams. I have seen scams that form a religion in order to avoid paying taxes. There are plenty of charity scams that involve 'charities' being formed and paid fund-raisers being hired. These fund-raisers are then paid a commission on all funds that they raise. However, I want to highlight another scam that has been going on for decades: the *book scam*."

I chuckled and said, "I don't think that I have heard of that before, Mike. How can publishing a book result in a scam? After all, books don't usually have a huge selling price."

Mike smoothly answered, "I was recently contacted by a well-known individual who wanted me to promote her book to the people in my database. Her e-mail promised to pay me for each person who bought her book as a result of my contact with those prospective buyers. The author promised me leads and promised to pay me for affiliates who have large databases for her to contact them. However, nowhere in the letter to me was there any discussion about what was in the book or why it would be a good book to read.

"In fact, her letter to me never mentioned why my contacts would even benefit from her book. She was solely interested in selling lots of copies during a one-week period in order to get on the bestselling list, and this author assumed that I couldn't care less about the quality of her work!"

Astonished, Matt asked, "Mike, does this happen a lot?"

Mike smiled which is rare for him, and said, "Yes, sadly this does happen a lot. Publishers are aware of this ploy, and some of them don't care how books are sold as long as people buy the books."

Matt then interrupted Mike and asked, "So, how do people avoid these false promotions and find out whether a book is really being recommended because of its quality and not because the person sending the recommendation is getting paid?"

Mike said, "Good question, Matt. You need to always be wary of folks who suddenly promote someone else's book when it first becomes published, or even worse, before it becomes available to the public. Don't assume that because a book made some bestseller list, it is necessarily a good book. In fact, I know authors who have purchased enough books by themselves, supplemented by hiring folks to buy enough books, so that they can make the bestseller list. It becomes an obvious fraud when the promoter wants everyone to buy the book within a set week or set time frame. Obviously, the promoter's goal is to make the bestseller list by making enough sales during some one-week period."

Identity Theft

"Mike, I want you address one of the biggest problems occurring today throughout the Internet, and that is identity theft. Please tell my readers what they can do to avoid it."

Mike steadfastly stared at us with the cold, stony eyes of a prosecutor and said, "Sandy and Matt, it isn't just on the Internet that this has become a huge problem. It is also a problem with wire transfers and credit cards. In fact, you weren't kidding when you said it was a big problem. It is quickly becoming the biggest problem worldwide.

"First, let's define what we mean by *identity theft*. This term refers to all types of crimes in which someone wrongfully obtains and uses another person's personal data in some way that involves fraud or deception, typically for economic gain.

"Sadly, unlike your fingerprints that are personal to you, anyone can use your personal data, social security number, bank account information, credit card number, or even telephone calling card number to personally profit at your expense. In many countries, people have reported that unauthorized people have taken funds out of their bank or financial accounts. In the worse cases, unauthorized people have taken over the victims' identity altogether, running up vast debts and committing crimes while using the victims' name. Not only can the poor victims incur a big financial loss but they also have to spend a lot of time and money restoring their name and credit."

Mike was really getting excited when he said, "This may surprise you, but identity theft wasn't even a formal federal crime until 1998. It became a crime as a result of a very notorious case in which a convicted felon not only incurred more than $100,000 of credit card debt but also obtained a federal home loan and also bought homes, motorcycles, and handguns in the victim's name. Even worse, he called the victim to taunt him saying that he could continue to pose as the victim because identity theft was not a federal crime at the time. In fact, the scamster also filed for bankruptcy in the victim's name."

Matt and I looked dumbfounded at each other.

Mike then continued: "What is most important is that most people don't even know how easily criminals can obtain their personal data without hacking into their computers or having to break into their homes. In public places, criminals can engage in *shoulder surfing*: watching people from a nearby location punch in their telephone calling card number or credit card number or listening in on people's telephone conversations in which they give out a credit card number.

"They might even be right next to you as you check into a hotel." Mike then quickly added, "In fact, they might use their cell phone to take a picture of your credit card and other identification.

"Some criminals engage in *dumpster diving*, which involves going through your garbage cans or trash bins to obtain copies of your checks, credit card accounts, or bank statements or other records that typically bear your name, address, and even your telephone number. These types of records make it easy for them to get control over accounts in your name and assume your identity. I should note that in many areas, dumpster diving is illegal; however, this still doesn't stop scammers from doing it."

Matt then chirped up and said, "Dad, I don't know if you knew this, but I had a vacation in New York City for a few days. When I got home the credit card company called me and said that there were two unauthorized attempted charges on my credit cards. Someone supposedly took my numbers and attached it to a credit card in order to make his own credit card. My card never left my sight, and I still have it. I have to say that it made me feel like a total jerk. I couldn't even tell you how they got hold of my credit card number. I guess no matter how careful we are, identity theft can still happen." Both Mike and I both sympathized when Mike said, "Matt, as I said, this can happen to anyone. It can't be totally eliminated."

How to Prevent Identity Theft

I interrupted: "Mike, this happened to me. I had an insect control guy in my home. He found a credit card slip on the kitchen counter of my home. Within one month, I had several thousand dollars of unauthorized credit card charges, and I had the Secret Service in my home conducting an investigation. It was very unpleasant.

"So what should people do in order to either eliminate or at least reduce the risk of identity theft?"

Mike took a few minutes to collect his thoughts and responded "I don't think that there is any way to guarantee that identity theft won't happen to you. However, there are some ways to significantly curtail the risk." Here are Mike's suggestions:

1. Do not give out any personal data or credit card information to anyone unless you have a very good reason to trust the person.
2. If you receive any preapproved credit card applications, tear them up into small pieces or, even better, buy a shredder and shred them.
3. Never give out information that a company with whom you are doing business should already know. Thus, if you have a password for your online banking or you need your pet's name, a bank employee shouldn't be asking for these personal items. This information should be in the bank's database.
4. Likewise, you should almost never give out your social security number to anyone. I don't even give it to medical offices.

5. If someone you don't know calls you and offers you a prize or credit card and wants personal information such as a social security number, have the caller send you a written application.

6. Don't give out personal information in a public place over the telephone. This is particularly true for hotels and airports. It is too easy for criminals to simply write down these numbers.

7. When giving someone your credit card while traveling, make sure that no one is looking over your shoulder.

8. Check your credit information monthly. Subscribe to a credit reporting service to monitor your credit. These services also look for new accounts that might be established in your name. Two popular services are Myfico .com or freecreditreport.com.

9. Read over your credit card statement carefully! Too many of us do not read these statements as carefully as we should. Always look for unauthorized transactions. Some of the "smarter" crooks charge only one or two minor things each month in the hope of not getting noticed.

10. If someone has managed to make unauthorized charges on your credit card or has taken money from your bank account, you need to immediately contact the credit card company or financial institution where you bank and report the transaction. You then need to place a *fraud alert* with both your bank and all credit reporting agencies. Of course, you should cancel any credit cards that have been compromised.

11. Always copy both sides of all credit cards that you have in your wallet. In fact, I even recommend copying your passport when going away on travel and putting this copy in a safe place in your luggage.

12. The real key, if you have your credit cards stolen, is to have the credit card companies' toll-free numbers handy so you know whom to call.

13. File a police report in the jurisdiction where your cards were stolen. This proves to credit card providers that you were diligent, and it can be the first step toward any investigation.

14. When writing checks to credit card companies, never put your social security number on your checks. (Duh.) In addition, just write the last four digits of your credit card on the "for" line of your checks. The companies have your credit card number. This way, people handling your check won't see your whole account number.

15. Request a copy of your credit report each year, and read it!

16. Buy a shredder, and shred every document, bill, invoice, or any other item that you discard that has any identifying information on it.

17. **Never, ever** send account numbers, dates of birth, or social security numbers by e-mail to anyone.

18. Never write down and leave your home computer login and password near your computer. Unfortunately most people leave this information right next to the computer. How much easier can you make it for the thieves?

19. Add your home number and home fax number to the Do Not Call list: https://www.donotcall.gov/.

What to Do If You Are a Victim of Credit Card or Identity Theft

"Mike, what should people do if they become victims of identity theft?"

Mike opened up some files and showed me the following checklist of what to do and whom to contact in case you are a victim of identity theft:

- Contact the Federal Trade Commission (FTC) to report the situation either by phone or online. The FTC has a toll-free number at 1-877-ID THEFT, which translates to 1-877-438-4338. You can also mail the FTC at the Consumer Response Center, FTC 600 Pennsylvania Avenue, N.W., Washington, DC 20580.
- In addition, you should contact the various credit reporting agencies:

  1. Call Equifax at 800-525-6285 and report the fraud.
  2. Call Experian to report the fraud at 888-397-3742.
  3. Call TransUnion at 800-680-7289.
  4. Call Social Security Administration fraud line at 800-269-0271.
  5. Contact all creditors with whom your name or identifying data have been fraudulently used. For example, you may need to contact your long-distance telephone company if your long-distance calling card has been stolen.
  6. Contact all financial institutions where you have accounts, and tell them that an identity thief has compromised your name and accounts or has created an account in your name without your authorization. You may need to cancel those accounts or place stop-payment orders.
  7. If you have had checks stolen from you or bank accounts set up by an identity thief, contact the major check verification companies such as Check Rite Systems at 800-766-2748; ChexSystems at 800-428-9623; or Telecheck at 800-710-9898.
  8. As mentioned above, file a police report in the jurisdiction where your cards were stolen. This proves to credit card providers that you were diligent, and it can be the first step toward any investigation.

Mike noted: "Some insurance companies, for a small fee, will provide identity theft protection. They not only will insure you for damage but will also provide an agent to handle your case and take many of the steps that I noted above."

Mike summarized by saying, "People can avoid identity theft, as well as all other scams, by paying attention to their surroundings, using common sense, and conducting their own research on any individuals or companies with whom they are interested in doing business. I hope the information in this chapter will prevent readers from becoming another statistic and that it will make their lives less taxing."

"Hey, Mike, that is my line," I quipped.

"Okay. Let me summarize what we said."

"There are a number of tax scams going on today, as listed below."

A Review of What You Have Learned

The Top 12 Tax Scams

1. **Phishing letters or e-mails:** Phishing scams involve your receiving valid-looking letters that ask for your personal information. Many times these letters allegedly come from the IRS or some other governmental agency.
2. **Economic Stimulus payments:** These communications allege that you need to give some personal information to get your stimulus check.
3. **Frivolous tax arguments:** Promoters cite a host of bogus reasons why you don't need to pay taxes or file tax returns.
4. **Fuel credits:** These are available only for off-road use of vehicles.
5. **Hiding income offshore:** Promoters falsely claim that Americans are not taxed on their worldwide income.
6. **Abusive retirement account arrangements:** Promoters falsely claim that you can transfer appreciated property in retirement plans.
7. **Claiming zero wages:** Promoters falsely claim that you can file returns claiming zero wages. This is just a variant of the frivolous tax argument scams.
8. **Filing false claims for refunds:** Promoters of this scam say that you can file a phony claim for refund and get back all of your money that you paid to the IRS.
9. **Return preparer fraud:** This involves falsely inflated or entirely made-up deductions and credits that were suggested by tax return preparers. In addition, IRS has gone after a number of tax preparers who have inflated credentials claiming they are CPAs, lawyers, PhDs, and other professionals, when they don't have these credentials.
10. **Disguising corporate ownership:** Promoters use fictional names and trusts to try to disguise the ownership of the assets and of the income received.
11. **Misusing trusts:** Promoters falsely recommend foreign trusts in order to avoid recognition of income. Americans and Canadians are taxed on their worldwide income.
12. **Abusing deduction allowances for contributions to charitable and nonprofit organizations:** In this scam, organizations are set up to avoid taxes. Many times they get tax-exempt status and encourage charitable contributions where the money is largely siphoned off to the promoters of the charities, and little money ever inures to the charity.

There is one more tax-related scam: Be careful of the tax reduction scams that promise to reduce taxes beyond what is actually possible.

Two Common Investment Scams

1. **Ponzi schemes:** Similar to Bernie Madoff's operations, Ponzi schemes use new investors' money to pay off previous investors.
2. **Stocks and commodities trading software scams:** Generally the promoters recommend very overpriced trading software that is sold at their seminars. The software programs usually don't work any better than cheaper versions that are available elsewhere. Remember, if you have a gold mine that gives gold nuggets, are you going to sell it or tell anyone about it for any price?

Seminar Schemes

These vary from trying to get large investments from you without complying with the SEC's requirements to Ponzi schemes to providing high-priced seminars that provide little content but lots of sales pitches.

Inheritance Scams

These are otherwise known as *Nigerian scams* because many seem to involve some Nigerian who wants to bring in a large amount of money to the United States but first needs some money to clear U.S. financial hurdles.

Pyramid Scams

There are two types of pyramid scams readers need to be aware of: illegal chain letter scams and illegal network marketing scams.

Advertised Products and Services

This is not a scam per se. However, generally no one should ever buy a product recommended by some celebrity who is paid to be a spokesperson. The celebrity's endorsement just inflates the cost of the products.

Other Scams Such as Book Scams

Promoters seem to recommend a newly published book, but their recommendation is not necessarily genuine because they are being paid to make it. Be wary of anyone who promotes a new book authored by someone else, especially if the promoter wants you to buy the book within a one-week time frame. In such cases, the sales pressure is the result of the author wanting to make some bestseller list.

Identity Theft

This is a major problem worldwide. Many criminals use shoulder surfing and dumpster diving to find out personal information. Paying strong attention to who might be listening to your conversations when you are in public and to shredding documents that contain your personal information can significantly reduce this problem. If you are a victim of identity theft, read over the steps above that you should take.

Notes

1. http://www.postandcourier.com/article/20120414/PC16/120419549&slId=6.

8

Homes and Mortgages

Home is where you hang your head.
        —Groucho Marx

However, if you don't know what you are doing taxwise, you can get your head handed to you by the IRS.

        —Sandy Botkin

What You Will Learn
- Pros and cons of homeownership
- What to look for in evaluating a home purchase
- Comparing 15- and 30-year mortgages
- Types of mortgages
- Advantages and disadvantages of the different types of mortgages
- How to avoid mortgage insurance
- Reverse mortgages

Pros and Cons of Home Ownership

Steven is the perfect person to interview for this topic. He has been a successful loan officer for many years and is a partner in a large mortgage banking operation. I met him when I spoke at a seminar. His knowledge was very impressive.

I took my son, Matt, with me instead of my wife, Lori. Matt is both a CPA and passed the Certified Financial Planner exam. He also has a master's in financial planning; thus, he has a lot of insight into financial issues that I might not have. In fact, Matt suggested that I add the reverse mortgage discussion to this book, which is a great, useful idea.

"Hi Steven. I brought my son, Matt, so that he can help with any topics that I might not think of. He just passed the CPA, and he also just passed the Certified Financial Planner exam.

Advantages of Homeownership

Steven responded, "Matt, it is nice to meet you. You surely do have an impressive résumé," which made Matt give one of his Cheshire cat smiles. Steven also added, "From what I can tell, you and your dad are going to have a seminal work for us baby boomers and generation Xers," which made Matt and me smile.

"Okay, Steven. Let's get to work. What are the main advantages of homeownership that renters don't get?" I inquired.

Steven responded, "Actually there are so many advantages to homeownership that I am surprised that anyone rents.

"First, as a homeowner, you get to deduct both your mortgage interest and property taxes. Renters don't have interest expense, and they usually don't pay the property taxes unless it is on a commercial property and their lease requires it. These deductions may significantly reduce the taxes for homeowners.

"Second, we all need a place to live unless we can find a nice, heated, free cave or igloo. Thus, we need to spend money on accommodations whether we rent or purchase a home.

"Third, as you know, if you sell your home, you have great tax advantages as well. Single people can avoid taxes on up to $250,000 of capital gain completely. Married people can avoid taxes on up to $500,000 of gain.

"Fourth, homes have historically provided tremendous appreciation upon retirement. I don't know if you knew this, but the majority of the equity for most retirees is in their own principal residence."

Matt perked up and noted, "Yes, we learned that in my graduate class. If I remember correctly, my professor said that for most people, their home was from 30 to 50 percent or more of their net worth."

Steven, obviously impressed with Matt, noted, "Yes, based on my experience, I would say that statistic is about right. I have also seen situations in which the vast majority of a retiree's net worth was in his or her home. In fact, I've seen it as high as 80 percent of a retiree's net worth."

Steven smoothly continued and said, "Okay, the fifth reason for homeownership is leverage. You can buy a home for as little as 10 percent down. And with loans from the Department of Veterans Affairs (VA), you can actually purchase a residence with no down payment."

Steven then tested Matthew by asking, "Do you know what I mean by *leverage*, Matt, and can you give me an example of it in effect?"

Matt smiled and responded, "Yes, *leverage* means using other people's money. Thus any appreciation is greatly magnified. If I put $10,000 down and borrow the remaining $90,000, my total purchase might be $100,000 even though I used only $10,000 of my own money. So if the house appreciates $10,000, I have made 100 percent on my money because my down payment was only $10,000."

Steven replied, "Are you sure that you are only age 25? That was a terrific answer. Your graduate training must have been terrific."

I said, "Now you see, Steven, why I brought Matt with me."

Steven then went on to note, "However, leverage works two ways. In recent years, many people have seen their house values drop. Since some of these folks have had very little down payment, especially in California, they have also magnified their losses many times over what they invested, which is why a number of people are sadly walking away from their homes.

"Sixth, buying a home results in a forced savings. You are building up equity in the form of both appreciation and the principal payments on your loan. I can't emphasize enough how it feels to own a home free and clear upon retirement. Renters end up enriching someone else forever."

I interrupted Steven by saying, "I use a great example in my real estate course in which I teach real estate brokers. Let's assume that you were to buy a home for $500,000. Even if you finance most of the price and the house never appreciates, you will eventually own the home free and clear. This means that through the forced savings of your payments, you have $500,000 of equity even if the house never appreciates!"

Steven then reiterated a benefit when he said, "Finally, when you own your home, you will eventually live rent free once the mortgage is paid off. The feeling of living mortgage and rent free upon retirement is amazingly uplifting." I silently cursed my county real estate taxes here in Maryland, which seem to always escalate.

Smiling, I interrupted and said, "Yes, we paid off our mortgages several years ago. I was so excited that I wanted to have a mortgage burning party. My wife, Lori, stopped me from doing this or even telling anyone about it because many of our friends were not the savers that we were. They still have a mortgage. In addition, some are still suffering from this economic downturn, and Lori felt that having this party would be rubbing salt into their wounds."

Steven noted in agreement with Lori.

Disadvantages of Homeownership: When Renting Is Better Than Buying

Matt then prodded Steven by inquiring, "I do agree that buying is usually much better than renting; however, aren't there situations in which renting is preferable? After all, people who have horrible credit might not have a choice. Likewise, people whose income is too low for the house payments might get financially overwhelmed."

Steven nodded and replied, "Yes. If they are not making enough income, they will probably not be able to get the credit that they need. Even if they do get the credit, they might find the payments tough to meet. Moreover, if they have horrible credit, buying a house will be tough. However, it won't be impossible. For example, they might be able to finance a new home using either VA financing or *seller financing*. Many sellers are willing to finance a buyer's purchase especially if they need to sell the home. Sellers typically aren't as savvy as bankers. They don't conduct the same credit checks that the banks do, although they should. The bottom line is, there are times when renting might be preferable.

"Another good example might be when people are moving every few years such as for military service. If someone is forced to move frequently, his or her closing costs could outweigh the property's appreciation. In fact, rarely do homes appreciate enough in a few years to pay off both the costs of purchases and of sales. Another example might be when someone has a tenuous job that could be lost at any time. Buying a home would be a risky maneuver."

What to Look for in Evaluating a Home Purchase

"Steven," I prodded, "what factors should my readers look for in evaluating a home purchase?"

Steven remarked, "There are several criteria that I would recommend. The first and foremost is location, location, location. If you have kids, you'll want to be near good schools. Not all schools are equal in most cities. You'll also want proximity to shopping and maybe even public transportation."

I interrupted Steven by saying, "Yes, here in Montgomery County, Maryland, we moved 10 minutes closer to Washington, DC, in order to get our kids into the Wootton School District, which is a top-notch school district. Our schools really do vary widely even within the same county."

Steven nodded with understanding and then noted, "You also don't want to buy the most expensive house in the neighborhood. You will have a hard time selling it. In fact, this may sound rather strange, but over time, many houses with the same number of bedrooms and bathrooms will equal out in price even if they are a bit smaller than the expensive models.

"Also, there are some good cosmetic improvements that significantly increase a house's value and make it sell quicker. Examples of these improvements are decks, fireplaces, solar panels, new kitchen cabinets, and granite, Corian, or other stone countertops. Having energy-saving appliances is also a nice touch."

Steven added, "I would also note that having a recent home inspection really does help in both making me feel better about a home and in the resale of the home."

He quickly interjected, "I should note that pools and hot tubs rarely increase the value of a house, and in many cases, they decrease the value because of liability issues and maintenance.

"Moreover," Steven added, "having fewer steps to climb especially in elderly communities can be a tremendous plus for resale. Finally, make sure that the house has enough rooms for expansion for more kids. Having only one or two bedrooms might not be enough. Likewise, having a two-car garage or even better, a three-car garage would be a nice addition."

I noted, "Yes, that is a good point, Steven. I have three kids. I needed to add a carport for my kids' cars. I have greatly wished that I had a three-car garage instead of my two-car garage and a carport."

"Finally, having a new paint job, new mulch, and new flowers in front of the house will make the house more salable," said Steven.

Comparing 15- and 30-Year Mortgages

I then asked Steven about an issue that has been asked of me many times. "Steven, I have been asked by many people if it would be better to have a 15-year mortgage or a 30-year mortgage. I've done a lot of research on the issue, and I've found even many financial writers disagree on which is better. Can you share your views on this?"

"Sandy, the reason that you have gotten some conflicting advice is that there are both pros and cons to having either type of mortgage.

"First, there is an obvious advantage of having a 15-year mortgage over a 30-year mortgage: you will save over half the interest. For example, a 5 percent, $200,000 mortgage payable over 30 years would produce monthly payments of $1,074 per month for which the total payments (which includes interest) would be $386,513. If the mortgage were for only 15 years, the payments would go up by about 50 percent to $1,582, which would result in the total payment over the 15 years being $284,685. A whopping $101,828 in interest would be saved by using a 15-year mortgage instead of a 30-year mortgage.

"Moreover, this was for a $200,000 mortgage at 5 percent. If the rate of interest was 6.5 percent or the mortgage was a lot more, say, $400,000, the savings could be well over $200,000 in interest payments!

"Thus, the general rule is the following."

Increasing your monthly payments by about 50 percent drops your total number of loan payments by half.

Steven continued, "Most people believe that you need to double your normal payment on a 30-year loan in order to reduce the loan amortization to 15 years. This isn't true. Simply increasing your payments by 50 percent will essentially cut your total number of payments in half."

Chuckling, I said, "This is why I took out a 15-year mortgage. I wanted to be debt free at retirement. I can tell you that the feeling of being debt free is indescribable! In addition, this was a great forced savings program for me. It was a lot better than if I had put the money in the stock market."

Steven reinforced my actions by saying, "Yes, I definitely see the allure of utilizing a 15-year mortgage exactly for the reasons that you mentioned, Sandy, and for the same reasons, I have no problem with some of my clients doing this."

Steven then went on and added, "However, generally a 30-year mortgage is financially preferable despite the interest savings."

I was a bit dumbfounded: "What is preferable about spending an extra $100,000 to $200,000 or more interest?"

Steven snorted and said, "There actually are several reasons that 30-year loans are preferable to 15-year loans. The first, as you know, is for tax reasons. You can deduct your interest in the United States if you itemize your taxes, which makes it cheaper to pay the interest. In fact, your favorite quote that you use in your seminars is 'Everything is cheaper if you get a deduction . . . cha . . . cha . . . cha.' Obviously, if you live in a country where home mortgage interest isn't deductible, such as Canada, this lack of deduction makes paying interest even more costly, and it might steer my opinion toward a 15-year loan."

Steven continued, "The main reason, however, why I like 30-year or even longer loans is flexibility. Let's say that interest rates drop. You can take advantage of the drop by refinancing your home. In addition, if you want to add an extra 50 percent to your payment, you can convert your 30-year loan to a 15-year loan anyway. Moreover, if you lose your job, it will be much easier to make lower payments on a 30-year mortgage than to make the much higher payments that a 15-year loan would require. This flexibility just can't be beat. This is why I recommend to most of my clients to take out a 30-year mortgage and to increase their monthly payments each month by what they can afford. This way they get the flexibility of lower payments if needed with the ability to pay off the loan in 15 years, not to mention the flexibility of refinancing."

I wagged my finger at Steven and said, "Yes, Steven. What you said may make sense. However, you know that most people are not going to voluntarily prepay their mortgage each month if they don't have to. In addition, adding additional funds to the monthly payments is a form of forced savings that a 15-year mortgage would provide. Finally, having no mortgage payment at retirement is just fabulous. Being debt free from the bank for many people could make a huge change in their lives at retirement."

Steven smiled and retorted, "Yes, this is why you have seen various commentators disagree on this issue. You certainly have a good point too. I guess it depends on the person. If people can be disciplined enough to pre-pay their loan, a 30-year mortgage would be preferable. If saving money is tough for a family and they can afford the higher payments, which would be the only savings they would have, a 15-year mortgage might be the way to go."

Matt chirped up and said, "You know, Dad, I would add one other factor. If people can make more interest than what the bank is charging on their mortgage, they should take out the longer loan. Let's face it: if I can make more money than the 5 percent that the bank is charging me, I might be better off buying stocks or other investments that give me a better rate of return while deducting the interest."

Steven looked dumbfounded at Matthew while I said, "See why I brought Matt with me? He has always been very savvy, even at a young age."

After overcoming his shock that a 25-year-old could be so financially mature, Steven replied, "Yes, Matt, you are quite right. However, it is a bit more than that. A lot depends on your tax bracket. *Tax bracket* means what you pay on the last dollar you earn. If you are in the 30 percent bracket (you need to consider both the federal and state income tax brackets), which is true for many people, then you benefit by a deduction to the extent of 30 percent. In other words, the government subsidizes your deduction by your tax bracket. Thus, if you are paying 6 percent interest and are in the 30 percent bracket, your actual cost, net of the government's 30 percent subsidy, will be 4.2 percent after taxes. If you are in the 40 percent bracket, which doesn't take that much income to reach, your actual cost will be 3.6 percent after taxes. Thus, if you can make an after-tax rate of return greater than these numbers, you would probably want a longer loan."

Matt nodded and said, "Yes, that makes perfect sense."

I decided to interrupt Steven to ask about the formula.

So the formula for my readers would be to take (1 minus the tax bracket) times the interest rate to calculate their actual after-tax cost, right?

I probed further: "So, if I am paying 6 percent on my mortgage and have a federal and state tax bracket of about 33 percent, which is common for many people, the formula would be the following, right?"

(1 – 0.33) × 6 percent = 4 percent

"This would be the after-tax cost to me of paying interest or the after-tax savings by not having a mortgage, right?" I asked.

Steven nodded and replied, "Yes, if you can earn substantially more than the net after-tax cost of your interest deduction, you shouldn't prepay the loan. Moreover, as you noted in Chapter 6 on getting out of debt, you would be better off paying off other loans that have a high nondeductible interest rate such as credit cards."

Steven then suggested helpfully, "It is also wise to prepay your mortgage when most of your payment is principal. The way the amortization tables work, most of your payments are interest in the first few years. Slowly, more of the payment becomes principal, and less of it is interest because your balance starts decreasing each year. A lower balance means less interest for that year. When you are in the last four to five years of your loan, most of the payments are principal. Thus, paying off the loan when you are in the latter few years of your loan would also be a wise move since you are not getting much of an interest deduction anyway."

I reinforced this point by stating, "Yes, that is exactly what I did. I took out a 15-year loan. When I got down to the last 3 years of the loan, I paid it off because I wasn't getting much of an interest deduction anyway."

Types of Mortgages

We decided to question Steven on an area that has been the source of constant questions from clients and participants at my seminars, which is this: What type of mortgage is best?

"Steven," I questioned, "there are many types of mortgages available for home buyers such as adjustable-rate mortgages (ARMs), fixed-rate mortgages, interest-only loans, and balloon mortgages. What are the advantages and disadvantages of each, and which one do you recommend?"

Steven breathed deeply before answering and said, "I knew that you were going to ask me this. First, let's make sure that your readers understand what the differences are between these mortgages."

Fixed-Rate Mortgages

"Fixed-rate mortgages are just that. Borrowers pay a fixed interest rate, and that rate never varies over the life of the mortgage. Thus, not counting property tax increases or homeowners insurance, the payments on these mortgages stay the same throughout the life of the loan, and these are the least risky types of mortgages for borrowers. These mortgages are riskier for the banks so their rates tend to be a bit more than the rates for other mortgages by about 1 percent."

Steven then added, "Moreover, there are various types of fixed-rate loans. You have the conventional fixed-rate loan with a financial institution that has no limit on lending other than your creditworthiness and the value of the underlying property."

FHA Mortgages. "There are Federal Housing Administration (FHA) mortgages that allow for loans to be made with less than 3.5 percent in the down payment. These loans are usually easier to get for those with poorer credit (although no one will lend money to people with severely impaired credit). In addition, these FHA loans have limits on the amounts of the loans."

VA Mortgages. "A final type of fixed-rate loan is a Veterans Administration (VA) loan. For these loans, you must be a veteran and get a certificate of eligibility. What is great about the VA loans is that they are assumable by the buyer when it is time to sell the property, and they don't require mortgage insurance even if your down payment is under 20 percent. However, the VA does have loan limits. To find out about VA loans, call 800-827-1000 or go to www.homeloans.va.gov."

Adjustable-Rate Mortgages

"Adjustable-rate mortgages came into being because people wanted cheaper monthly payments in order to afford their loans. Thus, banks offer lower initial rates that vary with various factors such as the prime rate. In addition, since banks can charge more interest as rates increase, these mortgages are less risky to the banks or financial institutions but riskier for the borrowers. These mortgages, however, do have a maximum increase on the interest-rate adjustment each year, and many have a lifetime cap. Thus, there is a limit to the borrower on the risk.

"The adjustments to interest are based on the type of adjustable rate loan. For example, a one-year adjustable-rate loan is adjusted each year. A three-year adjustable-rate loan remains the same for three years but may change every three years."

Interest-Only Mortgages

"Interest-only loans provide lower payments because no principal is being repaid with the payments. Each payment is solely interest. Thus, 10 years down the road, you owe the same amount on the loan that you started with."

Balloon Mortgages

"A balloon payment mortgage typically charges a low interest rate for a period of years, or it charges only the interest for a period of years. This type of loan is typically written for between 5 and 10 years. At the end of the term, the note must be either paid off or refinanced."

Advantages and Disadvantages of the Different Types of Mortgages

Steven continued: "Each of these types of loans has its own advantages and problems. Fixed-rate loans tend to have the highest interest rates among them all. However, these loans also impose the lowest long-term risk to the borrowers. Adjustable-rate loans tend to be riskier because the rates can go up.

The Subprime Mortgage Crisis of 2003 to 2007

"In fact, adjustable-rate loans might have been a big factor in the subprime mortgage meltdown. Here is what happened. Interest rates started going up to the point that many folks with adjustable-rate loans couldn't afford the payments. This started causing more foreclosures, which decreased the sale prices of many homes. This in turn made it harder for folks whose home values had fallen below the amount of their loans to refinance their loans. It was a bad situation."

I agreed and said, "Yes, I have seen a number of people lose their homes."

"Exactly," Steven said. Even worse were the balloon payment and interest-only mortgages that suddenly came due when the interest rates rose. For these homeowners too, like the people who had the adjustable-rate mortgages, the falling values of real estate meant that they couldn't get a bank to refinance their mortgages because their outstanding loan balances were more than the value of the property!

"The worst, however, were the negative amortization loans. These loans provided lower initial monthly payments for several years over what the homeowners would have paid with 30-year loans. Thus, if the normal amortization monthly payment was $1,800, folks who took out these negative amortization loans might have paid only $1,200 per month for the first 3 years. The $600-a-month difference was then added to the total amount of the loan. Thus, the borrowers would have a larger loan balance at the end of 3 years. After this 3-year period was over, the payments would increase to amortize the whole loan including those payments that were added to the loan balance."

Matt interrupted: "Why would anyone agree to a balloon mortgage or interest-only mortgage or even worse, a negative amortization loan? Didn't people realize how dangerous these loans were?"

Steven responded, "You have to understand, Matt, that financing in the 1980s, 1990s, and even in early 2000s was a wild and woolly situation. Financial institutions could get away with a lot. For example, California banks were writing 100 percent loan-to-value mortgages, and sometimes they were lending even more than the value. The lenders were allowed to do this partly because the regulators didn't do their jobs properly, in my opinion, but also because housing prices were solidly increasing. Moreover, home buyers wanted to buy the properties, and they needed funds to do so. These buyers didn't care about the terms. Historically, nothing appreciated as readily or as consistently as real estate appeared to. People concluded that real estate loans were not that risky due to the appreciation in property values that was constantly occurring, especially in some areas of the country like California. In addition, our country had a policy of trying to get as many people as possible into home ownership. Anything that encouraged people to buy homes was considered good for the country."

What to Look For in Evaluating Mortgages

"Okay, Steven," I said. "What are the recommended best mortgages? And none of this 'it depends' nonsense."

Steven laughed and said, "Sandy, it really does depend. Certainly, I can say, now that I have a lot of hindsight, people should stay away from balloon mortgages and negative amortization loans especially in this tight money environment. To me, balloon mortgages are like neutron bombs: they leave the property but can kill the people. In addition, I would stay away from interest-only loans too. You really want that increased equity in your home by paying off your mortgage.

"As for adjustable-rate mortgages, it really does depend on the situation. In some situations, you don't have a choice. For example, adjustable-rate loans are usually the only financing available for commercial property. Moreover, if you are in a period of declining interest rates, starting off with an adjustable-rate mortgage would be ideal since your payments will automatically decrease. In addition, if you want to refinance the adjustable-rate mortgage, you can, and at lower rates especially if interest rates are decreasing.

"My overall recommendation, however, is to get a fixed-rate loan. Normally these are the best, absent a climate of decreasing interest rates. You might pay an extra 1 percent interest or so, but this rate will never increase. Likewise, if the rates drop considerably, you can refinance these loans too. Thus, if rates go up, you are locked in with lower rates. If rates go down considerably, you can refinance and obtain the new rates. It is a win-win for the borrower. The only downside is that there are costs of refinancing every time you refinance, and you start off with a slightly higher interest rate than that of an adjustable-rate mortgage."

"Yes, Steven, I think you are right. I would also add one more caveat. I would not take on an adjustable-rate loan solely because the initial interest rate makes it affordable. If someone can't pay the maximum rate, assuming rates do increase, these loans can be too dangerous," I added.

Both Steven and Matt agreed with my statement, which always makes me feel a bit smarter.

"Steven," I inquired, "are there any other topics regarding mortgages that you want to mention before we move onto the topic of reverse mortgages?"

How to Avoid Mortgage Insurance

"Yes. First, most borrowers should avoid mortgage insurance, which is a charge made by a financial institution in order to insure that you will pay off your loan. A bank is supposed to require a 20 percent down payment in order to make a loan fairly risk free. If it takes less than that, say, 5 percent, it will require the borrower to pay mortgage insurance. The insurance will pay the bank the remaining part of the 20 percent equity if the borrower defaults. Thus, you are insuring the financial institution against its risk."

Steven added, "The cost for this insurance depends on your down payment. Generally the cost can be as low as about $60 per month, but it can run as high as several hundred per month depending on the amount of the loan and the amount of your down payment."

The lower the down payment, the higher the premium for mortgage insurance.

"The good news is that if you put at least 20 percent down as a down payment, you will not be charged mortgage insurance. Likewise, when your home value increases so that your equity in your home is at least 20 percent of the loan, you can ask to have the mortgage insurance removed."

Reverse Mortgages

"Steven, I see a lot of commercials on television about reverse mortgages for the elderly where folks can get their equity out of their home and use it for retirement. What do you think about these types of mortgages?" I inquired.

"First, we need to outline what a reverse mortgage is. These are designed for older folks, usually age 62 or older (and preferably age 70 or older). With these mortgages, the banks pay the homeowners instead of the homeowners paying the bank, as they would for a normal loan. In effect, the banks are lending the homeowners the money on the basis of their home equity, and the proceeds from the loans are generally tax free. Generally, the older the homeowners, the more they can borrow.

Advantages and Disadvantages of Reverse Mortgages

"What is good about these loans is that you generally don't need to pay them back until you either die or sell the home or move out of your home. Furthermore, you can usually stay in the home till you pass away or need to move as long as you keep your home insurance in force and pay your property taxes.[1] These loans are also *nonrecourse*, which means that if the bank doesn't sell the home for the amount of the loan, it cannot go after you the borrower for the difference."

Matt inquired, "What happens when the borrower dies and the bank sells the home?"

Steven replied, "The bank will sell the home for what it can get. If that is more than the loan, the family of the borrower will get the difference. If the house doesn't sell for the amount of the loan and accrued interest, the bank gets paid by the government for the difference and the family gets nothing."

"Wow," I exclaimed. "These reverse mortgages seem quite good."

Steven composed his thoughts for a minute and said, "Yes, they do have their benefits. However, there are a number of hidden drawbacks that folks should know about."

"Matt and I are all ears, Steven," I teased.

FHA Insured Reverse Mortgages. "First, there are several types of reverse mortgages, and some are better than others. Among the better types are the *FHA insured reverse mortgages*. These are best if you are 70 years or older since the older you are, the more you can get each month. You also get a 60-day rate guarantee. If rates decline during the first 60 days from the time of your application, you get the lower rates. In addition, like most reverse mortgages, the proceeds are nontaxable, and the loans are *nonrecourse*, which means that the bank can't go after the borrower if the house doesn't sell for the amount of the loan. You also don't have to ever pay anything back for as long as you are living in the house and own the house. Thus, if you live till age 100 or more, the bank cannot foreclose on your house or force you to move.

"One downside to this type of mortgage is that, at the time of this interview, the maximum loan amount is $625,500 or your home equity, whichever is less. In addition, costs involved in this type of loan can be as high as 4 to 5 percent of the loan, which is a bit more than that of uninsured loans. Moreover, all interest keeps compounding on the loan balance. Thus, the borrower's heirs may have no equity left upon the death of the borrower.

"Finally," added Steven, "since the mortgage interest is accruing and not being paid, the mortgage interest is not deductible for income tax purposes. However, even if the homeowner did pay the interest, the deduction for the mortgage interest would be limited since this is not considered *acquisition indebtedness*, which could make the interest nondeductible even if it were being paid!

Lender Insured Reverse Mortgages. "The second type of reverse mortgage is the *lender insured reverse mortgage*. Again you get paid monthly based on your home's equity and your age. The interest can be at a fixed rate, or it can be adjustable. Like the FHA insured mortgages, these are nonrecourse loans, and they do not have to be paid back until either the borrower dies or the borrower moves out or fails to keep up the home insurance or property tax payments.

"With these types of loans, some lenders even provide an annuity for borrowers who move out of their home. In addition, borrowers can usually get more of their home equity in payments than they can get with an FHA insured reverse mortgage."

Steven then added, "The main downside of this type of mortgage is that the loan costs tend to be higher than those associated with an FHA insured reverse mortgage."

Uninsured Reverse Mortgages. Steven went on: "The final type of reverse mortgage, which isn't one I recommend, is the *uninsured reverse mortgage*. This type of mortgage is very different from the other two. First, it is available to you if you are age 62 or older. Second, you get payments for a fixed period of time. Third, although you can get a higher loan than you can get from the other two forms of reverse mortgages, your loan isn't guaranteed. Fourth, the loan costs tend to be lower than they are for the other two types of mortgages.

"The biggest problem with uninsured reverse mortgages is that the loans become due after a set period of time regardless of whether you are alive. Thus, the home might be foreclosed from you, which means that you could lose your home. It is primarily for this reason that I do *not* recommend uninsured reverse mortgages."

When to Use Reverse Mortgages and When Not To

"Steven, all of this information is really making my head spin. What is your bottom line on when to use reverse mortgages and when not to?"

"Okay, here's a list of the disadvantages of reverse mortgages."

- Compound interest works against you. You are constantly accruing interest.
- These mortgages involve high fees, which can be from $6,000 to $13,000 up to 2 percent of the fair market value of your home. Thus, the overall fees can be as high as 5 percent of the loan balance.
- There are also origination fees of $2,000 or more in addition to the other high fees.
- And if this isn't enough in fees, the banks have additional options for charging fees for servicing the loans.
- Because of the high fees, these types of loans should be used only for long-term loans. This usually means more than five years. For short-term loans incurred with reverse mortgages, the loan costs could be equivalent to paying 40 percent interest, which is why you want to take advantage of these for the long term.
- The interest that accrues is not deductible for income tax purposes.
- Even if you do pay the interest and don't let it accrue, then the deduction for the interest may be limited or even nondeductible depending on use of the received funds.
- You must keep the home, keep it insured, keep it in good condition, and keep paying all of your property taxes. You *cannot* rent it out or change the title.

Steven gave us the following list of conditions for when a reverse mortgage is ideal:

- The borrowers are over age 70.
- The borrowers' homes have appreciated a lot, and the borrowers have few liquid assets.
- The borrowers income needs are great.
- You want tax-free payments when you receive them. Thus, they don't affect social security or Medicare.

Steven concluded: "There are some final comments I want to make to everyone: Do *not* use a reverse mortgage to gamble in the stock market You also don't want to use these types of mortgages if you want to leave a legacy for your kids. The costs and accrued interest will quickly eat up all of the equity. There are cheaper and better ways to get money out of your home equity than using reverse mortgages."

Matt added, "You also don't want to use these mortgages to gamble at a casino," which made Steven and me chuckle with agreement.

An Alternative to a Reverse Mortgage: A Sale Leaseback

"Steven, I can think of a good technique that I teach in my course that is a lot less expensive than a reverse mortgage and that will keep the home as a legacy for the family. Folks can use the *sale leaseback technique*. Here they can sell their home to their kids and lease it back at fair market value. This way there are no costs or commissions, and the parents still can get their equity out of the home. I discuss this in depth both in my home study course and in my book *Lower Your Taxes—Big Time!*, both of which are found on my website at www.taxreduction institute.com.

Matt perked up at this and interjected, "Dad, I would LOVE to buy your home once I get financially situated. In fact, maybe you can just give it to me," which made me laugh.

I responded, "I don't think your brother and sister would approve of my giving you the house; however, I might be inclined toward the sale leaseback if I felt you could easily afford the payments. I don't want to have to foreclose on my own son," which caused Steven to laugh but made Matt a bit nervous.

Before we finished, Steven asked Matt, "What type of firm do you want to work for?"

Matt's response was vintage Matt, "I want to work for a financial planning firm to hone my skills and to become partner!" Steven looked at me and winked, which echoed his appreciation of Matt's goals.

"Sandy and Matt, let's see what you learned."

A Review of What You Have Learned

- Owning a home has a lot of major benefits and should be attempted by most people instead of renting a home. These benefits include the following:
  - You can take advantage of tax benefits in deducting your mortgage interest and property taxes.
  - You would need to spend money on a place to live anyway.
  - Upon sale, you can avoid taxes on up to $250,000 of capital gain if you are single and up to $500,000 if you are married.
  - Historically, real estate has appreciated tremendously.
  - Owning a home can provide you with lots of leverage, which requires relatively little down payment.
  - A mortgage can be a kind of forced savings as you make your loan payments.
  - Eventually you will live rent free when the mortgage is paid off.
- However, renting might be preferable for those with poor credit, for those who move a lot, for those who don't make enough money to cover their loan payments easily, and for those who have an insecure job.

- In evaluating whether to buy a home, you should consider the following factors in order to maximize the appreciation potential:
  - Look at the home's location, location, location in relation to nearby schools, shopping, and public transportation.
  - Don't buy the most expensive house in the area.
  - Make good, cost-effective cosmetic improvements such as solar panels, decks, Corian or granite countertops, and energy-saving appliances.
  - If you are in an elderly neighborhood, get a house without steps.
- Generally a 30-year loan is better than a 15-year loan due to its flexibility. However, prepaying the loan by paying more each month would be a smart idea:
  - Generally adding an extra 50 percent per month in payment reduces the overall number of loan payments by half. Thus, a 30-year loan would be converted to a 15-year loan by adding an extra 50 percent to each month's payment.
  - If you have a hard time saving money, having a 15-year loan might be a good, relatively cheap way to force yourself to save money regularly.
- Generally a fixed-rate loan is much more preferable to an adjustable-rate loan unless mortgage interest rates are clearly declining.
- Never use a balloon mortgage or negative amortization loan. They are like neutron bombs: they kill the people while leaving the property.
- Always consider an FHA and especially a VA loan because of their lower down payment requirements and borrowing costs. In addition, VA loans are assumable. However, both have limits on how much you can borrow.
- Reverse mortgages have their benefits. You can get your equity out of your home on a tax-free basis through monthly payments, and you don't have to pay back the bank unless you move out, die, fail to keep up the insurance or property taxes, or fail to keep the property in good condition. Also, reverse mortgages are nonrecourse loans, which means that the bank can't go after the borrower if the house doesn't sell for the amount of the loan. There are three types of reverse mortgages:
  - FHA insured mortgages do not have to be paid back till the borrower either dies or moves out. Although all reverse mortgages have high costs, this type has among the lower costs, and it has a 60-day guarantee on the interest rate from the date of the borrower's application.
  - Insured reverse mortgages provide payments based on your equity, similarly to FHA mortgages. However, they have slightly higher costs. Like FHA mortgages, the bank does not get its money back until the borrower either moves out or dies.
  - Uninsured reverse mortgages tend to provide more money and have lower loan costs. However, they usually pay out for a set period of time before the bank wants its money back, which could cause the borrower to lose the home if he or she is still alive. Thus, these types of mortgages are not recommended.
- All reverse mortgages are very costly. They can easily cost from $6,000 to $13,000 to more than that just to get the loan; plus there is the cost of the accrued interest. These types of loans can be very detrimental to people who want to leave a legacy to their family. If borrowers have other money to live

on, they should generally avoid these due to their high costs. Other ways to get money out of the home equity can involve the sale of the home or a sale lease-back.
- People who are ideal for reverse mortgages are the following:
  - People who have few resources outside their home but who have lots of equity
  - People who are age 70 or older
  - People who don't want to leave a legacy for their family unless the reverse mortgage will be for a short-term life expectancy

Notes

1. A problem that most people don't realize is that over 10 percent of the people who take out reverse mortgages lose their homes because they can't afford the property insurance or property taxes, which in many states keep escalating. This is a huge problem that all potential borrowers should plan for.

9

Investing, Part I

In investing money, the amount of interest you want should depend on whether you want to eat well or sleep well.
—Kenfield Morley

> **What You Will Learn**
> • Ten common investing mistakes
> • Investing in gold

Matt and I couldn't wait to see my friend Jeff again. Jeff is one of the more renowned financial planners and investment advisors that I know. He has a huge number of clients and manages over $200 million of people's money.

When we got to his house, I was reminded that although his house was a good sized white house, which reminded me of the presidential White House, it wasn't as big as I would have thought a successful financial planner like Jeff would have had. He has always been frugal, which should give you a clue about his life.

Ten Common Investing Mistakes

Wasting no time, we sat down to business. "I first want to focus on what people should *not* do, which sadly many people ignore. Thus, we will start our discussion on investment mistakes."

1. Buying Stocks Based on the Latest TV Commentary on Them

Jeff said, "There was a study, conducted many years ago, by Wall Street firms to find out the best way to make a return on investment of a solid 20 percent or more. Here is what they found."

- Sell investments and make commissions.
- Or tout stocks on TV and take a position in those stocks before recommending them on TV.

"Today, they can still tout stocks and have a position in them as long as they disclose it.

"The problem," Jeff noted, "is that these stocks tend to move up for a very short period of time and then go back to their original price or even below their original price at the time of the tout."

Jeff smoothly continued, "This is why most people who have bought a stock right after it was touted by Cramer, Ludlow, and other TV analysts lost money." So the rule is simple:

Never buy a stock right after some TV commentator touts it.

2. Buying High and Selling Low

"The second mistake is to avoid buying high and selling for a lower price."

"Wait a minute, Jeff," I teased. "Doesn't everyone try to buy low and sell high?"

Jeff smiled and said, "You wouldn't believe how many people buy high and sell low. They do the exact opposite because they act emotionally."

Matt then asked, "Why do you think most people buy high and sell at a lower price?"

Jeff smirked a bit and said, "The reason is a combination of fear and greed. They buy a stock usually for the wrong reasons. The stock starts going up, and they might even buy more. Since the stock market is cyclical, the stock might then start dropping. Now they get worried, but they say to themselves that things will be fine. However, the stock keeps dropping, and now the fear sets in. They read in the media about the terrible economy, the rising unemployment numbers, jobs lost, Greece's default on its debts, alligators eating people, and so on. The further the stock market drops, the more fearful they get. They begin to fear that they won't have a retirement or college fund left. At some point when the stock gets low enough and pain of loss becomes too great, they sell. Thus, they sell for a low price.

"Now, eventually, the stock starts going up, but they don't buy it back because they aren't sure that this is a real rally. They keep reading negative news in the newspaper or keep seeing negative news on television. However, the stock keeps going up and up until they become 'sure' that a rally is in full swing, and then they repurchase the stock at a high price. This happens all the time."

3. Using Short-Term Trading Strategies

Jeff further noted that despite the fact that mutual funds have averaged an incredible, long-term, compounded rate of return of 9 percent, most mutual fund investors have lost money because they didn't keep the funds long enough and gave into their fears.

"This leads us to our third mistake: Don't be a day trader. Only buy stocks, mutual funds, exchange-traded funds (ETFs), and real estate investment trusts (REITs) for the long haul.

"A large number of people are buying trading software and trying to beat the market using short-term trading strategies based on daily market or stock movements. Sadly, the vast number of people that try this lose money. The software that is usually sold to the public doesn't really work well. Even worse, the commissions will eventually eat up any profits that you might have made."

"Jeff," I said, "I know someone who was a short-term trader in options. He bought or sold options that expired in less than one month. He made a huge amount of money for years. However, during the one year when the economy tanked, he lost all of the profits that he had earned over the last five years."

Frowning, Jeff responded, "You don't need to warn me about the pitfalls of trading. Yes, short-term or day traders almost always lose money over the long term. I wish people understood that. Sadly, they all think that they will be the exception."

4. Using Full Service, High-Commission Brokerages

"The fourth investment mistake is investing through full-service brokers and high-load mutual funds.

"Two of the full-service brokers are Merrill Lynch and Morgan Stanley. They can easily charge 2 percent or more for each buy and sell if you do not request a discount. If you are going to buy individual stocks, you should almost always use a discount broker. Don't be a sucker. Many of the same analytical services are now available to discount brokers. If, however, you are going to have an advisor manage your portfolio, always pay the advisor an asset management fee, and never retain the advisor on a commission basis unless the commission is based on yearly results."

5. Being Underdiversified

"Don't be underdiversified." Jeff continued, "You can never be diversified enough. I have rarely met anyone who is diversified enough. Owning a few stocks or bonds is *not* right for most people. Instead, I would suggest that the average person should own at least 50 or more different types of stocks from many sectors and even from foreign countries. This means owning some growth stocks, income stocks, foreign stocks, bonds, cash, and some real estate or real estate investment trusts.

"Remember the following important point."

Concentration of funds can make you rich, but diversification can keep you rich.

"In fact, the best way to become diversified is through mutual funds and exchange-traded funds."

Being a bit perplexed myself, I asked, "What is an exchange-traded fund?"

While smirking, Jeff asked Matt, "Can you answer your dad, Matt?"

Matt smiled and said, "Sure. An *exchange-traded fund* (ETF) is a form of mutual fund that owns a basket of securities that are all listed on a particular stock exchange. The fund might own a group of stocks that mirrors the list of stocks in the Dow Jones Index, which is 30 stocks, or in the Standard & Poor's 500 Index stock listing. These funds replicate those indexes perfectly since they actually own the stocks that make up the index, and they receive and pay to investors dividends too. In addition, because there is very little management in ETFs, management fees are much lower than those found in traditional open-end mutual funds."

Jeff was awestruck with Matt's answer as was I. Jeff then said, "Matt, make sure you see me when you are ready to start your financial planning career."

Jeff then regained his composure and said, "I would always recommend either mutual funds or exchange-traded funds, especially for a small investor or one who is just starting out. Interestingly, funds can also own bonds, foreign stocks, and even have cash, such as money market accounts. In fact, they can even own real estate in the form of real estate investment trusts (REITs). Buying individual stocks is a very risky move for most investors because they need a lot of time to manage their investments. They also need strong financial and math knowledge.

"The key," Jeff added, "is to be diversified enough.

"In fact, let me give you an example, Sandy. Let's say that I have the following three different types of investments."

Investment A will give a guaranteed 4 percent rate of return tomorrow.
Investment B will give a guaranteed 10 percent rate of return tomorrow
if it rains or snows and give nothing if it doesn't rain or snow.
Investment C will give a guaranteed 10 percent rate of return if it is
sunny and give nothing if it rains or snows.

"Sandy, which investment would you take without checking on the
weather forecast?"

I was a bit taken back by this and said, "I would take the guaranteed 4
percent investment, which is Investment A."

Jeff smiled and said, "You would be wrong. The best answer is to put
half your money into Investment B and half into Investment A. This way
you will guarantee yourself a 5 percent rate of return no matter what happens to the weather."

Jeff felt he was on a roll and excitedly continued, "This summarizes the
principle of diversification in a nutshell. Being very diversified will actually
cut your risk and increase your long-term rate of return."

"That was a great example, Jeff. However, I want to add one more item
to this discussion. Diversification also means diversifying your planners.
If I am worth substantially more than $500,000, I would never have one
person or one firm managing everything. I believe, due to the $500,000
of security protection available to investors, that investors should have
only the greater of 10 percent of their portfolio or $500,000 with any one
broker or planner. This way if a Bernie Madoff situation happens, they are
protected.

"Also, to even get insurance for theft, which normally covers $500,000
for thefts of securities and $250,000 for thefts of cash, the firm must be
a Securities Investor Protection Corporation (SIPC) member firm. The
investment firm will note this protection in its literature. If it doesn't have
SIPC insurance, I would advise investors to avoid that firm.

"Some firms have even more protection that they have purchased
with Lloyd's of London. For example, Raymond James, a full service
brokerage firm (which I am not necessarily endorsing) has purchased
an additional $750 million of coverage with a sublimit of $1.9 million
per customer for cash above the basic SIPC for the wrongful theft of
customer funds. This protection also applies if the firm fails financially
and is unable to meet its obligations. However, this protection does not
apply to losses due to market fluctuations. Other firms might have also
increased their protection above the SIPC limits. Thus, investors using
these firms should always inquire whether the brokerage firm has additional protection against theft or losses resulting from the firms' failing
financially."

Jeff winced at that but said, "Well, I would never tell my clients that, nor would any other planners, but you do have a point. In my case, I am very honorable and certainly would never do what Bernie Madoff did, and it wouldn't be a problem, not to mention that the firm that I use, which is Raymond James, has higher protection limits."

6. Failing to Pay Off High-Interest Credit Cards

Jeff continued, "One of the best investments that most people can make is to pay off any high-interest credit card balances. I am shocked at folks who want to invest money in the market while they are incurring 18 to 24 percent interest on some debts. Pay off the high-interest debts! It is definitely one of the best investments anyone can make. Doing so provides a guaranteed, high-yielding, safe return."

Jeff then pursed his lips, narrowed his eyes, and grimly noted, **"However, paying off debts does not work as a strategy if you simply borrow money to pay off the debt and then run up the credit card balances again."**

7. Failing to Have a Reserve Account

"I am astonished at how many people are living from hand to mouth each day. The average person can live without a paycheck for less than a month. People should have solid reserves for unemployment and emergencies, and they should maintain approximately one year's worth of earnings. This reserve should be in risk-free funds and easily accessible."

I grinned and said, "Jeff, Chapter 2 is devoted to this subject, and I wholeheartedly agree with you."

8. Failing to Consider Personal Aversion to Risk

Jeff said that another prevalent investment mistake is failing to invest in accordance with the investor's risk tolerance. "I know someone who is very rich. He has all of his money invested in the stock market, against my wishes. Every day he stresses out about the market's fluctuations. Slight drops in the market make him want to sell. He would buy high and sell low if I didn't counsel him. He probably shouldn't be invested entirely in the stock market given his investment fears."

Jeff patiently continued, "Folks need to understand their tolerance for risk. If they are very risk averse, they should have very little exposed to fluctuating investments. Generally, the younger you are, the longer you have to recoup from a bad market. However, simply because you are young does *not* mean that you should have all of your funds in the stock market."

9. Failing to Have at Least Some Money in the Stock Market

"Sandy and Matt, there is a basic principle that everyone needs to understand. In the long run, owners make more money than creditors. This means that the stock market should outperform the bond market over the long term. It always has and probably always will. Let's face it: who would borrow money unless they could earn more than the interest rate that they are paying? This means that everyone should own some stocks. However, the proportions of stocks in investors' portfolios have to be balanced with their age investment horizon and risk tolerance. A rule of thumb is the following."

100 – age = percent of portfolio in stocks

"I vary this by using the following formula *for those investors who are willing to undertake some risk.*"

110 – age = percent of portfolio in stocks

Let's see what this means.

Jeff asked Matt for his thoughts on the following hypothetical situation: "Using the original (first) formula, if you are age 25, what percentage of your investment portfolio should be in stocks (which might include real estate)?"

Matt answered, "The proportion should be 75 percent because I am age 25."

Jeff said, "Correct." Jeff then continued: "If you were more aggressive, which I would recommend at your age, I would say closer to 85 percent (which is 110 – your age). This tells us how much of your portfolio would be exposed to market fluctuations. This would include mutual funds, ETFs, and real estate. The other 15 percent might be in bonds, utility stocks (which are like bonds), and cash."

"Do you both understand this?" asked Jeff.

I nodded and said, "Yes, this all makes sense. However, what if I am older and am getting risk averse? What if I have a college fund that will be needed for college in a few years? How does this change the equation?"

Jeff responded, "If you are more risk averse or you have need for the money within a few years, then more of the money should be placed in a risk-free investment. The preceding formula applies to funds that you won't need within the next three years or so. This is why folks who set up a college fund by investing in the stock market should convert their investments to risk-free money a few years before college starts. Ideally, they should have a systematic structure in place to reduce the risk associated with college funds that make the investments more conservative as the child approaches college age. Some Section 529 plans will do this automatically."

Matt interrupted here and said, "C'mon, Jeff. What you said might be good ideas, but do most people do this?"

Jeff grinned, looked at Matt, and said, "Well, my clients do this. The key is to have a good manager who knows about this need and can undertake more conservative investments as the time approaches for big expenses such as college costs or weddings.

I also want to add one more idea to this discussion. The above formula that we mentioned is a general guideline for most people. However, some older investors might never need their portfolios to supplement their retirement income due to a substantial pension. If their risk tolerance allows it, they may wish to have a higher allocation to stocks because the investment horizon is longer (based on the assets passing to children and grandchildren).

"Sandy and Matt, there is a basic principle that everyone needs to understand. The stock market is a great hedge against inflation. It has usually not only kept up with inflation but has historically out performed it!"

I decided to tease Jeff: "You're saying that people should usually have some money exposed to stock market risk regardless of risk tolerance. But wait a minute: earlier you just said that our investable portfolio should be based on our risk tolerance. Isn't that a conflict?"

Jeff retorted with the question, "Sandy, did you ever hear the phrase 'going broke slowly?'"

I responded, "Yes, I have, but I want you to explain it to my readers," to which my son chuckled.

Jeff complied with my request: "'Going broke slowly' means investing in something relatively safe where your after-tax rate of return doesn't keep pace with inflation. Let me give an example. There have been some time periods when rates on a certificate of deposit or savings account were 1.5 percent or even less (such as in 2012), which is fully taxable. Let's say that you pay 33 percent of this in taxes, which leaves you with a meager 1 percent after taxes. If we have a 3 percent inflation rate, you are slowly going broke because your nest egg is being eaten away by inflation.[1] **Thus, if your after-tax rate of return is less than the inflation rate, you are going broke slowly!**

"Lou Gehrig earned $100,000 a year as a ball player. At that time, having $100,000 in salary was enormous. You could have bought a house for cash, eaten out every day, and had most of your money left over. Today, $100,000 won't buy most houses. In fact, in many areas of the country, you need more than that simply for the down payment. This illustrates the impact of inflation over time. It is vital that people make enough in earnings, after taxes, to provide for their living expenses and for inflation. Historically, only the stock market and real estate have accomplished this. This is why everyone should have at least some of their money exposed to these investments."

10. Trying to Time the Market

"The final investment mistake is thinking that you can time the market correctly. If you were to see a graph of how well the market performed among various sectors of investments, you would find no correlation. I will say it and hopefully people will take this to heart: **you cannot time the market.** This is why most short-term or day traders don't make money over the long term. This is why you can't pull your money out when you think it is a good opportunity."

Getting even more excited, Jeff added, "As I mentioned, mutual funds earned a compounded rate of return of over 9 percent over the last 40 years. However, this didn't occur every year. In fact, most of this return occurred during a few of the last 40 years. If you had taken your money out at the wrong time, you would have had a significantly lower return. In fact, if you had bought and sold at the wrong times, you may even have had a negative return. Taking a long-term perspective for stocks, mutual funds, and real estate investments is the only really clear way to go for most people."

Investing in Gold

"Jeff, before we move onto a discussion about specific investments, I wanted to ask you about gold. Many people are buying gold bullion as an inflation and currency hedge. In today's economy, people don't know where to put their money so gold seems like a safe place. After all, it has performed amazingly well recently. What do you think of owning gold bullion?"

Jeff smiled and said, "Yes, gold has done well in inflationary economies; however, owning gold bars or bullion is a silly investment. First, you make no income on the gold. Gold doesn't pay dividends. Moreover, it actually costs you to own the gold. You have to pay storage costs as well as commissions for buying and selling gold, and those fees are higher than they are for stocks. In fact, you may also have to pay to have the gold certified and weighed when you want to sell it."

Now being on a roll, Jeff smoothly continued, "However, I do believe that folks should own some type of gold or hard assets as part of being diversified. The secret is *not* to own gold but to own gold or precious metal stock funds. These funds may also have earnings that will be distributed. The value of the funds will also go up with inflation. Finally, the cost of owning these stocks or funds is much lower than owning the physical commodity.

"I want to make one final comment about gold ownership. If you are going to ignore my advice about buying gold bullion, at least buy only gold coins, such as the South African Krugerrand. Although the commissions are high and there are storage costs, you do not need to pay fees for weighing and certifying the gold."

Matt then decided to tease Jeff a bit by adding, "So I shouldn't get my girlfriend a gold ring or gold jewelry? I would love to tell her that she shouldn't ever get these items based on your recommendation."

Rolling his eyes, Jeff said, "Matt, yes, buying gold jewelry or diamond rings aren't good investments in themselves. However, they can provide a lot of dividends with the person that you gave that gift to." At which point, Jeff winked at me and we all chuckled.

A Review of What You Have Learned
Ten Common Investing Mistakes

1. **Buying stocks based on the latest TV commentary on them:** Never buy a stock right after some TV commentator touts it.
2. **Buying high and selling low:** Avoid buying high and selling low.
3. **Using short-term trading strategies:** Only buy stocks, mutual funds, exchange-traded funds, and REITs for the long haul.
4. **Using full-service, high-commission brokerages:** Avoid full-service brokers.
5. **Being underdiversified:** Don't be underdiversified. Being diversified lowers your risk and raises your rate of return.
6. **Failing to pay off high-interest credit cards:** Pay off your high-interest debts and credit cards before you invest in anything else.
7. **Failing to have a reserve account:** Maintain adequate reserve accounts to cover your needs in case of unemployment or emergencies.
8. **Failing to consider personal aversion to risk:** Invest in accordance with your risk tolerance.
9. **Failing to have at least some money in the stock market:** Failing to invest some money in inflationary investments such as stocks or real estate may result in your "going broke slowly." Use the formula 100 − your age = the percentage of your investable portfolio that should be in stocks and real estate. Failing to have some money invested in the stock market and/or the real estate market can expose your portfolio to losses due to inflation.
10. **Trying to time the market:** Thinking that you are some special person who can time the market correctly can cause you to lose money.

Investing in Gold. If you are going to invest in gold, own a precious metal stock fund. If you are going to ignore that advice, then at least buy only gold coins such as Krugerrands. This will avoid the costs of certifying and weighing the gold.

Notes

1. Inflation data can be obtained from these two sites: http://inflationdata.com/inflation/inflation_articles/calculateinflation.asp and http://inflationdata.com/inflation/Consumer_Price_Index/CurrentCPI.asp.

10

Investing, Part II

Money is like manure. You have to spread it around or it smells.

—J. Paul Getty

It was a rainy, overcast day when Matt and I saw Jeff again at his home. We were simply overwhelmed by everything Jeff had said, and we needed a break. Accordingly, we arrived a bit later on the next day than we had promised. Jeff, however, was eagerly expecting us and was full of energy and enthusiasm.

What You Will Learn
- Why most people who manage their own investments lose money
- Why constant earnings usually outperform widely fluctuating earnings
- Possible investment risks
- Bonds
- Annuities
- Gold and other precious metals
- Equities

Why Most People Who Manage Their Own Investments Lose Money

Jeff wagged his finger at us for arriving late. He then spontaneously exclaimed, "Sandy and Matt, do you know why most folks fail in managing their investments?"

Matt smirked and answered, "Yes. Here's the problem," Matt soundly reasoned. "People who want to invest their own money need a lot of time to both manage their investments and handle the strong math and accounting that it takes to choose investments wisely. As we noted in Chapter 9, this lack of experience causes most people to accomplish the opposite of what they want. They end up usually buying investments for top dollar and selling at a much lower price. It is a great strategy for failure and for going broke."

Jeff stared at Matt in disbelief and said, "Really, Matt, when you are ready to start your practice, come see me."

Why Constant Earnings Usually Outperform Widely Fluctuating Earnings

Jeff then composed himself and said, "I am going to give you an overview of the pros and cons of various investments. This won't be an exhaustive discussion because you would need to devote your whole book to this," which made me chuckle. Jeff then continued and said, "However, I will be covering some of the more common investments including some of my favorite and most recommended approaches. Before we discuss all this, there is one more principle I first want to share with you. The question is simple: "Are you better off with constant earnings or fluctuating earnings?"

I was a bit confused and asked Jeff, "What do you mean by this?"

Jeff responded, "Let me give you an example. Let's say that you have a choice of two stocks. Stock A will provide a 20 percent return in year 1 and nothing in year 2. Stock B will appreciate 10 percent per year each year during the first two years. The question is, which is the better investment?"

Let me illustrate this question with this example:

	Stock A	Stock B
Year 1	20%	10%
Year 2	0	10%

My initial reaction was, "I think you would be better with Stock A."

Jeff smirked and said, "And you would be wrong, Sandy. If you had a $100 investment, you would have $110 at the end of year 1 with Stock B and $120 with Stock A, right?"

"Yes," I said.

Now in the second year, Stock A would still be worth, assuming no dividend, $120. Yet, Stock B would be worth $121." Jeff reiterated that the principle of this is simple:

You are usually better off over the long term having constant earnings over widely fluctuating earnings.

"Do you see this," asked Jeff?
Both Matt and I nodded in agreement.

Possible Investment Risks

It was at this point that I asked Jeff, "Do all investments have risks, and how do we measure what these risks are?"

Jeff snickered, which is the only way I can describe his response, and said, "Sandy, actually you are asking a good question. There are effectively two types of risks. The first are considered *systemic risks*. These risks affect almost all investments. They involve things like interest rate changes, foreign currency changes, and inflation risks. The second are considered *nonsystemic risks*. They involve risks associated with individual investments such as business failures."

Jeff continued, "I have mentioned these because there are two key principles that everyone must keep in mind about risk."

Generally the higher the risk, the higher the potential rate of return. The lower the risk, the lower the potential rate of return.

"Although this isn't an absolute correlation, it is a pretty good bet that for most investments, this first principle applies."

Jeff then quickly added, "The corollary of this principle also applies."

Investments that promise or imply a higher rate of return also have potentially higher risk.

"Thus, you have to be careful of any investment opportunity promising above-market rates of return."

I then interrupted Jeff with, "Wait a minute, Jeff. Some investments have very low or even no risk such as bank CDs, savings accounts, and even cash."

Jeff then quickly blurted out, "Yes, and they pay almost nothing these days. In fact, they aren't risk free either."

Chuckling, I quickly retorted, "How can you have any risk with a savings account or with cash?"

Jeff eagerly pressed on by saying, "You have two major risks with cash and savings accounts. The first is that the bank might go under, although you do get up to $250,000 of insurance with the government. The bigger risk, however, is inflation. Putting all of your money in CDs, savings accounts, or even in your mattress is a great, guaranteed way to 'go broke slowly.'"

Matt noted that this important concept of 'going broke slowly' was discussed in yesterday's meeting and in Chapter 9, "Investing, Part I."

With a twinkle in Jeff's eye, he responded, "Yes, we did. This is why everyone has to take a certain amount of risk or inflation will erode their lifestyle. This leads us to the second basic principle of investing."

You have to understand your risk tolerance, and you should balance your investment with enough risky investments to overcome taxes and inflation but to not exceed your risk tolerance.

Being a bit confused, I asked Jeff to elaborate on the second principle.

Jeff excitedly responded, "If you can't sleep at night because most of your money is invested in the stock market, you have to lessen your risk a bit. If you will need the money within a few years for your kids' college tuition, you shouldn't have those funds exposed to stock market risk. Investors have to balance their tolerance for risk by looking at their personal comfort and the time frame for their investment goals."

Both Matt and I agreed with Jeff's sound reasoning.

Bonds

At this point, Matt and I needed a break. Jeff offered us some soft drinks and lemonade. Most people don't realize that Maryland is a very southern state. We are not as fast paced as our northern brethren, and we thus tend to take a more relaxed view of life. However, outside is a different view than southern warmth. It was a cold November day with a cold, soaking rain. However, it did make for a very conducive work environment since neither Matt nor I wanted to be outside in this weather.

Once we finished our refreshments, we retired to Jeff's home office in order to further our discussion. Jeff then said, "All of our prior discussion in both today's and in yesterday's discussions leads us to what I want to discuss now, which is the types of investments that are available and the types of investments that are best for most people."

Matt and I both got ready to focus on these important points.

Jeff then noted, "The first types of investments which we will discuss are basically fixed income investments such as certificates of deposit (CDs), bonds, fixed annuities, and savings accounts. These are promises made by entities: CDs are from banks, annuities are from insurance companies, and bonds are from companies or the federal or a state or local government.

"With one exception that I will get to, these all provide fixed payments of interest. The interest is usually fully taxable as ordinary income. The problem with bonds and to some extent long-term CDs is that not only is the rate of return fixed but also the value of the bond varies as interest rates change. Thus, if interest rates go up, the value of the bond goes down, and vice versa."

Matt interrupted Jeff and said, "However, if investors hold the bonds to maturity, they don't have to worry about interest rate fluctuations, right?"

Jeff responded with some probing of his own and said, "Yes, that is true. However, what happens if investors need the money before maturity? They might have to take a penalty if they withdraw the money early from a CD, or they might have to sell the bond when the value is below the maturity value."

Jeff excitedly continued: "Moreover, you are tying up your money for a long time. If you are getting only 1 to 4 percent while having to pay taxes, you might not have enough to cover inflation. The key with bonds is to be protected against defaults and interest rate fluctuations. There are several ways to achieve this."

Bond and CD Ladders

"The first way is to create a bond or CD ladder," according to Jeff.

I was a bit puzzled and asked, "What is that, Jeff?"

He smoothly responded, "You set up a *bond ladder* when you buy bonds with varying maturities. Thus, you might have five bonds where each one matures in a different year during the next five years. Thus, Bond A would mature next year while Bond B would mature in two years, and so forth. The advantage here is that you are always having bonds mature. At maturity, you can then invest the bond proceeds at the new current interest rate. Thus, if interest rates increase, some of your later maturing bond values may decline in value, but you will have cash to buy the higher yielding bonds at the higher interest rates with the proceeds from the bond that matured."

"Okay, Jeff," I said. "I think I understand. By layering bonds and CDs to mature successively over a period of years, we are reducing the risk of increasing interest rates because we will be having bonds mature each year. Those bonds will provide us with cash to protect against market declines associated with higher rates, right?"

Jeff smiled and said, "Sandy, that is exactly the reason for bond and CD ladders. People who invest heavily in bonds should certainly consider this strategy."

Jeff then continued, "However, one important point is to *not* buy only one type of bond." Jeff then probed Matt by asking him, "Matt, do you know why you shouldn't buy only one type of bond, especially one type of corporate bond?"

Matt smiled and excitedly said, "Yes, because of diversification. All investments, even bonds, should be diversified. In the case of corporate bonds, for example, if the company has severe problems, it can default. In fact, defaults are not limited just to corporations. States, counties, cities, municipalities, and even other government entities can also default. Although default is the worst event that can happen to a bondholder, a bond may also lose its value if the entity issuing the bond has its rating downgraded."

"Right you are, Matt. This is why we have a second way of investing in bonds: bond mutual funds.

"Most bond funds have a variety of maturity dates that provide some degree of interest rate protection. Bond funds also provide some amount of protection against the possibility that a particular company or state or even a federal bond becomes downgraded. The catch is that these funds involve management costs, and they aren't usually as laddered as many people might want."

Jeff then added, "However, investors need to be careful when reviewing bond funds in particular. Bond funds can be categorized as short, medium, and long term. Investors concerned about rising interest rates would not want to invest in long-term bond funds.

"In addition," Jeff noted, "investors need to pull out a calculator and run some numbers. Many bond funds have projected yields that are greater than what the investors will actually receive."

At this point I was confused, so I quizzed Jeff by saying, "I don't get this. How can an entity project a yield greater than what the investors would actually receive? Can you give us an example?"

Jeff smiled and said, "For example, assume a bond fund owns one bond. This bond is selling for $110, which is 10 percent over the bond's original *par value* or, put another way, it is 110 percent of the par value. Assume that it will mature in five years and has a *bond coupon rate* (interest rate that is payable on the bond) of 4 percent. The coupon rate is always based on the par value of the bond when issued. The bond fund would, in this case, quote a yield of 3.64 percent, which is calculated by showing the current yield of 4 percent divided by the current market value, which is $110. However, the investor would not receive a 4 percent yield or even a 3.64 percent yield!" He turned to Matt and said, "Matt, do you know why?"

Before I could comment, Matt responded by saying, "Yes, the bond will mature in five years. Thus, the investors who buy the bond today at $110 will lose $2 per year since upon maturity the bond will pay out only the par value, which is $100."

Jeff then said, "Matt, you understand what *many* investors fail to understand when buying bonds or bond funds. The most important consideration when looking at yield is what is known as *yield to maturity*. This calculation takes the interest rate that is payable annually and adds or subtracts any loss or gain in the value of the bond upon maturity. In the example given above, the bond was paying $4 for each $100 of par value. However, it was losing $2 each year as the bond was maturing since upon maturity the bond issuer would pay only the par value, which was $100. Thus the real approximate yield to maturity would be 1.64 percent."

This made me wonder how many individual investors take the time to run these calculations, and how many investors make bad decisions because they do not understand these calculations and do not take the time to calculate their true return. Getting a bit excited about this, I noted, "So, Jeff, the really important question concerning bonds, besides the rating or risk of default, should be what the yield to maturity is, and *not* what the interest rate is?"

Jeff smiled and said, "Yes, that is exactly the important point in evaluating the return on investment for a bond."

Jeff quickly continued, "There is one other way to limit your risks of default and interest rate fluctuations, which is to buy short-term bonds that all mature within a year or two. This way, if interest rates rise, your bonds will be shortly coming to maturity and you will be able to take advantage of interest rate increases. However, the big problem with buying short-term bonds is that usually they pay less interest than the longer maturity bonds pay. Thus, the benefit of using bond ladders with a combination of bonds having both short- and medium-term maturities and using various types of bonds from a variety of companies provides you with a diversified bond portfolio."

Matt and I both liked Jeff's reasoning, and his thinking is probably why he is so successful.

Federal Government and Government Agency Bonds

I then quizzed Jeff about government bonds. I said, "Jeff, who should own government bonds, and what types of bonds are there?"

Jeff thought for a minute and said, "There are two main types of U.S. government securities. The first are those issued by the federal government, and they are listed below."

Treasury bills: These mature in usually less than 6 months, and they can be bought directly from the Treasury or financial brokers.
Treasury notes: These are medium-term obligations that mature from 3 to 10 years after issue and pay semiannual interest.
Treasury bonds: These mature from 10 to 30 years from date of issue.

"In addition," Jeff added, "there are a variety of government agencies that issue bonds too."

Jeff then noted, "A very important point to note for most bonds is that the longer the maturity dates, the higher the interest."

I asked Jeff, "Can you elaborate on why this is?"

Jeff responded, "Longer-term debt has greater risk. Although with U.S. government bonds, there is no risk of default, you do have interest rate risk, inflation risk, and the risks of possible bond rating downgrades.

"Let me give an example. If the interest on bonds issued at one particular time is 2 percent and later on bonds are issued at a higher rate of 6 percent, the 2 percent bonds won't be as much in demand as the newer bonds that pay higher interest. Thus, if you want to sell the 2 percent bonds in order to buy the newer 6 percent bonds, you will have to take a loss because their value will have fallen.

"Long-term bonds have a much greater risk of interest fluctuation if you want to sell them before maturity.

"In addition, you have inflation risk with bonds. When you get back your original principal, it is paid in future dollars, which probably won't have the same amount of buying power. Thus, inflation risk is a risk inherent in all bonds, which is one of the reasons that they pay interest."

"Good point," I said with a bit of a chuckle.

Jeff then added, "There are other types of Treasury obligations. For example, there are the Series EE bonds that are bought for 50 percent of their face value as well as the Series I savings bonds that are bought for 100 percent of their face value."

I then asked about Series HH bonds that I heard something about.

Jeff responded, "These bonds used to be issued by the United States. However, due to lack of investor demand, the federal government has stopped issuing Series HH bonds."

I then quizzed Jeff by saying, "Jeff, if longer-term bonds have interest rate risk and inflation risk inherent in them, is there any way to avoid these problems other than with bond ladders?"

Jeff smiled and replied, "Yes! This brings up my favorite Treasury security, which also is very little known. This type of security is called TIPS."

I was taken aback by this since I had never heard of them. I therefore inquired, "Jeff, I have never heard of TIPS. What are they?"

Jeff responded, "TIPS is an acronym for Treasury Inflation-Protected Securities."

I immediately teased Jeff by saying, "I already like the name of that."

Jeff laughed and said, "There is a reason that I like these. With TIPS, the principal (par value) increases with inflation but also decreases with deflation, as measured by the Consumer Price Index (CPI). When these securities mature, you are paid the adjusted principal or original principal, whichever is greater.

"TIPS pay interest twice a year, at a fixed percentage of the inflation adjusted principal. Since this rate is applied to the adjusted principal, interest payments rise with inflation and fall with deflation. TIPS can be bought directly from the Treasury in $100 increments, and they mature in 5, 10, or even 20 years. You can even buy mutual funds that own these securities. In essence, you are getting not only interest but potentially inflated interest and principal that are designed to keep up with the risk of inflation."

I had never heard of TIPS. Thus, I told Jeff, "If TIPS provide for inflation, they really do seem to be a good deal for many people. I am glad you mentioned them."

Looking a bit concerned, Jeff added a note of caution in saying, "Investors need to be aware of one more aspect of TIPS. If the principal value of the bond is increased because of inflation, the increase in value is subject to taxation at ordinary income rates just as interest income is."

I stopped Jeff and said, "Wait a minute. The investors aren't receiving any cash for this increase, and they will not receive cash until the bond matures, right? Thus, they have to pay taxes on the increased value without having the cash?"

Jeff said, "Tax law treats the increase in value as current income subject to income tax. Because of this tax consequence, TIPS are attractive investments to hold in tax qualified retirement accounts such as IRAs, 401(k)s, and pension plans."

Municipal Bonds

We took another short lemonade and soft drink break before I broached the next topic. "Before we leave the concept of bonds, I want to discuss municipal bonds. Due to the tax-free nature of these bonds, wouldn't they normally be considered better than most other types of bonds including federal government bonds?"

Jeff anticipated my question and responded, "Municipal bonds, otherwise known as *munis*, do have some problems. Yes, they are usually free of federal taxes if they are *general obligation (GO) bonds*. They also are generally free of your home state's taxes. However, the interest you earn on another state's bonds might be taxable to you for your home state's income tax purposes. Also, many municipalities are in financial trouble. Thus, if a municipality defaults, your bonds will have questionable worth."

I was a bit taken aback by this and said, "I didn't know that states and cities are in as much trouble as you have intimated."

Jeff gave me a deadpan look and said, "Yes, sadly, many are in trouble. They can always raise taxes in order to make up for shortfalls. However, the current estimates of the total U.S. shortfall for municipalities are as much as $2.9 **trillion.** At least the federal government can print money."

Jeff's last remarks left me a bit chilled.

Formula for Comparing Yields for Taxable and Tax-Free Bonds

Jeff felt that he was on a roll, and he excitedly added, "Moreover, sometimes having a fully taxable bond might be better than a tax-free municipal bond *if* the taxable bond pays a lot more in interest." Jeff then asked Matt, "Matt, do you know the formula for deciding how to figure out whether a particular taxable bond would be better than or equal to a particular tax-free bond? What is the formula for figuring out the taxable equivalent of a tax-free yield?"

Matt smiled and said, "I sure do. If you have a tax-free interest rate that you want to compare to a taxable equivalent, there is a formula that shows what an investor would have to earn on a taxable investment in order to match the yield on a tax-free investment. Here is the formula."

> **Tax-free yield/(1 – the marginal tax bracket) = Taxable equivalent bond rate**

"Thus, if you can get a tax-free interest rate of 3 percent but you are in the 40 percent tax bracket, you would take the 3 percent and divide it by (1 – 0.4). Thus, you would figure 3 percent/0.6, which would give you 5 percent. This means that any taxable bond that pays 5 percent would equal a 3 percent muni bond yield. If it pays more than 5 percent, it would be better than a 3 percent tax-free municipal bond."

Jeff smiled and said, "Okay. Then what formula should I use to determine the tax-free equivalent of a taxable yield? In other words, if I have a taxable bond rate, what would be the tax-free equivalent?"

Matt looked at me and smiled and responded, "If you start off with a taxable yield and want to know what type of tax-free bond would be equivalent to that yield, the formula would be (taxable yield) × (1 – marginal tax bracket). Thus, in our example, if we had a 5 percent corporate bond that is fully taxable and we were in the 40 percent tax bracket, our formula would be 0.05 × 0.6 = 3 percent." Matt then used his Cheshire cat smile on Jeff.

Jeff just gaped at Matt with astonishment. "Matt," he said, "when you get out of school, come see me. You have a guaranteed job offer from me."

Jeff tried one more time to trick Matt: "What about state income tax rates?"

Matt said, "This is important too. The state rate has to be added to the applicable federal rate." Matt then thought he would turn the tables on Jeff and coyly asked, "Are all municipal bonds federal tax free?"

Jeff didn't take the bait and responded, "Some bonds are not tax free. Moreover, some bonds might not be subject to the ordinary income taxes, but they are subject to the alternative minimum taxes. Therefore, investors need to check to see what the tax consequences are before they buy the municipal bonds."

When to Get Taxable Bonds Rather Than Tax-Free Bonds

Jeff continued: "I want to summarize a few more points as to when taxable investments would be, in my opinion, better purchases than tax-free bonds."

"First, investors who are considering municipal bonds should be at least in the 25 percent tax bracket or higher. If you are not paying much in taxes, you probably don't want to be investing in municipal bonds because municipal bonds generally pay a much lower interest."

Matt and I both agreed with this logic.

"Second, in qualified plans such as IRAs and pensions, always buy taxable bonds because they pay a higher interest rate, and any money coming out of these plans is fully taxable anyway even if the income came from a normally tax-free bond.

"Third, if you really need to live on the interest because you are retired or disabled and you are in a fairly high tax bracket, you are generally better off with tax-free bonds, although you still want to use the formulas that we discussed above.

"I should note that I always believe that most people should have some municipal bonds, as well as some taxable bonds, in order to have a well-balanced portfolio."

Corporate Bonds

"Okay, let's talk about corporate bonds for a moment. These usually provide higher interest than do government bonds because the corporate bonds are riskier. First, they have the same interest rate fluctuation problems that I noted above. In addition, unlike government bonds, there is a greater likelihood of default with corporate bonds if the bond issuing company experiences severe economic difficulties. Corporations can't raise taxes, nor can they print money. Finally, and this is something that many people may not realize, there is the risk that the bonds will be called."

I was a bit perplexed when I asked Jeff, "Can you explain what you mean by *calling the bonds*?"

Jeff grinned yet cautioned prospective corporate bondholders: "At today's interest rates, we all assume that interest rates will go up over the life of the bond. Although today we have unusually low rates, bond rates have been known to drop. Normally investors would at first seem happy about this because lower interest rates typically increase the value of the bonds. However, many corporate issuers want the ability to refinance the bonds should interest rates drop. Therefore, many corporate bonds contain a call feature whereby the corporation can redeem the bonds and pay off the investors. This way, the corporation can pay off the investors at the face value of the bonds and *not* at the current market value, and then they can issue new bonds with a lower rate."

Scowling, I said, "This really isn't fair to the investors, is it?"

Jeff casually responded, "This may not be fair, but it is the general rule with corporate bonds. It is the same general rule for homeowners who have the right to refinance their houses and take advantage of lower rates. Thus, you need to check whether the bonds that you are getting have this feature. It really does limit the profit that investors can make, especially for higher yielding bonds."

Jeff went on and said, "This leaves us with one more option that is included on some corporate bonds that I like, and that is a conversion feature. *Convertible bonds* offer investors the combined advantages of owning a bond and owning stock in the company. You get a fixed interest rate, but if the underlying stock price rises, you can convert your bonds to stock if the value of the stock that it could be converted into would be greater than the value of the bond. The bondholder then benefits from the rising stock prices. Who says that you can't *have your cake and eat it too*? However, these bonds may also be callable, so you have to be careful with them.

"This is why I usually recommend either a diversified bond ladder or a bond mutual fund that also includes convertible bonds. This way, the overall risks associated with bonds can be reduced.

"Here's one final point about bonds before I move away from our discussion of them," Jeff noted. "Generally, it is better for the broker rather than the investor to keep possession of all the bond certificates. Folks can lose them, have them destroyed by fire, or have them stolen. Keeping them with the broker is a much safer alternative."

Matt and I both nodded in agreement.

Annuities

Jeff then continued: "I want to discuss one other investment, and that is *fixed annuities*. These are akin to bank certificates of deposit, but they are provided by insurance companies. Unlike that of a CD, the interest isn't taxable each year in which it is earned. However, it is taxed when you withdraw the interest from the annuity. Moreover, the interest provided by annuities usually pays more than bank CDs. The key here is that the investor should be cautioned to check the financial status of the insurance company since there are no federal guarantees with annuities."

Teasing Jeff a bit, I said, "So you would strongly recommend annuities to our readers?"

He bristled at this and said, "Actually, I rarely recommend annuities despite the advantages noted above," which was an extreme statement that took both Matt and me by surprise.

I thus followed up with the obvious question: "So why do you feel so strongly about not investing in annuities?"

Jeff quickly responded, "Insurance companies are known for insurance and *not* investments. The two should never meet. You almost never buy insurance products for investments. The reasons are simple: They charge a *lot* of costs and commissions for their products. Annuities, for example, have costs incurred when you first get it because these investments have to be sold to customers by agents.

"Even worse, some of the surrender charges don't expire for 10 years or more. Thus, you don't really have access to the cash without paying a sizable penalty. At least with CDs, you can get your cash at any time, but you might lose some or all of the interest. Moreover, if you get a *variable annuity*, which is one that has a stock portfolio attached, you will be paying much higher commissions. In addition, unlike that of bank certificates of deposit, you can't take the interest out of the annuity without a sizable penalty until you reach age 59½."

Wagging my finger at Jeff, I said, "One thing I have learned about teaching the SATs is that whenever the answer is 'never,' it probably isn't the answer. There must be some circumstances in which you would recommend annuities?"

Anticipating my question, Jeff smoothly responded, "Yes, if a person is a true spendthrift and can't be trusted to manage money and needs an income for life and is in the 28 percent tax bracket or lower, an annuity might be beneficial. This type of annuity is known as an *immediate annuity*, and it can work well to fund a lifetime need for income while protecting the principal from the tendency to spend."

Jeff cautiously added, "However, even then, the annuity payment stays stagnant. It never increases. Thus, inflation will eat away at the income over the years to the extent that the income eventually won't be that beneficial, which is another reason why I don't like annuities."

At that point, I just gave up on this and gave Jeff an exasperated look.

Seeing the look on my face must have triggered some thought in Jeff because he added, "Annuities can also be useful for some specialized planning scenarios. There are some examples in which annuities are helpful. For example, annuities become particularly useful for college funding because all assets in annuities are generally not counted in the Free Application for Federal Student Aid (FASFA) formula in computing need-based financial aid. Thus, monies in annuities as well as cash value insurance policies are not counted as assets for financial aid. Annuities can also be of some benefit for elder planning and for professionals in high-risk occupations (think lawsuits) who might benefit by having some funds in annuities because insurance products in many states are exempt from creditors."

Gold and Other Precious Metals

Jeff then stared coolly at us and said, "I know that we discussed gold regarding diversification yesterday, but I would like to touch on the subject again. You see lots of folks running to buy it. There is almost a frenzy to buy the bullion due to the economic turmoil, which is why gold is appreciating so rapidly. You already know that I think owning gold is a *very* silly investment."

"I do remember that, Jeff, but I thought that most top planners were recommending some gold for their clients as a hedge against inflation?"

Jeff responded, "I do recommend some gold for my clients. But as you know, I don't recommend owning the bullion or gold coins for the reasons I mentioned yesterday. There is a very high commission to purchase gold bullion or coins compared to buying equities, so you have high costs to both buy and sell the gold. Then there are the storage costs as well as the fees to verify its authenticity and weight. And finally, gold doesn't pay dividends or interest."

Jeff then smoothly continued while smiling and said, "How would you like the benefits of owning gold while paying less in commissions and costs, paying no storage fees, and paying no verification charges while receiving yearly dividends?"

I looked at Matt, and we both nodded excitedly in agreement.

Jeff chuckled and said, "The best way to own gold is to buy either mining stocks or, even better, to buy mutual funds that specialize in owning mining or gold stocks. This way, you avoid all of the pitfalls of owning gold yet get most of the same upside inflation potential benefits. Even better, these funds usually pay you (in dividends) rather than your paying ownership costs such as storage fees."

Matt and I both really appreciated that comment and wrote this suggestion down for our future investments. I commented, "It is amazing that most people never think of this. It is a great idea."

Jeff smiled and said, "This is one reason why a good financial planner is worth the money."

I had one final question for Jeff about this: "Jeff, how much gold should a typical investor own?"

Jeff's response was, "I usually recommend about 5 to 10 percent of the amount of bond allocation. Thus, if investors own $500,000 in bonds, their gold equity holdings should be around $50,000. If they don't own bonds, then I recommend that about 5 percent of their net worth be in gold mining funds.

"I do want to add one more concept to this discussion, which is, what should investors own if they are expecting a recession?

"The answer is that during recessions, certain things drop in value such as stocks, bonds, collectibles, and real estate, which is what we saw during the 2008 to 2011 economic downturns. What tends to do well in recessions are natural resources such as gas, oil, minerals, and forest products, although in this recession, these investments didn't do that well either. The only really safe places were bonds and cash.

"Bottom line: Gold is certainly a mineral, but as I noted, I wouldn't own the gold itself. I would recommend mining stocks or mutual funds that specialize in mining."

Equities

Jeff then started his discussion on stocks. "Let me make the following point that most people overlook."

Owners, long term, do much better than creditors.

"What this means is that stocks will usually, on a long-term basis, outperform bonds. I know that in recent times with our economic difficulties, this wasn't the case. However, over the long term, stocks will outperform bonds. Here is an interesting example. If you bought a bundle of stocks for $10,000 in 1926, guess how much it would be worth?"

My answer was, "About $2 million."

Jeff chuckled and said, "You are way off. The value would be about $11 million today!"

Matt and I both were stupefied. We both dropped our jaws.

"There are four reasons that equities will generally outperform bonds," Jeff wisely noted. "First, stocks have a potential for long-term growth.

Bonds will go up only if either the interest rate drops or if folks own convertible bonds for which the underlying stock has appreciated. Remember, interest rates can fall only for so long. Eventually, the bonds will mature at par value.

"Second, stocks can provide income like bonds in that they pay dividends. Even better, the dividends have the potential to increase due to the profitability of the company.

"Third, stock dividends give better tax advantages than interest under current income tax law in the United States. Interest, as you know, is treated as ordinary income and taxed like any other form of income such as salaries. Qualified stock dividends currently have a maximum tax rate of 15 percent, which is very nice.[1]

"Finally, stocks, unlike bonds, have the potential for inflation protection. They do tend to keep up with and even exceed the rate of inflation. Most folks think that this applies only to precious metals, but a good diversified portfolio of stocks will do well in inflationary times."

Chuckling I said, "Yes, I agree. Stocks can be a great long-term inflation hedge. I guess many of these gold buyers don't understand that."

Jeff nodded in agreement.

Tax Advantages of Equities

After hearing about the advantages of equities, we wanted to discuss the tax advantages of owning stocks and mutual funds. I started the discussion by saying, "Jeff, as you know there are many great tax advantages to owning stocks and mutual funds that I want to get into for our readers. First, you get lower capital gains taxes on gains. With income from interest and rent, you pay taxes at ordinary income rates. With stocks and funds held for more than one year, you get a maximum capital gains tax rate of 15 percent plus state taxes. Even better, if investors are in the 15 percent bracket anyway—which means that their taxable income is less than $35,349 if they are single taxpayers and less than $70,699 if they are married taxpayers filing a joint return—their long-term capital gains tax rate is incredibly zero!"

Jeff nodded and said, "That is certainly a big deal."

I went on, "In addition, qualified dividends also get the benefit of these long-term capital gains rates."

Jeff continued with his sound reasoning: "There is one other big benefit of owning stocks. You don't pay tax on any gain until the stock is sold. Thus, there is no tax on the appreciation until a sale is made. Interest, however, is taxed each year it is received. This is why people are taxed each year on their CDs."

I wagged my finger at Jeff adding, "But, Jeff, if stocks were such a perfect investment, everyone would do it. You know as well as I that there are downsides to equity investments."

He quickly responded, "Yes, stocks and other equity investments do have downsides. Certainly you usually have more fluctuation in values than with bonds. In fact, stocks have had several down cycles during which their value dropped more than 50 percent. In addition, like bonds, you have business risks that the company will start losing money and go out of business. You have legal risks too if a company incurs large lawsuits for big damages and cannot pay dividends."

Investment Tips for Equities

Jeff then added, "There are several steps that all investors should take in order to maximize their equity investments.

"The first is rarely, if ever, use a full-service broker. This is a broker that charges 1.5 percent commission or more for each trade, whether it is a buy or sell. Discount brokers can save you a *lot* of money, but they don't usually give the same level of investment advice.

"Another alternative," Jeff said, "is to hire a fee-based advisor to whom you pay a fee rather than commissions. This would mean that the advisor would not be rewarded for making trades on your behalf."

Jeff then continued with his sound reasoning by saying, "Second, always buy stocks in lots of 100 shares for cheaper costs.

"Third, *always* take the dividend reinvestment option offered by the underlying company until you need the cash flow. This lets you accumulate additional shares without any commission, and it is a great way to save money.

"Fourth, take advantage of the *qualified tuition plans* that we discussed in prior chapters and of Roth IRAs. The accumulated profits and income can be tax free in these plans.

"Finally, *always* diversify your investment. This includes some bonds, stocks in various industries, and even global holdings. I can't emphasize this enough."

Matt nodded in approval at this and said, "Yes, I honestly believe that people can't be diversified enough." Jeff agreed with Matt.

Jeff excitedly added, "The problem is that most people don't diversify enough because they don't have enough money to buy all the different types of equities that they need. The best investments to have in order to diversify your holdings are mutual funds, exchange-traded funds (my favorite), and managed money. I will discuss all of these."

This made both Matt and me start taking copious notes since this seems to be the key to proper diversification.

Just then, Jeff's wife, Amy, came in with a tray of some cool lemonade and some homemade cookies, which my cookie monster son started to gobble up. I had to growl at him in order to have a few for Jeff and me.

After we finished our snack, Jeff continued: "Let's start with managed money. This can bring about the best results because the manager can continually take the client's risk into account with what is happening in the market. Be aware that it can be expensive, and costs can be as much as 1 to 2 percent of assets. However, there are no charges for buying and selling investments. Another problem with using a personal money manager is that you need a fairly large minimum portfolio, generally $100,000 or more."

I interrupted Jeff by asking, "Wait, Jeff, can't we achieve the same diversification and risk management by using mutual funds, which have a lot lower costs?"

Jeff's response was interesting. "Sandy," he said, "first, mutual funds have a lot of management costs built into the funds. Second, a money manager might use funds as part of the portfolio. What the manager does is to make sure that there is a proper allocation each year. Thus, if one segment of the diversified portfolio has greatly appreciated, the manager might sell off part of this and allocate more money to other areas. Likewise, if the manager thinks that the allocation might be better off in certain funds based on existing events, the manager will allocate the funds accordingly.

"Thus, managed funds ensure that there is proper diversification for the client in accord with the client's age and risk tolerance. Most people don't do this for themselves. However, since you mentioned mutual funds, let's discuss them as a great way to achieve diversification."

Mutual Funds and Exchange-Traded Funds

Jeff pressed on eagerly saying, "**In my opinion, the best way for most people to achieve a cost-effective, diversified portfolio is to put their money in mutual funds and exchange-traded funds (ETFs).**

"There are many advantages to investing in these investment vehicles. First, they are affordable. You can get access to literally dozens or even hundreds of stocks for a small amount of money when you buy shares in these funds.

"Second, as I noted above, you achieve a lot of diversification since these funds own lots of different types of stocks and/or bonds.

"Third, you get professional management, at least for the mutual funds, that manages these funds and, in some cases, tries to minimize taxes that would be owed by holding the underlying stocks a sufficient amount of time to garner long-term capital gains. Brokers refer to funds that take taxes into account as *tax-advantaged funds*."

I interrupted Jeff by asking what the differences are between mutual funds and exchange-traded funds."

Jeff replied, "Exchange-traded funds are similar to mutual funds except that they own all of the stocks of a given stock index. In other words, like mutual funds, they invest in a basket of stocks. Thus the S&P 500 exchange-traded fund would own all of the stocks included in that index. Most of these pay dividends; thus, owning shares in this fund would ensure an investor's portfolio diversification, long-term growth, and income."

Jeff went on to say, "In fact, there are a number of advantages to exchange-traded index funds over mutual funds as follows."

- Exchange-traded funds give investors precise tracking because the fund owns all of the stocks and/or bonds in that index.
- ETFs are more tax efficient because they don't buy or sell stocks other than to accommodate more investors joining the fund or to reflect rare changes in the list of companies whose stocks and bonds underly the index.
- ETFs give a broad range of market coverage.
- Most important, ETFs charge *much* lower fees than do mutual funds because ETFs require less management.

"Jeff," I quizzed, "if ETFs are so good, why doesn't everyone own them?"

"That's a good point," Jeff said smiling. "Most people don't know about them. Also, there are some downsides. First, you can own them only by using a broker who generally charges $10 to $15 for each purchase. Second, ETFs are better for those who make large investments and/or use dollar cost averaging where people would invest a fixed amount into the fund each month regardless of the share price. Third, an ETF will precisely track its underlying index, but it will never do better than its underlying index. Finally, there aren't nearly as many choices for diversification among ETFs as there are for mutual funds. However, I really like them for most people's portfolios primarily because of the diversification that they provide and because of the tremendously low cost for both getting into the ETF and for running the ETF. In a number of cases, ETFs have outperformed most mutual funds primarily for these reasons."

Types of Mutual Funds. I then quickly quizzed Jeff by asking, "What other types of mutual funds are there?"

He replied, "If you can think of it, there is a fund for it. For example, there are funds that invest in Ginnie Mae (GNMA) mortgages, which is a way to participate in real estate investing without owning real estate. There are short-term government security funds. There are long-term bond funds for both U.S. securities and corporate bonds. There are global government funds, and there are municipal bond funds that invest only in municipal bonds. There are junk bond funds that have a portfolio of low-graded bonds that achieve high rates of return. There are balanced funds, which contain a mixture of stocks and bonds and can be a great safety hedge in return for a slightly lower long-term rate of return. There are even gold and precious metal stock funds. There are also my favorite funds, which are global funds that invest in both U.S. and foreign stocks. This gives a very broad range of diversification."

Real Estate Investment Trusts. Jeff then pressed on eagerly saying, "There is one other type of fund that I want to discuss. It is a real estate investment trust."

At this point my son, Matt, was grinning from ear to ear and said, "Yes, I know about them. They are like a fund, but they own various real estate investments."

Jeff corrected Matt by saying, "Yes, that is one type of real estate investment trust (REIT). There are two other types though. There are those REITs that own mortgages, which lost significant value when the subprime mortgage market collapsed. The third type is the hybrid type that owns both real estate and mortgages."

Excitedly, Jeff continued: "REITs must distribute 90 percent of their income and capital gains to comply with federal tax law. Thus, they become great investments for people who need an income flow. Moreover, they can be very diversified by owning a large number of different real estate properties and mortgages.

"What is also interesting about REITs, which is also the reason that I recommend them to clients, is that they usually run counter to the stock market, although with the recent downturn, they did just as badly. They also provide reinvestment opportunities just as mutual funds do."

Matt then chirped up and said, "Then you would recommend them to most people as part of their portfolio?"

To which Jeff responded, "Yes, but I would stay away from mortgage-only REITs. I like the ownership of the underlying real estate. I don't have problems with hybrid REITs though. Also, due to diversification, I would not recommend that more than 10 percent of a portfolio be in REITs alone. Real estate can fluctuate in value, as we have seen in this recent downturn."

Taxation of Mutual Funds. I smiled and said to Jeff, "This is one area that I know about, but it is one area many people overlook. You pay taxes on any appreciation above your basis. Your basis is not only your cost of the shares but also any dividends that get reinvested. Thus, people who own mutual funds must keep a record of reinvested dividends as well as any fund purchase costs."

Matt interrupted me to say, "Dad, this is true for stock purchases as well," to which I nodded in agreement.

I then added, "Moreover, there are several methods of figuring your basis too. One is to average out your total cost plus dividends reinvested divided by the total number of shares. The second is to keep separate records on the dividend reinvestments and treat those shares separately. In addition, you can choose a wide array of options as to which shares are sold such as specifically identifying shares or selling the first shares purchased. A good accountant will know what to do here."

Factors to Look For in Mutual Funds. I then asked Jeff, "What factors would you look for and what factors would you avoid in choosing a mutual fund for clients?"

Jeff hesitated a bit before responding. "One key element that everyone should investigate is the load and expense charges of the fund. There are many charges that can occur in a fund that investors should ask about. First, there is the possibility of *front-end load*. This is a commission charge to get into the fund. A fund can be a no-load fund, or it can charge as much as 8.5 percent and anywhere in between. Sadly, many brokers are more interested in their own pocketbook than that of their clients. For example, there are brokers and planners who don't utilize the discounts available for large transactions. Some brokers split transactions to avoid price break discounts. Some fail to give discounts for new accounts."

Jeff excitedly continued, "In addition to the possibility of front-end loads, there could be back-end loads with surrender fees that can be as high as 6 percent, although these usually decline by 1 percent for each year that the client stays in the fund. Finally, you have the management fee within the fund that usually is between 0.5 and 2 percent of fund assets.

"All fund managers need to be paid, and there are a number of costs involved in the fund. However, my recommendation is this: **absent some special circumstances, the lowest loaded funds tend to give the best rates of return to the clients.** Thus, I like no-load funds. I would rarely, if ever, recommend a front-end load fund. I also like exchange-traded funds due to their low operating cost and high level of diversification.

"In addition, I look for a good track record among management. I would suggest *not* going into a new fund for example." Jeff then quickly added, "Also, don't think that because a fund did phenomenally well last year that it will do well this year. Funds, like athletic teams, have varying results from year to year. However, you are generally better off with management that has a long, good track record of success."

Since Jeff was on a roll, he said, "Guys, there are a few more points that I want to give about investments and equities that I think would be very beneficial to your readers. I know that this chapter is probably going to be long, but do you mind if I add some important information?"

Matt and I didn't know what to expect, but we both nodded in agreement.

"Okay. First, ETFs and especially mutual funds are long-term investments. They are meant to be held for as long as possible until you might need the cash. They should not be used for short-term investments. This also means that you shouldn't be selling these investments when the market is low. You wait till the market is relatively high if you need the money. Don't let fear and greed prevent you from holding onto these investments.

"A good example of the importance of making these investments into a long-term hold is found in a study of investors. Mutual funds and ETFs during almost any 5-year period made a profit for the investors 90 percent of the time. However, during any 10-year period, they made a profit 96 percent of the time. Even better, during any 15-year period or longer, they made a profit for investors almost 100 percent of the time!"

Both Matt and I were shocked in amazement at these statistics.

Jeff went on: "Second, whatever you do, don't try to time the market. Say this five times.

"Third, whenever possible, take advantage of dividend reinvestment plans. With these plans, the stock or fund takes the dividends and reinvests them in more shares instead of distributing the dividends to you. There are no costs or commissions involved, and it is a great way to save money.

"Fourth, whether you buy shares of stocks or mutual funds, always buy in lots of 100 because doing so will lower the commissions. The only exception would be those shares purchased through dividend reinvestment since there are no commissions involved.

"Fifth, mutual funds and ETFs are particularly good for *dollar cost averaging* by which you invest a fixed amount of money each month or year. This is a great way to both save money and provide a relatively safe harbor during price fluctuations.

"Sixth, even retirees should have some stock or fund investments in order to avoid erosion from inflation."

"Jeff," I asked, "regarding the sixth statement, how much should people have at risk in the stock market? In other words, what percentage of their portfolio should people such as retirees have in stocks or mutual funds?"

"Sandy," Jeff answered, "that is a great question, which we discussed before in Chapter 9. Just to reiterate, the general rule is to take the number 100 and subtract the investor's age. This is the percentage of the investor's portfolio that should be in stocks and/or stock funds or ETFs. Thus, if you were age 65, under this formula, you should have 35 percent of your portfolio in the stock market. If someone is a bit of a risk taker, I would change the formula, particularly for younger people, to 110 minus their age. Thus, if you weren't totally risk averse, I would recommend for someone age 65 to have 45 percent of his or her portfolio in stocks and funds (110 minus 65).

Matt then asked Jeff, "Can you give sample allocations for aggressive portfolios versus moderate portfolios?"

"Sure," said Jeff. "Here is what I would normally recommend for aggressive and moderate investors."

Aggressive Portfolio

- S&P 500 Index funds: 30 percent
- Small-cap growth funds: 35 percent
- Foreign stock funds: 15 percent
- REITs: 5 percent
- Precious metal mining stock funds: 5 percent
- Intermediate-term bond fund or bond ladders: 10 percent

Portfolio for Moderate Risk

- S&P 500 Index funds: 35 percent
- Global large-cap value funds: 25 percent
- Small-cap funds: 5 percent
- Precious metal mining funds: 5 percent
- REITs: 5 percent
- Short-term bond funds or bond ladders: 10 percent
- Intermediate-term bond funds or bond ladders: 5 percent
- Foreign fund or growth funds or balanced funds: 10 percent

Jeff then concluded: "I do want to add one final wrinkle for people who are relatively sophisticated investors, and it is a plan that your dad does, Sandy. This is to buy quality stocks that are recommended by the analysts that also pay dividends and then write a call option on the stocks. A *call option* is a right to buy 100 shares of a stock at a fixed price.

"Let me give you an example. Let's assume that you own a stock worth $40 per share (which was also your cost) and you sell a one-month or three-month call option for $45 per share. (Longer call options are available, but I do not recommend writing an option for the longer period.)

"The buyer would give you about $100 to $200 for each call that you write, which you would bank immediately. This, by the way, is known as *writing a call on your stock*. If the stock goes down, you have the call option premium to help subsidize the stock drop. If the stock goes up significantly, you make the call premium *plus* you make the extra $5 per share since the call option strike price is $45 in this example. If the stock stays about the same price and doesn't reach the call strike price, you get to keep your premium, and you can write another call when the first one expires. Typically, this type of investing has made clients about 10 to 20 percent annualized returns."

Jeff added, "However, there are some downsides to doing this. First, you should do this only with at least 10 different stocks in order to help ensure some diversification. Second, if the stock appreciates significantly, you are limiting your gains to the strike price of the call. However, it can be a nice way to achieve a much larger amount of income for relatively low risk. Finally, this is for people who are sophisticated about investing."

"Jeff, this whole subject of investments was not only fascinating but amazingly instructive. Matt and I want to thank you for your time and great knowledge."

Jeff warmly shook our hands and led us out to the blistery winds that were presaging the start of winter.

A Review of What You Have Learned

These are some of the notes I took while we were talking about investing.

- People lose money usually due to inexperience and due to fear and greed. Emotion cannot get in the way of making a logical investment.
- Constant earnings usually outperform widely fluctuating earnings.
- Generally the higher the risk of an investment, the greater the potential return.
- There are several risks that can occur:
  - *Systemic risks* such as interest rate fluctuations and currency fluctuations.
  - *Nonsystemic risks* such as company bankruptcies.
  - *Inflation risks*: If returns aren't higher than the rate of inflation, then you are going broke slowly.
- *Formula for investment goals:* Returns should exceed inflation and taxes.
- You should balance your investments with enough risky investments to overcome taxes and inflation but still be within your risk tolerance.
- Types of investments:
  - **Fixed return investments** such as bonds, CDs, and annuities. Use bond and CD ladders to reduce impact from interest rate fluctuations. Or invest in mutual funds that have varying bond maturities, or invest in short-term bonds and/or CDs.
  - **U.S. government bonds** are state tax free.

- **Municipal bonds** are federal tax free and can be state tax free for the state of issuance.
  - Formula for converting the tax-free yield to taxable yield is as follows: the tax-free yield / (1– the marginal tax bracket).
  - Formula for converting the taxable yield to the tax-free yield is as follows: the taxable yield × (1 – the marginal tax bracket).
  - If you are going to buy corporate bonds, consider convertible bonds, and watch out for call features in all corporate bonds.
- **Treasury inflation-protected securities (TIPS):** These are government bonds that give more interest if there is inflation. You are taxed on any bond interest increase due to inflation even though the bonds may not have matured. Thus, they are ideal for retirement plans.
- **Annuities** are issued by insurance companies and generally should be avoided. They do have some special applicability for professionals involved in high-risk occupations and for college funding.
- **Precious metals** are good for portfolios, but investors should own precious metal mining stock funds over owning the bullion. This will avoid storage charges and will result in much lower commissions.
- **Equities, including mutual funds,** are long-term investments. Owners do better than creditors. Thus, stockholders will usually earn more than bondholders over the long term.
  - Great tax benefits with equities. First, if the stock or fund share is held for more than one year, you get the 15 percent maximum capital gains rate. The same rate applies to dividends too. Also, you are not taxed on appreciation until you sell the shares.
  - **Mutual funds:** many types. Great for achieving diversification and management.
  - Unless unusual circumstances exist, try to get the lowest loaded funds. No-load funds are best.
- **Exchange-traded funds (ETFs):** Great for diversification, and their costs and loads are lower than they are for mutual funds. Great for most portfolios.
- Investment tips:
- Don't use a full-service broker.
- Always buy stocks in lots of 100 shares unless your purchase is through a dividend reinvestment plan with the underlying company.
- Always take the dividend reinvestment option offered by the underlying company or mutual fund unless you need the cash flow. This lets you accumulate additional shares without any commissions, and it is a great way to save money.
- Take advantage of qualified tuition plans noted in this chapter and of Roth IRAs. The accumulated profits and income can be tax free.
- Always diversify your investments. This includes some bonds, stocks in various industries and even global holdings, and some precious metal holdings such as precious metal funds.
- Always have some real estate investment trusts (REITs) in your portfolio unless you already have some significant real estate holdings. REITs are great ways

to own real estate and have an income flow without the hassles of real estate management.

- All investors should own some stock, even retirees. The formula for the percentage of stock or equities that should be in a portfolio is 100 minus your age. If you are a bit aggressive or are younger with many years ahead to recoup stock losses, the formula would be more like 110 minus your age.
- If you are a sophisticated investor, consider owning a variety of dividend paying stocks and writing some calls on the stocks owned. This is a relatively risk-free way to substantially increase your rate of return to 10 percent a year or more.

Notes

1. As of the writing of this book, it has been proposed to raise tax rates on dividends and capital gains to 20 percent, which might take effect in 2013.

11

Insurance, Part I

What You Will Learn
- Four ways to deal with risk
- Disability insurance
- Long-term care insurance
- Homeowners insurance
- Vehicle insurance
- Health insurance

Today is an Indian summer day. It's the beginning of winter, but people are out jogging and bicycling in the nice 70 degree temperatures. Even the plants seem to be confused between going into hibernation and flowering. I thought this would be a great day for Matt and me to meet Mike, who is NOT the same guy that I mentioned in Chapter 7. This Mike is a successful elder law attorney. Thus, I thought he would be a great person to interview. In addition, he is probably one of the nicest guys that I know.

When we arrived at his house, I was really taken aback. Mike is a very unassuming person, yet his house was at least twice the size of mine. It easily qualified as a minimansion. Who says being an attorney doesn't pay?

When we got to the door, Mike was there to give us a great, warm greeting. Mike already knew my son, Matt, so I didn't have to introduce him. Mike ushered us into a conference room in his home that was lined with oak and mahogany walls.

"Mike," I said, "as I told you on the phone, Matt is working with me on a financial planning book I'm writing, and we want to give readers some inside information that most insurance agents and accountants are *not* telling their clients. With your experience and obvious success, I thought you would be a great person to interview about all aspects of insurance." It always helps to butter up my interviewees before I conduct the interviews. It makes them feel better, and they open up comfortably on the subject at hand.

"Sandy, thanks for including me in your interviews. I will certainly try to give you the best information that I know. Although if I let you pick my brain too much, my kids will tell you that I will have nothing left." Matt and I smiled at this remark since that is a line that I have been using with my kids for years.

Mike started in by saying, "Let's first understand the primary role for insurance, which is to cover a financial loss . . . period. Say that again five times. Thus, it would be good to cover your lost income in case of disability or loss of your spouse's earnings or for lost services in case your spouse dies or gets disabled. It wouldn't be good, however, to cover the earnings of kids unless they are making a significant contribution to the household expenses."

Four Ways to Deal with Risk

"Essentially, the following are four ways that we can deal with a major risk such as fire or lawsuit."

1. Avoid the risk by not going anywhere and building a self-sufficient fortress similar to what was found in the Middle Ages. Sadly, even with this, it won't stop all risks such as fire. The black plague affected nobles in their castles just as much as it affected the commoners.
2. Accept the risk and pay the damages.
3. Reduce the risk as much as possible with some lifestyle changes.
4. Transfer the risk, which is the purpose of insurance.

"The key concept that everyone should know," Mike added, "is that one big event can wipe out all of your life's work! If people get into an accident and the breadwinner in the other car is seriously injured or killed, the resulting lawsuit can easily wipe out their lifetime's work. A fire or flood or earthquake that destroys an uninsured home can be devastating. If you are not prepared for it, becoming disabled so that you can't work can easily devastate your entire family. This is why transferring the risk to insurance makes a lot of sense. Do you both agree?"

Both I and Matt nodded in agreement.

Disability Insurance

Mike began, "Let's start with the concept of disability and the need for disability insurance. First, Sandy, what would you say is your greatest asset?"

My initial reaction would be to say "My home," but upon further thought, I said, "My ability to speak, write, and earn money."

Disability Statistics

Mike reinforced this response by saying, "Yes, your earning power is your number one asset. I did a lot of research on disability as part of my job, and I thought I would share my findings with you and your readers. Here are some startling statistics:[1]

- Nearly one in three Americans ages 35 to 65 will become disabled for more than 90 days.
- A 35-year-old has a greater chance of becoming seriously disabled than he does of dying before he reaches age 65.
- Once an individual has been disabled for 90 days, the average length of disability is two years.
- A fatal injury occurs every five minutes, and a disabling injury occurs every two seconds.
- More than 20 million Americans suffer disabling injuries each year.
- Two-thirds of disabling injuries suffered by American workers in 2004 were off-the-job, meaning they weren't covered by worker's comp.
- Many people buy life insurance so that if they die, their families will have a way to pay the mortgage. However, the odds of mortgage foreclosure due to disability are 16 times greater than the risk of foreclosure due to death.
- Moreover, 25 percent of today's 20-year-olds will become disabled before they retire.[2]
- Over 36 million Americans are classified as disabled; this is about 12 percent of the total population, and most of them became disabled during their working years!
- Here is a very startling statistic: one in eight workers will be disabled for five years or MORE during their working careers![3]
- In fact, medical problems from a sickness or accident contributed to almost half of all home foreclosures.[4]
- Despite these alarming statistics, only 15 percent of the U.S. population has disability insurance.

"Mike, these statistics are very sobering. I didn't realize that there were that many people whose lives will be ruined because they didn't have disability coverage," I suggested ominously.

"What most people don't realize," Mike interjected, "is that the cost of disability insurance is quite low. The annual cost is only about 1 to 3 percent of the income to be replaced. Thus, if you want to replace $5,000 per month of lost income (which would be $60,000 per year), the annual cost for the disability insurance would be between $600 and $1,800 per year."

Mike then added, "I think the reason many people don't have this type of insurance is that they think that they will be covered by social security. This is very faulty thinking for two reasons. First, social security doesn't pay that much if you are totally disabled. Second, it is the old golden rule, 'He who has the gold, makes the rules.' To be eligible for social security disability, a person must be qualified in the following ways."

> The disability has lasted or is expected to last for at least one year or to result in death. In addition, the worker must be unable to do the work that she did before, and/or she must be unable to adjust to other work because of her condition. The real kicker is, however, <u>that the person must not be able to do any type of gainful work that can produce at least $720 per month in the first nine months of disability and no more than $1,010 per month afterward.</u> If the person is self-employed, the earnings limit is $720 per month, which is net of all business expenses.

"Thus, a disabled dentist who can wait tables won't qualify unless he earns less than $720 a month! As you can see collecting disability payments from the social security program is very tough."

"Even worse," Mike added, "many people opt for the cheapest disability policy they can find. Here's a tip about insurance companies."

> Policies are cheaper when the insurance company knows that there will be little chance to pay out. The general rule is that the cheaper the policy, the greater the risk on the insured!

Key Considerations in Analyzing Disability Insurance Policies

"Okay, now that we understand how important disability insurance is to the lives of most people, we need to discuss the important factors that everyone should know about when analyzing disability insurance policies and companies.

"Clearly the single most important consideration is the conditions in which the policy will pay off. This is determined by the policy's definition of disability. The best definition, which is also the most expensive, is one that pays if you can't perform the duties of your own occupation. Thus, the dentists who can't continue to practice dentistry or the auto mechanics who can no longer fix cars would receive benefits even if they were working in another field.

"Second, all disability policies have a waiting period. This is the period during which a person must wait, while being disabled, before the policy starts paying. The longer the waiting period, the lower the premium because long waiting periods decrease the risk to the insurance company. The key is to get a waiting period that you can live with and have sufficient funds to fuel your lifestyle until the policy payments kick in. Generally having a 90-day waiting period gives the best bang for the buck. An important note to remember is that you aren't being paid during the waiting period, and you should have enough funds to fuel your lifestyle during this period.

"A third provision that you want is an inflation provision. You should always try to get a policy that increases each year with inflation, or you will eventually find that inflation will degrade your payments over the years and not leave you with a secure life."

Mike then added, "Moreover, you want a noncancelable, guaranteed renewable policy that must stay in effect as long as you continue to make payments and one for which the premiums will be level for the life of the policy.

"In addition, you want to try to get a *future increase rider* without medical exams. This allows you to buy more disability insurance if your income rises. Again, the purpose of disability insurance is to protect your earnings. If your earnings rise substantially from the date that you purchased your policy, you probably want to get more insurance to cover this increase.

"Also, if you can get a policy that has a *partial disability clause*, this would be worth getting. This type of clause kicks in when you can do the duties of your own occupation but you can't work full time. Thus, you have a decrease in earnings due to the limited time that you can work. The policy will pay a portion of the disability payment based on how much of your earnings that you are losing.

"Finally, if you have a business that you own, you can get *business overhead disability insurance* that will pay your overhead while you are disabled. This is particularly beneficial for firms that are service oriented and dependent on a certain worker's performance or hours worked. Thus, a single firm owned by a doctor or dentist or lawyer would be ideal for this type of extra insurance."

Matt said, "This is great information for individuals, but what about the group disability insurance that some workers have?"

"Good question, Matt. *Group disability insurance* is much cheaper per person than a good individual disability insurance policy. Thus, based on my rule noted above, it isn't nearly as good as a good individual policy. There are a lot of reasons for my saying this.

"First, group insurance can be canceled by either the insurance company or the employer.

"Second, group insurance is lost if you leave the company, and the premiums go up with age, unlike that of an individual disability insurance policy for which premiums are usually level for life.

"Third, group insurance usually has an inferior definition of disability compared to individual plans. They rarely offer an *own occupation* definition.

"Fourth, group plans usually integrate with social security plans. Thus, if you receive social security, the group plan pays less. An individual plan pays regardless of the social security payments the policy owner collects."

"Mike," I quizzed, "how much disability insurance can people get? What I am really concerned with is how much of their income can they insure?"

He responded with, "The general rule is that insurance carriers will insure between 60 and 80 percent of your earnings."

"Mike," I interjected, "are there any other points that you want to add regarding disability insurance before we move onto a discussion of long-term care insurance?"

Mike thoughtfully added, "Yes, a couple of points and an observation or two. As you can tell, I don't like *group* disability insurance. Although it is better than not having insurance, it really benefits the insurance company and the employer more than the worker. If people can get supplemental, individual disability coverage, it would be very beneficial for most of them.

"Also, people should get disability insurance to last to at least age 65 and preferably for life. Moreover, people shouldn't be cheap regarding these types of policies. The definition of disability is crucial. Getting an inflation rider, getting the ability to buy more coverage without medical questions, and having a partial disability rider are all essential in my opinion.

"Finally, if you don't have any disability insurance coverage, get it now. Don't wait. Don't procrastinate. Get it now while you are healthy and can get it."

I turned to Matt and said, "The minute you start your own practice and start making money, you must get this insurance. I have had this all my life and have always been glad to have it."

Matt agreed wholeheartedly.

Here is a summary of desired provisions that you should have in disability insurance policies:

- Get a strong <u>definition</u> of disability that covers your <u>own occupation</u>.
- Generally get a <u>90-day waiting period</u> unless you don't have the funds to survive for 90 days.
- Always get a policy whose benefits will increase each year due to <u>inflation</u>.
- Get a <u>noncancelable, guaranteed renewable</u> policy, which will guarantee that the premiums won't increase unless the company increases the premiums for everyone.
- Take any <u>future increase riders</u> that allow you more disability coverage without medical exams.
- Look for a policy that provides a <u>partial disability rider</u>.
- If you own your own business that is very reliant on your ability to work, consider getting business <u>overhead disability insurance</u>.

Long-Term Care Insurance

Mike then changed gears and started discussing long-term care insurance. "The reason I am discussing this after our disability insurance discussion is that this type of insurance is essentially disability for retirees. Many people believe that this insurance is only for nursing homes. That is not the case. This insurance allows people to live at home while getting the necessary in-home care. This type of insurance is needed in case people live too long, which is what is happening today."

Long-Term Care Statistics

"Here are some interesting statistics." (Mike is great at both remembering and spouting off statistics, which is probably why he is so successful.)

- Life expectancy in ancient Greece was 20 to 30 years of age.
- Life expectancy in the 1500s was 45 to 48.
- Life expectancy now is over 77!
- Over one-half of women and one-third of men who reach age 65 will need some form of long-term care lasting over 90 days.
- Here is an ominous statistic: more than 7 out of 10 couples can expect at least one partner to use a nursing home during their lifetime.
- According to the U.S. Department of Health and Human Services, 2 out of 5 people (which is 40 percent of the U.S. population) who reach age 65 will need long-term care. Of these, 10 percent will need this care for 5 years or longer.

I turned to Matt and said, "Did you know that the chances of needing long-term care were that high?"

Matt chillingly said, "Yes, the statistics are even getting worse as the U.S. population ages and as costs go up for this type of care."

Key Considerations in Analyzing Long-Term Care Insurance Policies

Mike agreed and then added, "There are two types of long-term care that insurance will pay for. The first type is *qualified skilled nursing care*, which means that the individual needs help from a chronic illness or medical condition. The second type of care that insurance will pay for is *custodial care*. However, this second type of care will pay benefits only when the patient needs help with at least two or more *activities of daily living*, which include the following."

- Eating
- Bathing
- Dressing
- Toileting
- Continence, which is the voluntary control of urinary or fecal elimination
- Transferring, which is the ability to get in and out of beds, chairs, and so on

Mike then quickly summarized by saying, "Long-term care pays off if the patient has a chronic illness and/or the patient can't handle by himself at least two of the activities of daily living. Thus, if you can't dress yourself and bathe yourself, the policy will pay its benefits."

How Much Can Long-Term Nursing or Home Care Cost?

"Mike," I asked, "how much does long-term care cost?"

He quickly responded, "I have the long-term care costs here in Maryland. In Maryland, homemaker services run about $44,044 per year. A private one bedroom can cost about $39,600. A semiprivate room in a nursing care facility can cost a whopping $83,000 a year!"

Both Matt and I gulped at how expensive nursing care can cost. I then quickly suggested, "Mike, it seems to me that as high as these costs are, if people are multimillionaires, they won't need these policies since they have the money to pay the costs."

His answer was, "Yes, that may be true, but don't forget that costs go up with inflation. People need to have a net worth of at least several million to not have to worry about these types of costs, or they have to be completely broke in order for Medicaid to kick in."

What to Look For in Long-Term Care Insurance Policies

"Mike," I probed, "what clauses and other factors should we look for in analyzing long-term care policies?"

Mike thought about this for a few seconds and responded, "Most long-term care policies pay benefits based on the same rationale that I mentioned. When you invest in a long-term care (LTC) policy, you are buying a set amount of daily income for a period of years. The longer the years and the higher the daily amount, the higher the cost.

"So the first consideration is that, based on actual costs, you want a policy that will pay at least $200 per day or more. You can get policies that pay as little as $50 a day to ones that pay up to $500 a day.

"Second, you also need to choose a lifetime benefit. These range from as low as $100,000 to as high as $300,000 or more. My recommendation is to take enough months to cover you should your cash run out. Usually, I recommend at least five years.

"Most long-term care policies offer an *inflation rider* of some kind. In a sense, this is akin to getting higher coverage on your home. With the cost of nursing home and home healthcare going up due to inflation, having this type of coverage is very important."

"Mike, if I may interrupt for a minute," I asked. "My home healthcare policy actually has escalating benefits as the years go on. Thus, I had initial coverage for $150 per day, and several years later the policy benefit rose to about $210 per day."

"Yes, Sandy, I think that is a good example of a rider people should be getting."

Mike then added, "Here is a summary of provisions that you would want in your nursing home insurance."

- There should be a payment of at least $200 to $250 per day.
- There should be at least a five-year payout and preferably longer.
- I would recommend a 100-day waiting period unless you can't afford the nursing care cost for this waiting period.
- There should be some inflation protection.
- No prior hospitalization should be required in order for you to receive benefits.
- The benefits should be payable for all necessary home healthcare; the benefits should not be limited to just skilled nursing care.
- There should be a waiver of any premiums while you are in a nursing home.
- You want policies that are *nonforfeitable* and *guaranteed renewable*. This means that the insurance company can't cancel the policy and

that the premiums will remain level unless the insurance company raises premiums for all policyholders, including new policyholders.

Mike also noted, "Remember, crime doesn't pay . . . literally. **You will not be paid by the nursing home insurance company if you were injured participating in a crime, insurrection, or riot.**

"A final observation about nursing home insurance is to call the Better Business Bureau (BBB) and check out the A.M. Best Company's rating of the insurer. The top rating is A+. The insurer should have at least an A rating. You can also check out Moody's ratings at www.moodys.com. The insurance company should have an AA rating or better."

Mike then pulled out a sheet that showed what the typical long-term coverage benefits are, which are reproduced below:

- Your home healthcare including skilled nursing care
- Occupational, speech, physical, and rehabilitation therapy, as well as help with personal care such as bathing and dressing
- Homemaker services such as cooking or housekeeping
- Adult daycare health center care
- Hospice care
- Respite care
- Assisted-living facilities
- Alzheimer's special care facilities
- Nursing homes

Mike went on to note what is *not* usually covered such as the following:

- Care or services provided outside the United States (However, a growing number of policies will have an international care benefit.)
- Care or services that result from war or acts of war
- Care or services that result from an attempt at suicide or any intentionally self-inflicted injury
- Care or services for alcoholism or drug addiction with the sole exception being an addiction caused by physician prescribed medication
- Care or services covered by Medicare or by any state or federal workers' compensation plan
- Convenience items such as televisions in the room and weekly hairdressing appointments

All of this led me to quiz Mike, "So, since this type of care is fairly common among Americans, how much will it cost? I do know that my policy is costing at least $2,000 per year for me and the same amount for my wife."

Mike responded, "Remember what I said: the higher the risk to the insurance company, the greater the premium. If there is a low risk of usage, the premium becomes lower. Nursing home coverage is used a lot. Moreover, the potential benefits can be hundreds of thousands of dollars. Thus, it isn't cheap. A typical premium for a 45-year-old might be $1,700 per year. A 60-year-old might pay $2,300 per year and up. If you are over 70, it could easily be $3,000 per year!"

Since I personally have this coverage for us, I was aware of these high costs. I then probed Mike by asking, "What strategies can people use to cut these costs and help pay for this type of insurance? Won't Medicare pay some of this? Let's face it, Mike, not everyone has several thousand dollars extra lying around."

Paying for Nursing Home Insurance

Mike sniggered at this remark and said, "Well, there are a number of strategies I and many elder law attorneys have used to reduce costs. First, people need to understand that they can self-pay the cost of nursing care and home healthcare. It could easily run $200 to $250 per day and even more. This translates to between $5,600 and $7,350 per month that could cost the insurance company. Moreover, inflation will easily raise these costs over the years.

"Thus, if you are rich and can afford $80,000 per year and up, you may not need this insurance. This would mean that if your investable net worth, including the value of your home if no one needs to live there, is over $2 million, you probably don't need nursing home insurance. Moreover, Medicare will pay up to 100 days of skilled nursing home coverage. The catch is that you must be hospitalized for three consecutive days. Moreover, the nursing home must be Medicare approved, which applies to only about 20 percent of the nursing homes."

Mike added, "If you are very poor, the government (Medicaid) will pay for the needed nursing home coverage but not usually home healthcare. Thus, if you are rich, you can pay for it. If you are very poor, the government will pay for it. The middle class, however, gets shafted. They are the ones that need long-term care insurance the most. Thus, anyone with an investable net worth of fewer than $2 million probably needs long-term care insurance."

Matt then chirped in, "What would you say is the best age overall to buy nursing home insurance?"

Mike thought that this was a great question and said, "Well, the lower the age, the cheaper the insurance; however, you are losing the cash for a longer period of time. We have been recommending that the ideal time to buy nursing home insurance is around age 55."

I then quizzed Mike, "Mike, can't you just give away your money to your kids so that you can be poor enough for the government to pay the bill?"

Mike said, "This sounds reasonable; however, the government recently instituted a *five-year look-back*. Thus, **any gifts given away to your family within the past five years, which is measured from the date you enter the nursing home, are counted against you**. The government won't pay anything unless you pay this amount back to the nursing home. The government will actually check for fund transfers by inspecting your bank balances and other transfers. Nice try though."

Matt then interrupted Mike with the question, "Mike, before we get into planning for the payments, what is the maximum amount that you think people can pay for nursing home coverage?"

Mike smiled at this question and said, "Sandy, you have a smart kid there. The answer is that the Insurance Institute recommends that the maximum payout for nursing home insurance should not exceed 7 percent of your expected retirement income, which includes interest and dividends and social security."

Planning for Nursing Home Payments

Mike was now getting excited because he was getting to the real planning that he and other elder law attorneys were recommending. "There are ways, however, with which you can generate enough money to pay for the nursing home.

"One technique is to sell your current life insurance to a buyer. This is called a *viatical settlement*. Generally, if you have a life expectancy of three years or less, you can sell your policy and get a nice settlement to cover your nursing home costs. Moreover, some of the recent life insurance policies provide that 2 percent of the face value of the policy will be paid to you *each month* for nursing home care and 1 percent each month for other home care. The catch is that you must be deemed by a physician to be terminally ill."

Ways Around the Medicaid Rules

Matt was thinking about all that was said and asked, "Mike, I know that there are ways that many planners recommend to get around the Medicaid rules. What have you been recommending to your clients?"

Mike responded, "That is a great question, Matt, and it is a key to keeping the wealth in the family. There are a number of planning suggestions.

However, keep in mind that any transfer of monies to family members within five years of entering a nursing home, which is usually calculated as the date of the Medicaid application, can be gotten back by the nursing home before Medicaid will kick in. We call this the *look-back rule*.

"In addition, before Medicaid will pay anything, you really need to have almost nothing. This includes jewelry over a certain amount in value, home equities of over $500,000, IRA monies, $2,500 in life insurance value, $2,500 in a prepaid burial fund, and some retirement accounts. However, if you are married, the house, up to $500,000 in equity, won't count in the computation and neither will the car, as strange as that sounds. You are also allowed to keep a limited amount of jewelry, goods, and a prepaid funeral policy of up to $2,500 in value. Even worse, the other spouse can earn only about $2,000 per month including social security income. Any excess will be considered available for the nursing home payment."

Rolling my eyes, I said, "Mike, the government really doesn't leave you with much, does it?"

Mike sniggered a bit at this and said, "With today's deficits, if the government is picking up the tab, it wants to make sure that you have almost no ability to pay the nursing home costs. Again, it is that golden rule, and they are putting up the gold."

Mike went on, "The first technique is that you can give away up to $13,000 per year per recipient without worrying about the look-back. If you are married, you can give away up to $26,000 per year to each recipient without worrying about the look-back. Thus, if you have two married children and some grandchildren, you can give them *each* between $13,000 and $26,000 per year depending on whether you are single or married.

"A second approach is to have the couple divorce so that the nursing home patient needs to turn over half the money to the ex-spouse. These funds are not pulled back into the estate for Medicaid purposes."

I turned to Matt with a deadpan face and said, "This won't work. Your mother would kill me before we could use this technique," to which Matt chuckled.

"A strongly suggested third approach, which elder law attorneys have been suggesting for years, is to transfer all assets to your family well before you go to the nursing home."

Matt then interrupted and said, "Wait a minute! You just said that there is a five-year look-back rule."

Mike responded, "You're jumping the gun, Matt. Let me finish. Here is the second part of the plan. You would purchase, obviously well in advance, nursing home coverage for up to five years. Thus, when you enter the nursing home, the nursing home insurance pays the costs for the full five years. After five years, the look-back period is over and Medicaid will kick in. Isn't this a cool plan?"

Matt, liking what he heard, wanted to reinforce this concept so that he would understand it.

So people should take out nursing home coverage for at least five years. Later on in life, when they find that they need to enter a nursing home, they would transfer all of their assets out of their estate to their family and have the nursing home insurance pay the costs for five years. This would thus avoid the five-year look-back, and they could then transfer all of their savings to their family instead of the government.

"If I got this right, this is an amazing planning feature!"

Mike laughed and said, "Yes, it is a fabulous strategy. The key point behind this is that the look-back period begins from the day that a person enters the nursing home. In addition, you don't want to do this *unless* you have an irreversible condition such as dementia, Alzheimer's, or some other incurable disease that will last you for the remainder of your life."

I thought this was very sound reasoning and said, "What other tricks do you have up your sleeve that can circumvent the Medicaid look-back rule?"

Mike responded, "There is one other technique recommended by attorneys, which is to create a private annuity for your family."

I was aware of this from law school and said, "Mike, I know what this is, but would you explain this in detail to both Matt and our readers?"

Mike chuckled and said, "To set up a private annuity, a person agrees to give others, such as family members, an income based on the person's life expectancy. The family would get immediate control of all assets of the person going into the nursing home, and in return the family would agree to pay that person a lifetime annuity based on IRS life expectancy tables. Thus, each year a set amount of income would be paid to the person or to the nursing home. The key here is that this isn't a gift. It is a *sale for consideration*, which is a fixed annuity payment. Thus, the assets such as the family home, business, and investments are kept in the family in return for lifetime payments.

"I should note that if the person transferring the assets for a private annuity is terminally ill, this may not work. It is ideal for those that don't have this type of diagnosis."

Before we finished up on this important topic, I asked Mike if there were any other alternatives to cutting nursing home costs.

He thought about this and replied, "One important thing that many people should know about is Meals On Wheels. This organization will deliver prepared meals to your home or apartment. These meals are already cooked. All you have to do is defrost the meals and eat them, although some of them might need to be warmed up in a microwave first. This service could allow some folks to stay at home and not need a nursing home."

Homeowners Insurance

We took a bit of a break since both Matt and I were getting hungry and thirsty. Fortunately, Mike's wife had some great sandwiches prepared with some diet sodas. Afterward, we sat down to business in order to discuss homeowners insurance.

Mike began: "Without question, homeowners insurance is one of the best types of policies around. It is very encompassing. It covers damages from fire, theft, tornadoes, and wind. It even provides liability protection from guests' falling on your property. However, although it seems to cover almost everything, it is important to note that there are many things that it doesn't cover unless you get a special rider. [These noncovered items are listed below.]"

- Earthquake damage or anything caused by geological or astronomical events is not covered. You may not have a lot of earthquakes here in Maryland, but one good one that occurs near your home can damage the foundation, which could cost tens or even hundreds of thousands of dollars to fix.
- Floods aren't covered.
- Hurricanes aren't covered. However, although homeowners insurance doesn't cover hurricanes per se, it does cover wind damage.
- Damage due to landslides isn't covered.
- Damage caused by slow deterioration isn't covered.
- Mold damage isn't covered.
- Sewer backups, which are considered like floods, aren't covered.
- Expansive soil problems aren't covered. This one area causes more damage than fires and storms combined. It happens when there is a lot of clay that can expand and contract when the clay gets wet. You really need to know if you are living in an area with a lot of clay beds.
- The coverage for jewelry and computers and other personal effects is limited to usually around $1,000 per occurrence.

Being a bit surprised, I confessed, "Mike, I really had no idea that your typical homeowners insurance didn't cover all these things, and I would bet many of my readers will be surprised too."

Mike chuckled and agreed.

He then continued, "Because having a house destroyed by a storm or having the house cleaned out by thieves can be so devastating, people should get the best homeowners insurance that they can get. The key is to figure out what to look for and *not* to focus just on the premium.

"First," Mike noted, "there are two types of homeowners insurance. There is the cheap crappier type, and I do not personally recommend it. The cheaper one covers the *actual cash value of your home*, which is the cost minus the depreciation. This is *not* the one that anyone should have because houses usually appreciate, not depreciate, over a period of time. Moreover, construction costs of new homes and improvements always go up with inflation.

"The best type of homeowners insurance is the type that will give you *replacement value of your home*. This is more costly, but it is very much worth the price. The key here is that you would name a value. If the house is destroyed, the policy will pay to rebuild the house—and here is the catch—generally up to 120 percent of the insured amount."

Matt then interrupted Mike by saying, "Thus, people should have their home routinely appraised and get the value updated for insurance purposes every year."

Mike smiled at Matt's insightful comment but corrected him by saying, "Yes, but I would suggest the following."

> **First, over time it is imperative that people update their coverage. I don't think that it has to be done yearly though. However, if you live in an appreciating real estate market, the real estate value should be updated every two or three years.**

"However, with this type of coverage, it *must* be done regularly. The sad fact is that many people who think that they have replacement coverage don't take the step of having their home's value reevaluated routinely. If a catastrophic event occurs that destroys their home, they will get a *lot* less than they thought they would.

"I know of a couple who had this coverage on a historic property in Bethesda. The house was completely destroyed by fire. However, the value insured was only $1.5 million, while the home was worth $4 million. It was a disaster for the family. This problem could easily have been avoided had they updated the insurance value every few years. Sadly, this couple had not updated their insurance for many years."

Mike listed the following additional important points.

> **A second major point about homeowners coverage is that if people are in a zone that is subject to earthquakes, floods, or one of the other non-covered calamities, they should get a rider covering damage from these items. Riders are usually available.**

Third, because personal item coverage is very limited with homeowners insurance, many people should consider getting additional specific coverage for their jewelry, computers, antiques, and other collections. This is named coverage that has to be specifically identified in the rider to the policy. It is important that you submit proof of purchase showing purchase prices. If it involves collectibles and jewelry, an appraisal should also be submitted so you can get the fair value of the items if they are stolen.

Fourth, if you have a dog, make sure that you are covered for dog bites. However, some dogs will not be covered such as Rottweilers, pit bulls, Great Danes, German shepherds, Siberian Huskies, and even temperamental dogs such as Chow Chows. People really need to know what dogs will be covered when they buy the dogs.

Fifth, always, always get an *umbrella policy*. This is a relatively cheap policy that covers many things, especially liability issues arising from your home, car, and even from issues such as slander and libel. The cost is a negligible: $200 to $300 per million of coverage. I would recommend at least $3 million of umbrella policy coverage. Moreover, if you can afford it, I would even suggest as much as $5 million.

Finally, make a video recording of your home and its contents every five years or more often if necessary. This shows what was in the home. Moreover, with a video camera or camcorder, you can dictate the serial number of any electronics. Thus, if your house is burglarized, you can have the police trace the equipment.

I decided to probe Mike a bit about reducing the costs of these policies by asking, "Mike, if people want to get this great coverage but at a lower cost, what should they do?"

Mike smiled when I asked that and responded, "People have a couple of choices. They can avoid covering some items and take risks. As long as they understand the potential loss from the risks and can afford them, they should be fine. There is, however, a better approach that many agents aren't telling their customers because the agents want a higher premium, which means a higher commission. Remember when I said that insurance is designed to cover your risks that you can't afford?"

Matt and I both nodded in agreement.

"The key then is to cover *unaffordable risks*. Thus, I would suggest increasing most people's deductible in order to reduce their premiums. Moreover, the deductible is what you would have to pay out of pocket. Thus, whatever deductible chosen, it is imperative that you can afford to pay this amount out of pocket. Thus, if you have a $5,000 deductible (which I personally have on my home), you would have to pay up to $5,000 due to an event such as fire or wind damage. If you have the money, it isn't a problem.

"However, if your house burns down without proper coverage, as I noted in my example above, now you have a catastrophe. **Thus, raise the deductible to a point at which you can afford to both pay the insurance and pay the deductible if a problem arises.** Raising the deductible from $250 to even a $1,000 can reduce the premium by as much as 20 to 25 percent.

"In addition, shop around. Check out good companies and see what they are offering. However, you want to compare apples to apples. Make sure you are getting all the items that I noted above.

"Finally," Mike added, "most companies will cut their homeowners insurance costs between 5 and 10 percent if you get a monitored burglar alarm. Of course, the cost of monitoring your home plus the installation may exceed the savings. However, you will get an annual savings by implementing this."

Vehicle Insurance

Mike wanted to touch upon vehicle insurance (and health insurance also, which he discussed with us later) so that folks can get a good bird's-eye view of the types of insurance available and know how to reduce their costs while minimizing their risk.

After a bit of a coffee break, Mike stated, "Okay, let's get started with vehicle insurance. You will notice that I said *vehicle* insurance. This type of insurance covers cars, trucks, and even motorcycles. Most vehicle insurance is divided into three parts: liability, collision, and comprehensive. I would bet, Sandy, that as smart as you are, you don't know the difference between collision and comprehensive."

Being a bit taken aback, I admitted that I really didn't know the difference.

Mike smiled and politely said, "Don't feel badly. The vast majority of Americans don't know the difference either. Here is what each does."

- **Liability** covers you when you are at fault. It pays for the other person's personal and property damage arising from an accident caused by you.
- **Collision** is used to fix your car. Thus, it covers your personal vehicle for car crashes with inanimate objects (such as other cars, trees, or buildings).
- **Comprehensive** covers damage to your vehicle from events other than accidents. It covers damage due to theft, fire, hail, wind, and so on, and it has a deductible.

"Understanding what these items entail is important for vehicle insurance planning. For example, you probably don't need any collision or comprehensive coverage if you have a car worth less than $2,500.

"In terms of liability coverage, my suggestion is to get only $250,000, which is usually the minimum required coverage in order to get an umbrella policy that we talked about before. The umbrella is what will potentially cover the vast amount of liability risks."

"Mike," I blurted out, "I don't mean to be pushy, but frankly, all car insurance is about the same in that the policies cover folks for the same damages. To me the key question that my readers will have is how to cut the cost of the vehicle insurance while maintaining relatively little risk." After all, it was nearing the end of the day, and Matt and I were starting to get restless.

Mike smiled knowingly and said, "Yes, you are right, Sandy. So let's get into the ways to reduce vehicle insurance costs. A lot depends on the coverage and deductible.

"First, as I noted above, you don't need collision or comprehensive for wrecks or for very old vehicles that aren't worth much.

"Second, there are certain types of protections that insurance agents try to sell folks in order to increase the agents' commissions. Personal injury protection is one of these. This pays for medical expenses arising from an accident. You don't need this if you have good health insurance."

Mike was really getting into the swing of things when he said, "If you want to reduce rates, you need to do the following."

- Raise your deductible to at least $250 and preferably $500 or more. This could drop costs 30 percent or even more. You don't need coverage for the small things unless you are living from hand to mouth. However, for big events such as major accidents, you really need the insurance.
- Get multicar coverage. If the insurance company covers all of your vehicles, you get a substantial discount on all coverage.
- Sometimes, if you also have your home covered, you can get even further discounts.

"I do want to discuss leased cars. Contrary to what the leasing companies tell you, your car insurance will cover any accident that you incur while leasing a car. The problem that most people may not know is that the insurance covers the depreciated value of the car and *not* the full value or the net loss of rent. Thus, if you are leasing a car, you should always try to get gap insurance as part of your policy. This covers the full value of the car rather than just the depreciated value, which could be quite less. Also, having good comprehensive coverage is mandatory for leased cars.

"Moreover, if you are traveling abroad, you may need to get special vehicle insurance for that travel. Check with your insurer about this.

"Finally, I want to suggest that everyone shop around. Check out the rates with all of the main companies and the coverage so that you are sure to compare apples to apples. You should check with the Better Business Bureau about complaints that other people might have made against the insurance company. It is useless to get a low rate with a company that tries not to pay claims."

Health Insurance

"That is all that I have to say about vehicle insurance." Mike then shifted the conversation to health insurance, which he considers an essential type of policy for everyone to have.

"First, I want to note that medical and hospital costs cause more bankruptcies than almost any other reason. A severe illness of a family member can easily cost in the hundreds of thousands of dollars. However, there are approximately 32 million uninsured people in this country. This is completely unacceptable. Part of the reason is that they can't get insurance because they have a severe preexisting condition. The main reason, however, is cost. Health insurance has a very high utilization. Moreover, although some of the top health insurance plans can be costly, there are various options with health insurance that can provide a variety of affordable costs and benefits.

"Sadly, many people look at health insurance as a luxury. In fact, studies have shown that people without health insurance have a lower life expectancy because they tend to stay away from doctors and hospitals.

"I am hoping to change everyone's mind to feel that it is an essential coverage. In fact, once the Affordable Care Act takes full effect in 2014, everyone will be required to have health insurance. Obviously, the government feels as I do."

While on a roll, Mike added, "Currently, before the Affordable Care Law takes full effect (although many of these points will still be in effect even after healthcare reform occurs), people should be aware of the different types of health insurance coverage, which are the following."

Health Maintenance Organizations

"Health maintenance organizations (HMOs) are the cheapest among all forms of health insurance, but many people, including me, consider them the worst of the bunch. However, an HMO certainly is better than not having any medical insurance.

"This type of insurance provides a specific doctor to monitor your family's needs. Besides being the cheapest form of health insurance, it does provide some advantages. Although HMOs are starting to charge a small amount for drugs, they usually provide free physicals and lab testing, and there are no deductibles for any care. Thus, there is no coinsurance by which you pay a portion of the bill, and there are no deductibles. Your premium is all that you pay.

"The main problem with HMOs is that you can't use a specialist unless your primary care physician refers you. Since insurance companies are in business to cut costs and save money, you can bet that they try to not refer people to specialists when they possibly can get away with this. The second disadvantage is that you must use a set, listed group of doctors. If you need a special surgery, you can't go to the best surgeon in the world unless that surgeon is on the list of approved physicians, which is usually a limited list. But, as I said above, from a cost perspective, HMOs are unbeatable."

Preferred Provider Organizations

"Among these plans there are some variations. The typical preferred provider organization (PPO) is a combination of a traditional fee-for-service structure and an HMO. Like an HMO, there is a limited number of doctors and hospitals to choose from. When you use those providers (sometimes called *preferred providers*, other times called *network providers*), most of your medical bills are covered.

"When you go to doctors in the PPO, you present a card and do not have to fill out forms. Usually there is a small copayment for each visit. For some services, you may have to pay a deductible and coinsurance. As with an HMO, a PPO requires that you choose a primary care doctor to monitor your healthcare. Most PPOs cover preventive care. This usually includes visits to the doctor, well-baby care, immunizations, and mammograms.

"A big advantage of a PPO over an HMO is that in a PPO, you can use doctors who are not part of the plan and still receive some coverage. At these times, you will pay a larger portion of the bill yourself (and also fill out the claims forms). Some people like this option because even if their doctor is not a part of the network, it means they don't have to change doctors to join a PPO. Moreover, you don't need a referral from a primary care physician to utilize the services of a specialist. Thus, it is the more flexible of the health insurance plans and consequently, the most expensive.

"Besides knowing the types of plans available, there are four terms and features that should be understood and analyzed for each company that you are considering, particularly if you obtain a PPO plan.

"The first is whether the plan pays **only reasonable and customary costs**. If there is a doctor who is part of the plan, the insurance company will have contracted amounts for payments. If the bill is more than those amounts, the doctor will reduce the fee to the amount stipulated by the insurance company. However, if you go outside of the network, the doctor might charge a lot more than what is reimbursed, which can cause you to have a much larger bill for services. Let's face it. One of the reasons doctors don't participate in some insurance plans, or in some cases all insurance plans, is that they want to charge more than the insurance contract allows."

I teased Mike by saying, "I would bet that the second feature that everyone should check out is the deductible."

With a deadpan look, Mike said, "Yes, that is exactly right. Policy costs become a lot cheaper as the **deductible** goes up because there will be fewer claims by the insured. This is why I normally recommend getting a much higher deductible because the main concern for most people should not be the small amounts that the doctor charges for a sickness but rather, the large potential expenses of major illnesses or injuries due to accidents."

Mike then quickly reinforced this statement by saying, "Now I know what everyone must be thinking. How high a deductible should people get?

"My suggestion is this: the deductible should be at least $1,200 for single people and $2,400 for families if they can afford it. The reason is that I recommend people getting health savings accounts (HSAs) that will cover the deductibles and other noncovered medical expenses. However, you must have at least a $1,200 deductible in order to get an HSA. Sandy, I know you have a lot of discussion about health savings accounts in your other book *Lower Your Taxes—Big Time!* Thus, I will defer any discussion on this to you and just suggest that the readers get your other book too.

"The third major term that everyone should analyze in their policies is the **coinsurance**. This is the portion that people pay once the overall deductible is met. It can be as little as zero with an HMO and as much as 20 percent or more of the bill per visit with other types of plans. In addition, there are prescription plans for drugs that have their own separate deductibles and coinsurance requirements too.

"Last but not least is the **stop-loss**. This is probably among the most important concepts that you should know about your policy. This is the total out-of-pocket costs that you will incur before the insurance company pays 100 percent of the remaining bills for the year. Thus, if your family's stop-loss is $6,500, you will not have to pay over $6,500 for the year . . . period, unless you use a noncovered physician who is out of the network.

"I should note that even when the Affordable Care Act takes full effect in 2014, those who have private medical insurance can keep it and won't have to switch to the government plan. This can be a big benefit since I can't imagine a government plan being better than a private plan. However, time will tell about this."

Mike asked Matt if he liked the sandwiches made for us. True to being vintage Matt, he responded, "Yes, I did like them. However, in the event that I get food poisoned, I have very good health insurance," which made both Mike and I laugh.

It was getting late, and we thanked Mike for all of the valuable information that he imparted. I thought Matt and I would go out to our favorite Italian restaurant for dinner. Matt did well, and I think he deserved it.

A Review of What You Have Learned

Four Ways to Deal with Risk
- Avoid the risk, by not going anywhere, which is very hard to do.
- Accept the risk and pay the damages.
- Reduce the risk with lifestyle changes.
- Transfer the risk with insurance.

Disability Insurance
- Most people should have it because a long-term disability is quite common.
- Don't depend on getting social security disability benefits. To qualify, you would have to be unable to do any type of work.
- The cheaper the policy, the less risk to the insurance company. Don't be cheap or look for the cheapest policy.
- When evaluating disability policies, look for the insurer's definition of disability. Get a policy that provides an own occupation definition to protect you if you can't fulfill the duties of your own occupation. Also get an inflation rider. Also get a policy that is noncancelable and guaranteed renewable. This means that you can't be canceled and the insurance company can't raise your premiums unless it raises everyone else's in your insurance class.
- For more affordability, increase the waiting period. Usually, 90 days will maximize the bang for your buck.
- Get a partial disability rider.
- Get a business overhead disability rider if you own a business and your services are critical to the income flow of the business.
- Don't depend on group insurance. They don't have great disability definitions, and you can lose your coverage if you are fired or you leave the company.

- Get a rider to purchase more disability insurance without needing a medical exam. This will help insure a higher income due to inflation.

Long-Term Care Insurance

- 40 percent of people will need this insurance by age 65. This can be critical insurance if you don't have the funds to pay for long-term nursing care. Your net worth should be several million dollars in order to minimize the need for this policy. Nursing care and home healthcare can easily cost between $40,000 and $85,000 per year depending on your needs and where you want to live.
- To qualify for benefits, you must not be able to meet two out of six activities of living such as these:
  - Eating
  - Bathing
  - Dressing
  - Toileting
  - Continence, which is the voluntary control of urinary or fecal elimination
  - Transferring, which is the ability to get in and out of beds, chairs, and so on

- The cost of the policy is based on daily benefits and years of potential payout. It is recommended that you get at least $200 to $250 a day for at least five years.
- Get a 100-day waiting period unless you don't have the money for the 100 days of costs. At that point, you might want to reduce the waiting period.
- Always get inflation protection.
- Get a policy that doesn't require a prior hospitalization for you to receive benefits.
- Benefits should be payable for all necessary home healthcare and *not* just for skilled nursing care.
- Get a waiver of premiums if you are in a nursing home.
- Get a nonforfeitable and guaranteed renewable policy so that the company can't cancel your policy and can't raise just your own premiums without raising everyone else in your policy's class.
- Check out the insurance company with the Better Business Bureau and Moody's.
- Here are some of your options for paying for long-term care:
  - Sell your life insurance policy using a viatical settlement. Some recent policies will pay you 2 percent of the face value per month if you are terminally ill. This can be good if you are terminally ill and you expect to die within three years.
  - Be completely broke so that Medicaid will pick up tab.
  - Be wary of the five-year look-back rule for prior transfers and gifts made to family. This five-year period begins at the start of your entry to the nursing home.
  - To reduce your estate, use annual gifts to family members, keeping your yearly gifts under $13,000 to each recipient if you are single and $26,000 to each recipient if you are married. These gifts don't count as part of five-year look-back. Other options would be to give most of your assets to your family well before the five-year period begins.
  - Get long-term care insurance to cover you for five years, and at the same time transfer to your family members all of the assets you won't need to pay for extra nursing costs. Thus, you will have your five years of coverage paid by

the insurance company, and you can then qualify for Medicaid. This way, your family will get your assets, and not the government. You want to do this only if you have an irreversible condition such as dementia, cancer, or Alzheimer's.
- Consider setting up a private annuity with your family in which you transfer your assets in return for an annuity. This annuity is for full value, and it should not be pulled back into the estate for Medicaid purposes. However, the annuity can be used by a nursing home to reduce Medicaid costs.
- Consider avoiding a nursing home by using Meals On Wheels.

Homeowners Insurance
- This type of insurance covers many things including, fire, wind, and theft of property and liability. However, it is important to know what isn't covered such as the following:
  - Earthquake damage
  - Flood damage
  - Sewer backups, which is considered to part of floods
  - Astronomical events
  - Expansive soil problems, which are prevalent where there is lots of clay in the foundation soil
  - More than $1,000 of the theft or loss of personal items
- Get riders to cover any hazards that might exist in your area such as floods or earthquakes.
- Get riders to cover specific jewelry or collections.
- It is important to get replacement coverage for the home, which is a more expensive policy, than getting the cost less depreciation of your home, which is a cheaper type of policy. If you do get replacement coverage, always have your home value reevaluated every few years. Too many people forget to do this.
- **Always** get an umbrella policy for at least $3 million or more. Ideally, it should be $4 million to $5 million.

Vehicle Insurance
- Know what each part of your insurance covers:
  - **Liability** covers accidents that were your fault.
  - **Collision** covers the fixing of your car. You don't need this if your car is worth under $2,500.
  - **Comprehensive** covers damages to your vehicle from events other than accidents such as wind, theft, or hail. This also isn't needed if the car is worth under $2,500.
- If you lease a car frequently, you will need collision and comprehensive to cover you for damage to the leased car.
- Raising deductibles to at least $250 or more can significantly reduce the premium. You want to be covered for the big accidents and problems, and not the small stuff.
- Vehicle insurance covers you for leased cars. However, if you enter into a long-term lease, you might want to get gap insurance to cover the difference between the depreciated cost of the car and its full value.

Health Insurance

- This is **vital** insurance. More bankruptcies occur due to medical costs than due to any other reason. Health insurance has a very high utilization.
- The two basic types of health insurance are these:
  - **HMO**: This is the cheapest. There is no deductible either. However, you can't see specialists unless you are referred to them by your primary care doctor.
  - **PPO:** This is better insurance, and it is therefore more costly. You can see specialists even if you are not recommended to do so by your primary care physician. You can use physicians outside of the plan, but doing so will be much more costly than using a physician who is a PPO member.

Notes

1. http://www.unum.com/disability101/WhyNecessary.aspx.
2. http://www.disabilitycanhappen.org/chances_disability/.
3. Ibid.
4. Ibid.

12

Insurance, Part II

*I have so much insurance that when I go,
so does the insurance company.*

—Jack Benny

When to Buy Life Insurance

In choosing an expert for our discussion about life insurance, I decided to find someone other than a life insurance agent. Agents are usually very knowledgeable but also very biased.

I therefore contacted Steve. Steve is another elder law attorney that I know, and he is also a financial planning professor. He has taught a number of courses for continuing education for financial planners, and he has written some successful books. He would be perfect for this important discussion, and most importantly, he would be relatively unbiased.

Matt and I met Steve at his waiting room; I was surprised at how lavish his waiting room furnishings were. Matt commented on the nice comfortable chairs and sofas. I guess as we get older, we need soft things to sit on.

We were then ushered into Steve's private office, which to our surprise was itself rather Spartan, although it was dotted with antiques. Steve was simply an acquaintance, and I am most appreciative that he took a fair amount of his time in order to help me with this book.

Being a no-nonsense type of guy, Steve started in immediately by saying that although life insurance is vital to many families and businesses, people usually don't obtain life insurance for the right reasons.

Steve went on, "There are two key rules that everyone needs to keep in mind and that will permeate everything that I will say today.

"**Rule 1** is that life insurance should be purchased for only two reasons. The first is to avoid a financial loss of income, and the second is to leave an estate such as a bequest to a college. Thus, having life insurance on children is ridiculous unless the parent is being supported by the adult child," Steve said disdainfully.

"**Rule 2** is that insurance and investments don't mix, especially due to the poor returns and high costs of insurance products. If you want insurance, it should be because you need insurance and for no other reason.

"The problem," Steve noted sneeringly, "is that agents are very well trained to mislead buyers by giving the insurance a name that seems applicable to the need. Thus, they might describe a policy as 'key man insurance,' implying that the insurance is some specially designed policy to cover key individuals when it is just normal life insurance. Likewise, I am sure that you have heard of 'mortgage insurance.' There is no such animal, but insurance agents coined this term to cover life insurance used to pay off the mortgage upon death. This is normal term or permanent insurance given a false name. These marketing practices apply to other coined names such as 'credit life insurance' and 'estate planning insurance.' In fact, just recently, I saw an ad for the Gerber Life College Plan. In my opinion, this is simply a savings plan with life insurance used to pay for college or pay off upon the death of the main wage earner. It is not some specialized college savings policy."

Matt then quickly interrupted Steve by saying, "Steve, shouldn't people have life insurance in order to protect the family upon the primary wage earner's premature death? After all, there won't be enough money to pay for college if this happens."

Steve quickly responded to Matt and said, "Yes, that is a good point. However, you don't need whole life insurance to accomplish this task when much cheaper term insurance can do the same job. Your mind is thinking faster than I can speak. Give me a few minutes, and I will discuss this."

Types of Life Insurance

Steve then clarified his points by saying, "There are several types of life insurance that everyone should know about. There are various types of permanent insurance and various types of term insurance. We will discuss term insurance first."

Term Insurance

"The first type of term insurance is *annual renewable term* (ART) *insurance*. This is the cheapest form of insurance. This policy simply covers the mortality risk of death. There is no cash value for this type of policy, nor are there savings. In addition, the premium increases each year with age since the risk of dying goes up with age.

"The second type of term insurance is *level term insurance*. This is simply term insurance with a savings plan that is designed to keep the premiums level for a period of time. This can be for 5 years, 10 years, or even 20 years. It tends to be more expensive up front than annual renewable term insurance, but as time goes on, it tends to be cheaper than ART insurance after the midpoint of the insurance term. Thus, a 20-year level term policy starts to have a lower premium than an ART policy at the midway point, which in this case would be around year 10. The problem is that you are paying a lot more up front for the insurance in order to build up the savings sufficiently to cover the premiums for the latter period of the insurance term.

"Finally, there is *decreasing term insurance*. With this type of policy, the premiums stay level, but the amount of coverage decreases. It is ideal to cover a liability that will be paid off over time such as a mortgage. If you are a good saver, it can also be ideal for you because you are slowly building up a savings side fund, and you may not need as much insurance as you did initially."

Permanent Insurance

Steve then said, "There are several types of permanent insurance. The first is *normal whole life insurance*. This is normal ART insurance *but with a savings feature built in*. It is very expensive, and it has the highest commissions and load costs found among any form of insurance. Basically, the first two full years of premiums are used for insurance company costs.

"A second type of permanent insurance is *variable life insurance*. This is the same as whole life in that you buy an ART policy, and the difference is placed in a savings account with a stock investment portfolio. If the market does well, this type of insurance can also develop some very decent cash value. However, if the stock market doesn't do well, the underlying portfolio doesn't do well, and it might require much greater premiums. Thus, the policy owner, who is usually the insured, bears the risk of investment returns in a variable life policy. If the stock market fluctuates, this could result in higher premiums, unlike that of a whole life policy for which the insurance company bears the investment return risk in exchange for much lower potential returns. Another problem with variable life insurance is that there are high loads and commissions. Those are the reasons why I don't like this type of insurance.

"Remember rule 2," which Steve reiterated: "Insurance and investments don't mix," to which Matt and I chuckled.

Steve then continued, "The third type of insurance is *universal life insurance*. Insurance companies implemented this type of insurance to address the constant criticism that insurance was too costly and that folks should buy term insurance and invest the difference in a savings plan. Thus, this type of insurance does just that: it is term insurance with a savings plan, somewhat similar to whole life. However, unlike whole life—which has many more guarantees built in and of course less of an upside—universal life is very dependent on interest rates. Agents can show their clients any projected result by using any assumed rate of return and premiums. Thus many policies have been sold on the basis of some very inflated assumptions. There is, however, usually a minimum guarantee of 4 percent interest, which isn't that much.

"Let me give you a great example. Years ago, around the early 1970s, interest rates were 18 percent . Many universal life policies used those rates in their calculations for premiums. When interest rates dropped, many people had to pony up a lot more money due to the original faulty projections."

The Type of Insurance That Most People Should Own

Matt thought about all this and asked, "Steve, so what type of insurance do you normally recommend?"

Steve knew this was coming and said, "For the vast majority of people, most financial experts will say that buying term insurance and investing the difference between the premium for the whole life policy and the premium for the term policy is by far the better alternative. Moreover, the mortality risk is the same whether you buy expensive permanent insurance or less expensive term insurance. If we have the same mortality, why not buy term insurance?"

Matt responded, "Buying term insurance and investing the difference between the premium for the term insurance and the premium for the whole life insurance seems to be the right way to go, but don't most people buy term and spend the difference?"

Steve quickly sneered at this comment that is used by many insurance agents and said, "Yes, Matt, you are right. Many people simply buy a term policy and spend the difference, and they don't generally save up money as the years pass.

"My favorite sales approach was started by a guy named Ben Feldman. Ben would argue as follows: Let's say that you have two accounts. One is a savings account paying 2 percent interest, and you can take money out of it at any time. Thus, if there is a 50 percent sale at Chico's, you can take money out to buy the clothes. If you want to go on vacation, the money can come out of the savings account. If your kids need extra money for college expenses, the savings account can fund that too. The second account is a tin can that is shut tight upon making a deposit. You cannot take money out of the tin can as easily as you can take it out of the savings account. He would then ask his prospect, 'Which do you think will have more money in the long run?' Of course, many people would say that it would be the tin can, which was his argument for whole life insurance.

"This is the argument that many insurance agents make. My take on this is that if folks can afford to pay the permanent life insurance premiums, they can afford to save the same amount of money by buying term insurance and investing the cost difference. Moreover, there are several serious problems with permanent insurance.

"First, it is a bad deal! Many financial experts advise against it because there are *huge* commissions and loads attached to permanent insurance. Moreover, you have to be very wary of all proposals offered by agents, especially those who deal with universal life insurance. Many times the policies don't live up to the projections. Let me give you an analogy of what permanent insurance is like, and you tell me whether you would buy something like this.

"Let's say that you want to buy insurance and you want to buy a savings plan. This combination is similar to a term insurance policy with a side savings plan. My company will manage your savings plan with the following conditions."

- My company will take everything that you pay for the first two years for ourselves.
- In future years, we will charge you each year for your deposits into the savings account, in addition to charging you for the insurance.
- We will let you borrow money from your savings account but will charge you significant interest when you borrow your own money.

- If you die while there is a loan outstanding on your savings account, we will decrease what we pay your beneficiaries by the amount of the loan and its accrued interest.
- If you fail to pay the interest on the money you borrowed from your savings account, the cash value of the policy might not generate enough earnings to cover the premiums. In that case, we will cancel the policy, and you will lose everything that you deposited.
- If you don't borrow any money, we will pay the face value of the policy and keep the savings for ourselves.
- You must buy life insurance whether you need it or not for us to manage your savings account.
- If you cancel the policy, which occurs in 26.3 percent of the cases within the first three years alone,[1] the insurance company pays nothing upon death. You end up losing all premiums paid to date other than the built-up cash value.
- Last but not least, you will get a fraction of what you could get in the market on your savings.

"Tell me, Matt, would you invest with me?"

Matt immediately said, "No way."

Steve smiled his crocodile smile and said, "I thought so, yet that is what most people get when they purchase permanent insurance."

Matt then asked, "If permanent insurance is such a bad deal, how is so much of it sold?"

Steve had to think about the answer to Matt's question, and then he responded, "Because insurance agents are adept at pulling at people's emotional heart strings in order to get what they want sold. Many agents are focused on increasing the money in their own wallet rather than increasing the money in their clients' wallet. Remember, there are no laws on agents' projections. They can use any assumed interest rate especially for universal and variable life insurance policies. Whole life proposals tend to be more realistic because of the higher built-in guarantees. However, even with whole life, there is a certain amount of 'flexibility' in the projections that agents show their prospects.

"Moreover, people need to know that the savings feature built into permanent insurance isn't really their money. If they borrow from it, they must pay interest. Upon death, the insurance company pays the higher of the savings cash value or the policy face value (which is usually higher)."

I then interrupted Steve and said, "Steve, there must be circumstances that justify whole life or some form of permanent insurance even with the high costs you've outlined."

Steve responded, "Yes, I guess that is true. Permanent insurance is something that should be kept forever. Sadly, studies have shown that as many as 41 percent or more of folks who get permanent insurance cancel it or let it lapse. This is one heck of a business model for the insurance company; they get their costs and profits built into the first two years of premiums. They get to charge high premiums, and in 41 percent of the cases, don't have to pay off. What a deal! Thus, the key with permanent insurance is that **it should be kept forever!**

"There are some 'forever needs.' One example would be to pay estate taxes. If you had an estate of over $5 million and you were single or over $10 million and you were married, you might want permanent insurance to pay the taxes. If you bought term insurance and you invested the difference between the cost of the term insurance and the cost of the whole life insurance in a savings plan, those savings could be part of the estate, but the insurance wouldn't be if it had been planned correctly. Thus, you could use the insurance to provide the liquidity to cover the federal estate taxes and state inheritance taxes.

"Another example of 'forever needs' would be if you had a significantly disabled child and you wanted to provide insurance regardless of how long you lived. In this case, permanent insurance might be useful. However, even in this situation, it would be better to buy term insurance and invest the difference in cost between the term and the whole life policies."

Steve then interjected an interesting parenthetical to this discussion when he said, "I should note that there is one type of permanent insurance that I do recommend for special situations. It is called a *modified endowment policy*. This is a form of permanent insurance; however, people normally don't buy this for the insurance, as strange as that may seem. It is used for special purposes. The key point is that most insurance cash values are exempt from creditors and from being counted as assets in the Free Application for Federal Student Aid (FAFSA) form used to determine college financial aid. You could have millions in cash value and still qualify for need-based scholarships.

"Thus, if you have a business with enormous liability potential such as an obstetrics and gynecology medical practice or some other high-liability medical specialty, you might want to consider putting large amounts of money into a modified endowment plan or even annuities, such as the Vanguard annuities, that don't have surrender charges. The costs are relatively low, and they might well protect you against liability judgments.

"In addition, if you have substantial assets or your kids have substantial savings for college, you might want to place all of those funds into a single-premium life insurance policy or a modified endowment policy or even an annuity. Doing so would mean that these funds would not be considered assets that would count against them in computing need-based aid. I have recommended modified endowment plans for those two circumstances.

"Certainly, you should evaluate their potential and costs in order to determine whether they are right for you. Also, use the specially designed modified endowment plans instead of the normal whole life policies or universal life policies. Otherwise, you will be paying the huge commissions and costs associated with normal whole life or universal life policies."

The Amount of Life Insurance Most People Should Own

I honestly began to see Steve's sound reasoning, so I asked, "Steve, I can see why you don't recommend permanent insurance, but you do recommend that most families who might incur a financial loss or businesses that might incur a financial loss should have insurance. This leads us to the question of amount. How much should most people have in life insurance for their families and businesses?"

Steve responded as follows: "Let me address business needs first. If the insurance is to cover a key employee, you need enough to make up for the loss of that employee and for the advertising costs to hire someone else and then the training costs to get that person up to speed. You might also need to know how much it would cost to buy out a partner or co-owner upon his or her death or disability. This insurance would prevent having to have the co-owner's or partner's relatives become unwanted partners.

"As for families, the key is to have enough, which would include their current savings, so that the family's lifestyle doesn't need to change. There are several ways to accomplish this.

"The first approach is called the *salary approach*. Here experts recommend at least 5 to 10 times the yearly salary. Thus, if a person makes $60,000 a year, that person would get between $300,000 and $600,000 of coverage."

Matt interrupted Steve by saying, "I don't like this approach because it doesn't take liabilities and future expenses such as college into account."

Steve replied, "Matt, you are remarkably smart for a young guy. Yes, you are right. That is a major drawback to the salary approach. This is why most people should use the comprehensive approach.

"The *comprehensive approach* takes several factors into account and adds them all up in order to come to a conclusive amount of insurance. The factors are the following."

- The current amount of liabilities including the home mortgage
- The expected amount of future liabilities such as college funding needs and charitable bequests
- Your current income or your current estimated yearly living expenses divided by a conservative interest rate such as 3 percent

"You would then subtract your current investable savings.

"Let me give you an example that will illustrate the above-noted formula," suggested Steve. "Let's say that I have a current mortgage and other debts totaling $300,000. In addition, I have two kids who will be going to college in eight years. I figure the cost will be at least another $300,000 for both kids by then. Finally, let's assume that I am earning the same $60,000 a year as noted above. If I take the $60,000 and divide by 0.03, I would get $2 million. Thus my total life insurance need adding everything together would be $2.6 million, before I subtract any accumulated savings. If I have $200,000 of assets saved up, my net insurance need, after taking savings into account, would be $2.4 million."

Matt whistled and said, "Wow, that is a huge difference between the salary approach that most agents use and the comprehensive approach."

Steve agreed. "This is why many agents use the salary approach. This way they can sell the higher-commissioned cash value insurance while ignoring the real temporary need of $2.4 million.

"By the way, this $2.4 million need isn't a permanent need. Once the mortgage is paid off and once the kids are out of college, the need drops. If the family can build up some good savings over the years, the salary loss needed for retirement will drop too, especially if the wage earner will qualify for a vested pension."

Planning for Life Insurance Ownership

"Steve," I suggested, "are there any particular additional comments about life insurance that you want our readers to know about?"

Steve laughed, "Yes, there surely are.

"First, when you get life insurance, always check to see if the policy has a *viatical settlement provision* if you don't have nursing home care insurance. This is a provision that will pay you monthly while you are alive but are expected to die within 24 months. It is usually tax free. Payments for chronic illness can also be tax free if the payments are either used for long-term care or services even if reimbursed from Medicare. These types of payments for chronic illness are usually capped at 280 days.

"Second, it is usually much less expensive to buy second-to-die policies. With these policies, both spouses must die before payment to beneficiaries is made. However, if one spouse can continue earning a nice salary, this type of insurance is ideal. It is also ideal for insurance used to pay estate taxes. Many agents don't recommend it because it is much cheaper than insurance on each life and therefore it pays less in commissions to the agents."

"By the way," Steve added, "I don't want to give the impression that all insurance agents are slimy and greedy. There are plenty of agents who are professional and try to make the client's needs a priority. However, there certainly are plenty of unprofessional agents who care more about their own pocketbook.

"Third, if you have a substantial estate worth over $5 million, you should usually not own the insurance individually. The ownership of the insurance should be an *irrevocable life insurance trust* for your family, otherwise known as an ILIT. This structure will avoid any of the proceeds being included in the estate for estate and inheritance tax purposes. If I may give a plug, seeing an elder law attorney like me would be essential in setting up this type of trust."

Matt and I both laughed and also agreed with Steve's comments.

Finally we finished our discussion. I thanked Steve profusely for his time. It is very reassuring that a professional like Steve would give his time freely to help others. Before we left, however, Steve wanted to make sure that we understood the material. I guess it was the professor in him, when he said, "Before you leave, let's review what we learned from this discussion." Going through our notes, we came up with the following.

A Review of What You Have Learned

- The two key rules related to life insurance:
  - Life insurance should be purchased for only two reasons. The first is to avoid a financial loss of income, and the second is to leave an estate such as a bequest to a college or charity.
  - Insurance and investments don't mix, especially due to the poor returns and high costs of insurance products. If you want insurance, it should be because you need insurance and for no other reason.
- Don't fall for misleading names given to insurance policies such as "college savings insurance," "credit" or "mortgage insurance," or "key man insurance." There are no such things. It is the same normal term or permanent insurance for all of these, just renamed to make them more palatable for the buyers.

- There are three types of term insurance:
  - Annual renewable term
  - Level term insurance, which has a level premium for a fixed number of years
  - Decreasing term insurance, for which the benefit declines over time. This type of insurance is ideal for a declining need such as paying off a mortgage.
- There are several types of permanent insurance:
  - Whole life
  - Universal life
  - Variable life
  - Modified endowment insurance
- For the most part, permanent insurance should be avoided other than to pay estate taxes. The reason is that they have very high commissions and costs.
- It is almost always better to get some type of term policy and to set up a side savings plan to reduce the need for insurance over the years.
- The one major exception is for specially designed single-premium policies, such as modified endowment policies, which are not used for the insurance. They are used for liability protection. In addition, cash value insurance doesn't count as an asset for need-based college aid. Only use these specialized types of policies. Don't just dump a lot of money into a normal whole life or universal life policy.
- Don't fall for insurance scams that use proposals that can project any returns using almost any assumed interest rates. This is particularly true for universal life insurance. Also, don't get insurance such as variable life insurance that is tied to the stock market. Remember, insurance and investments don't mix. You want a secure insurance policy. Do your own investing on the side.
- In case you do buy some form of permanent insurance, keep it forever; otherwise, you are paying high premiums and costs for nothing. It should thus be used for needs that last forever such as paying estate taxes or even for providing a fund for severely disabled kids. Even then, it is usually much better to have enough term insurance and then to invest the difference between the cost of the term insurance and the cost of the permanent insurance in a side investment for your family or disabled kids.
- There are two ways of figuring how much insurance you should have.
  - The salary approach assumes 5 to 10 times the current year's take-home salary.
  - The comprehensive approach takes the amount of all current debts plus future needs (such as college costs) plus the salary divided by 0.03 and subtracting out any investments that you have. This is the better approach.
- When you buy life insurance, check to see if it contains a viatical settlement clause in case you become terminally ill.
- Always consider second-to-die insurance, especially to leave bequests or to pay estate taxes.
- If you have a substantial estate worth over $5 million, you should usually not own the insurance individually. The ownership of the insurance should be an *irrevocable life insurance trust* for your family, otherwise known as an ILIT. This structure will avoid any of the proceeds being included in the estate for estate and inheritance tax purposes.

Notes

1. http://www.freeby50.com/2010/12/lapsed-policies-cost-whole-life.html.

13

Social Security

The key to Social Security reform is to take the security out of it!

—Jay Leno

> **What You Will Learn**
> - What is the full retirement age?
> - What are the penalties for taking social security benefits before the full retirement age?
> - What are the survivor benefits for spouses?
> - What are the tax implications of receiving social security benefits?

Matt and I decided to visit my friend Marvin who is a retired social security administrator. He is the most knowledgeable person I know on this subject.

Marvin greeted us expectantly with a warm handshake.

"Marvin," I said, "this is my son, Matt. He is a CPA, and he has passed the Certified Financial Planner (CFP) exam. I thought I would bring him along because he will be helping me with the book."

Marvin smiled warmly and said, "It is always great to get the younger generation educated about social security benefits. Too many people don't understand them, and consequently they make wrong choices regarding their benefits, sometimes to their irrevocable detriment."

Marvin's wife came in with some coffee and some homemade cookies, which my son, Matt, eagerly gobbled up. I really like southern hospitality.

What Is the Full Retirement Age?

"Okay, Marvin," I suggested, "let's get started. Let's start with the key question about social security. What is the age at which we should take our benefits?"

Marvin chuckled and said, "This isn't an easy answer because there are some factors that affect that decision, and they are things that everyone should know.

"Certainly, if you feel that you don't have a long life expectancy or you desperately need the income, you can take social security up to four years before your normal full retirement age.

"For people born between 1943 and 1954, this means that they can take it as early as age 62, with their normal full retirement age being 66. People born in 1955 get a later normal full retirement age of 66 years and two months. People born in 1956 get a normal full retirement age of 66 years and four months. Thus the normal full retirement age goes up in two-month increments each year for people born in 1956 through 1960, and for people born in or after 1960, the normal full retirement age is 67."[1]

See Appendix D for what your normal full retirement age would be based on your date of birth.

What Are the Penalties for Taking Social Security Benefits Before the Full Retirement Age?

I immediately interrupted and asked, "Why shouldn't people take the benefits early so that they can have the use of the money for several years?"

Marvin gave me a thoughtful look when he said, "Yes, you are right, Sandy. Many people take earlier retirements when they are very sick or when they don't think that they have a long life expectancy. In fact, I have a surprising fact for you. Over half of all Americans take their social security early."

That certainly surprised me.

Marvin smoothly continued, "However, taking benefits before the full retirement age is usually the wrong thing to do for many reasons. The first reason is that people who take their social security at age 62 through age 65 lose $1 of benefit for every $2 they earn above $14,160. This number does increase a bit with inflation. Thus, someone who makes $34,000 loses about $10,000 of their benefits. If they make $54,000 of adjusted gross earnings, they lose $20,000 of their benefits. In addition, if they are working while receiving social security, they must still pay social security on their earned income, which usually comes as a big surprise to many people. Even worse, they might get taxed on the remaining benefits that they receive, which we will discuss later.

"Also surprising is the fact that if they take social security during the year of their normal full retirement age, which for most baby boomers will be 66, but before their birthday, they will lose $1 for every $3 dollars of earnings over $37,680. The following chart will explain this:"

Maximum Earnings Before Social Security Benefits Are Reduced	
Before full retirement age:	Lose $1 for every $2 earned over $14,160
Year of full retirement age but before hitting full retirement birthday (which could be age 66 or 67 depending on your year of birth):	Lose $1 for every $3 earned over $37,680
After full retirement age:	No limit on earnings

"Marvin," I interrupted, "let me see if I understand what you just said. If my full retirement age is in 2014 and assuming my birthday is in September, if I receive social security benefits in 2014 but before my birthday, I will lose $1 of benefit for every $3 of earnings over $37,680. All benefits paid after my birthday in 2014 will not result in a reduction of benefits regardless of my income. Is that correct?"

Marvin leaned back and smiled while saying, "Yes, you are absolutely correct, although the phaseout threshold might change from $37,680 to something else due to inflation. Many people are not aware of this potential reduction in benefits."

I turned to Matt and asked, "Matt, were you aware of these benefit phaseouts that occur when people take their social security at age 62?"

Matt smiled and said, "Yes, and even worse, it can significantly affect spousal benefits, which few people even consider."

Marvin almost dropped his jaw at Matt's response and said, "Sandy, you have one smart kid," to which Matt smiled from ear to ear.

Marvin then regained his composure and continued: "Yes, Matt is exactly right. Most people don't consider the effect that a reduced social security benefit will have on the spouse. The spouse gets whichever is greater: his or her own benefit or 50 percent of the spouse's benefit. So spouses who didn't work end up with 50 percent of their spouse's benefit. Thus, if the primary wage earner gets a reduced benefit, that might affect the spouse's benefit forever. However, once the spouse hits their own full retirement age, they can elect to use their own earned benefit. Thus, they would get the greater of their own earned benefit at full retirement age or 100 percent of the spouse's benefit whichever is greater thereafter.[2]

"Did you know that for most women, who normally survive their husbands, 40 percent of their earnings at retirement come from social security? If they were to receive the full benefit that they would be entitled to if the husband waited for normal full retirement age, almost all of them would be earning above the poverty line. However, for surviving widows who receive benefits based on taking social security before the normal full retirement age, which is currently age 62, most fall below the poverty line."

Both Matt and I shuddered.

What Are the Survivor Benefits for Spouses?

"Marvin, you are raising a great point. So what are the survivor benefits for spouses?"

Marvin got out some papers and noted the following:[3]

- Survivor spouses <u>at full retirement age</u> get the higher of what they would have gotten on their own past earnings or 50 percent of their living spouse's benefits, even if the survivor spouse never worked.
- Widows or widowers at full (survivor's) retirement age or older, generally receive the higher of what they would have gotten from their own earnings or 71 to 99% percent of their deceased spouse's benefit if the widow or widower is at least age 60. Once they reach full retirement age, they can continue getting what they were receiving or they will get benefits based on their own earnings or 100 percent of their spouse's full benefit whichever is greater. This continues for the rest of their life.
- If a widow or widower has a child under age 16, he or she will receive 75 percent of the worker's benefit regardless of the age of the widow or widower. This will last until they have no remaining dependent children under age 16.
- Benefits are also payable to unmarried children under age 18, or under age 19 if they are attending high school full time. The child receives 75 percent of the worker's (deceased parent's) benefit. Moreover, benefits are payable to children of the deceased parent at any age if the child was disabled before age 22 and remains disabled.
- Here is one I bet you didn't know: An ex-spouse who was married for at least 10 full years gets a benefit based on the greater of his or her own earnings or 50 percent of the ex-spouse's earnings. If the couple

was married less than 10 years before divorcing, the divorced spouse can rely on only his or her own earnings!

I thus decided to probe Marvin further: "So, for retirement planning, spouses will be receiving some social security even if they never worked?"

Marvin responded, "Yes, they will either eventually get their own benefit based on their earnings, or they will get between 50 and 100 percent of their spouse's benefit depending on whether their spouse is living or not."

Matt then jumped in saying, "Marvin, can't people wait past their normal full retirement age and receive more money?"

Marvin had anticipated this question and quickly responded, "Yes, here is the rule."

For every year that you delay receiving benefits past your normal full retirement age, your yearly benefit increases at the rate of two-thirds of 1 percent a month. This translates into an 8 percent increase in benefits for each year that you wait. However, there is a maximum increase of 32 percent, which means that folks born between the years 1943 and 1954 should not wait past age 70 to receive benefits.

I then asked Marvin, "So at what age should people take their social security benefits?"

Marvin thoughtfully responded as follows.

The answer for most people is that they should at least wait until their full retirement age. If, however, they are in great health and are making substantial earnings from a pension and/or interest and dividends and they don't really need the social security for their lifestyle, they might want to wait until age 70. If, however, they believe that they have a short life expectancy or they desperately need the money, then they probably should take the benefit as early as possible.

What Are the Tax Implications of Receiving Social Security Benefits?

Marvin reinforced his opinion by saying, "Now you see why I recommend not taking social security benefits before the normal full retirement age. The reason is that doing so not only reduces your overall benefits for the rest of your life but it could also reduce your spouse's benefits for the rest of his or her life too."

Marvin added, "In addition, if this weren't bad enough, social security benefits can be taxable. In fact, there are three possible outcomes with social security benefits. They can be tax free, 50 percent of the benefits can be taxable, or as much as 85 percent of the benefits can be taxable based on your earnings. How's that for tax simplification?"

Matt and I chuckled at Marvin's quip.

Marvin continued, "First, you need to know your *modified adjusted gross income* (MAGI). This figure is not just your earnings. It includes your adjusted gross income, plus all tax-exempt income, and one-half of the social security benefits. If your MAGI is under certain threshold amounts—$32,000 for people who are married and filing joint returns or $25,000 for people who are single—no part of the social security is taxable. If the threshold MAGI earnings are between $32,001 and $44,000 for joint filers or between $25,001 and $33,999 for single filers, 50 percent of the social security benefits are taxed. If you earn over these amounts, 85 percent of the social security benefits are taxed." Marvin then pulled out a very useful chart that looked like this:

Amount of Modified Adjusted Gross Income (MAGI) That Causes Social Security to Be Taxable[4]		
	50% Taxable	**85% Taxable**
Married filing jointly	$32,001–$44,000	$44,001+
Single	$25,001–$34,000	$34,001+

Being quite impressed with all this, I said to Marvin, "These are great charts. I wish the Social Security Administration had these on their website. I think my readers will find them very useful," which made Marvin chuckle.

Appendix E at the end of the book shows how much your benefits will decrease if you start receiving your benefits before your normal retirement age. Appendix F shows how much your benefits will increase if you start receiving your benefits after your normal retirement age.

Marvin then continued: "I want to add a few important points to what has been said here."

First, when you want to start receiving social security, plan to file for benefits at least three months before the month in which you desire to start receiving them.

Second, if you are currently working, don't collect any benefits before your normal full retirement age.

Third, when you do file for social security benefits, you will need copies of the following:

- Social security card
- Proof of age, such as a copy of your birth certificate
- Your W-2 for the previous year or your Schedule C for yourself
- Marriage certificate if you are making a claim based on your spouse's work record
- If you are applying for survivor's benefits, proof (a death certificate) of the death of the worker

Fourth, make sure that you have at least 40 quarters of earnings. You should check out what social security has listed for you by going to www.ssa.gov. Also, as you know, Sandy, you have a great social security benefit calculator on your web site found at www.sandybotkin.com.

Elaborating on the fourth point, Marvin said: "Moreover, the Social Security Administration, due to budget issues, has announced that it will no longer send out yearly statements with the exception of those statements sent out just prior to most people's full retirement age. This makes you feel nice and fuzzy, doesn't it?

"You can review your earnings at the Social Security Administration's website, which I highly recommend that everyone do. Errors do occur."

I then asked Marvin, "Once people have taken these benefits and they realize that they took them too early, can they change their mind?"

Marvin responded, "That's an excellent question, Sandy. The answer is that once you start taking benefits, it becomes an irrevocable election. However, there is a little-known rule that allows people to pay back the benefits received if they do so within 12 months of initially receiving the benefits and if they delay benefits to a later year. Other than that one exception, you are irrevocably bound by when you take your benefits.

"The following point is also very important."

Even if you delay taking social security, you should register for Medicare when you are 65. Don't delay on this, or Medicare can cost you a lot more.

Now that we had finished our discussion, I asked Marvin if he had any parting words. He responded by saying, "Everyone who is reading this should take this topic to heart. Social security is usually 20 to 25 percent of most people's retirement income, and it could be as high as 40 percent. It could make the difference between having a good lifestyle and having to live on dog food, which has occurred."

Matt and I thanked Marvin for his invaluable information, and Matt thanked him for the cookies and asked for another cookie. It figures that food would be on the forefront of a young adult's mind.

A Review of What You Have Learned

- You get 100 percent of your normal social security benefit if you wait until your full retirement age, which is age 66 for people born between 1943 and 1954. If you were born after 1954, depending on the year of your birth, the normal full retirement age increases up to age 67. See also Appendix D.
- If you take your benefits at age 62, you irrevocably lose 25 percent of your normal benefit. This will also affect what your spouse could receive. See Appendix E for the percentage reduction in benefits that you would get if you took your benefits before your normal retirement age. This election becomes irrevocable, although you do have 12 months from receipt of your benefits to pay back the money you received in order to delay benefits for a higher lifetime payout.
- For people born in 1943 and later, if you take your benefits later than your normal full retirement age, you will get an extra 8 percent for each year that you wait up to age 70. See Appendix F for more information on this.
- Moreover, if you take benefits before your normal full retirement age, the benefits get phased out based on your modified adjusted gross income (MAGI), which includes your adjusted gross income plus tax-free income plus one-half of your social security taxes. Benefits start phasing out before normal full retirement age at $1 for every $2 earned over $14,160. Moreover, for benefits received in the year that you turn 66 but before your birthday, these benefits phase out at the rate of $1 for every $3 earned over $37,680.
- Spouses receive the greater of 100 percent of their own benefits earned or 50 percent of the worker's benefits even if the spouse didn't work. This will be true as long as they wait for their normal full retirement age. If they do not wait for their normal full retirement age, their benefits will be reduced.
- Normally it is best to wait until you reach your normal full retirement age to take social security benefits. However, there are some exceptions:
  - You are earning enough money from a pension or other source that is sufficient for you to maintain your lifestyle and you are in good health. In this case waiting until age 70 might be the better choice.
  - If you desperately need the money or you have a reasonable belief that you have a short life expectancy, taking the benefits earlier might be the better choice. However, even in this situation, you have to consider that this action will reduce your spouse's benefits.
- Social security benefits will be tax free if you are married and filing jointly and your MAGI is less than $32,000 or if you are single and your MAGI is less than $25,000. The benefits are taxed at 50 percent if you are married and filing jointly and your MAGI is between $32,001 and $44,000 or if you are single and your MAGI is between $25,001 and $34,000. Any MAGI over these limits will result in 85 percent of your social security being taxable.

- Even if you delay taking social security, do *not* delay filing for Medicare past age 65.
- When you file for social security, make sure you have a copy of your social security card and a copy of your birth certificate. Also, you should have your last year's W-2 if you are an employee or your Schedule C if you are self-employed.
- You should ensure that the Social Security Administration has correctly noted your earnings by going to www.ssa.gov. In order to check how much you and/or your spouse will get in benefits, go to the tools section of my website at www.sandybotkin.com and check out the social security calculator. It has options for both married and single taxpayers.

Notes

1. http://www.socialsecurity.gov/retire2/agereduction.htm.
2. http://www.aarp.org/work/social-security/info-02-2011/social_security_mailbox_survivor_benefits.html and http://www.ssa.gov/pubs/10084.html#a0=2.
3. http://www.ssa.gov/pubs/10084.html#a0=2.
4. http://www.irs.gov/newsroom/article/0,,id=253957,00.html.

14

Estate Planning

Good fortune happens when opportunity meets with planning.

—Thomas Edison

We returned for another meeting with Steve about estate planning. This is one area that most elder law attorneys are particularly adept in. After being ushered into his office and after being offered some coffee with some great Dunkin' Donuts, which are my favorite, Steve got right down to business. I guess I really like no-nonsense types of professionals.

"I want to note that estate planning really consists of several areas that we will discuss separately.

"First, there is *planning for special circumstances* such as for disabled kids or for newly merged families.

"The second area we will discuss is *planning for probate*, which affects everyone regardless of the estate.

"The final area will be *planning for estate taxes*, which isn't as useful now as it used to be before the estate tax exemption was raised to $5 million. However, for those with sizable estates, this is a very important area in which planning can save millions. Moreover, many people even with smaller, mod-

What You Will Learn (Cont.)
- How to reduce or even eliminate estate taxes and inheritance taxes
- What the superwealthy are doing for their families in order to reduce estate taxes and provide a lifetime income

erate estates might be hit with the state inheritance taxes because many states have much lower exemption amounts for their state inheritance taxes."

Who Needs Estate Planning?

My first question to Steve was, "Exactly which group of people should be concerned with estate planning? Let's face it, not many of us are worth over $5 million."

Steve's response is that everyone needs it. For example:

- People who have property that they care about (such as carpenters who want their tools intact) need it.
- Parents who want to provide for their children need it: Who will raise the children upon the death of their parents, and who will manage their assets?
- People who are likely to incur a lot of probate charges upon the death of a loved one need it. These charges can be easily avoided!
- People who want to make organ donations upon their death or make bequests to charities need it.
- People who have potential spousal problems need it: normally spouses get one-half of the estate in community-property states and one-third in most other states. If people want to change the distribution of their estate, they need to plan for that.
- People who have a business and want to leave that business intact for their relatives.
- People who have a lot of illiquid property, such as valuable paintings and real estate, and want to leave these items intact to their relatives.
- People who live in certain states that have low inheritance tax exemptions need it. These states include Maryland, New York, Massachusetts, Oregon, New Jersey, Ohio, Rhode Island, and about 15 other states.

Steve then quickly added, "What is interesting is that most estate problems, even estate and inheritance taxes, can be either completely avoided or significantly reduced with proper planning. However, due to ignorance, procrastination, and/or just plain cheapness, a lot of problems arise for families. In fact, here is an example of plain ignorance and cheapness.

"I have a limo driver who has several siblings. One of the siblings was taking care of their invalid grandmother. In order to facilitate care, the grandmother put all of her bank account funds in joint name with this granddaughter in order for her to pay grandma's bills. The grandmother, however, had a will that provided that all of her estate would go to her one remaining daughter and not to any of her granddaughters.

"Sadly, when granny died, all of the jointly owned property went to the joint account holder. Jointly owned property passes outside of the will, and it is not controlled by the will. The granddaughter kept the money and created irrevocable animosity among the family members, and she even alienated her own mother who was supposed to inherit the funds. It was a nightmare for the whole family and a huge tragedy. With a little planning by an estate or elder law attorney, this problem could have easily been rectified. However, the grandmother didn't want to spend the $1,000 necessary to plan the handling of her affairs and to create the correct documents, and/or she didn't want to take the time necessary to meet with a lawyer."

Both Matt and I shook our head with sadness at this situation.

I then said, "Yes, Steve, death really does affect families strangely and can easily cause irrevocable rifts among friends and families. Your example was a great illustration of what can happen with bad planning.

"This is why it is vital to get a proper will. Sadly, many people are cheap; they try to go to LegalZoom.com and create their own will, or they use some other service that gives out prepared wills without a lot of individualization. This can be a big mistake! I can't emphasize this enough. Wills are critical documents that can make or break the fortunes of families, which is why I highly recommend that people use a professional estate planner or elder law attorney and get their will personalized as much as possible."

Wills and Necessary Provisions in Wills

Steve nodded in agreement and said, "Okay, let's start with our first topic: wills. We are going to start off with some of the more important, elementary provisions that should be in all wills. I will not be mentioning the tax provisions that will be the subject of our estate tax discussion."

Matt and I understood and agreed that this was fine.

Steve went on: "What is interesting about having a will is that if you don't have one, the state draws up a will for you. This is called *dying intestate*, which means dying without a will. This might result in leaving assets to someone other than those that you would prefer. For example, for most individuals who die intestate, the states usually leaves one-third of the estate to the spouse, unless you live in a community property state.[1] In that case, the state will provide that about one-half of the estate go to the current spouse. Moreover, many times property is left to siblings or parents. However, if you have a significant other, that person might not inherit one dime without a proper will.

"Certainly, if you have minor kids," Steve added, "you should always have a guardianship provision as to who will be their legal guardians and how their assets will be managed. Consideration must be given to the health of the guardians, their religious views, their knowledge of the kids, and how financially secure they are. After all, you don't want the guardians to have to raid the kids' accounts because they need to pay for their own living expenses.

"While we are talking about kids and guardianships, I want to note that IRAs, pension plans, and life insurance distributions are *not* controlled by the will. They have their own transfer rules that are controlled by the pension or life insurance documents. However, you should *never* leave IRA money or life insurance money directly to minor kids because this creates problems. At the least, they usually don't know how to handle the money, and they might go on a spending spree. In addition, they might get divorced later in life too. **I strongly recommend that IRA monies and life insurance proceeds be left to a trust, which can be used to manage and conserve the funds. It can also serve as protection against liabilities incurred by the kids, and it can protect these assets in case of divorce.**

"Another point I want to mention about wills is, **do *not* create a family war**. I have seen all kinds of expensive litigation and irrevocable animosity among family members simply because there was a lack of communication between the deceased parents and the kids. Tell your family about items that you own so they can see what you are doing and what your intentions are. If some kids want specific items, such as mom's rings or some antiques, let them make their intentions known so that everyone will be on board with it. I'll say it again: communicate with your family.

"This is why **I also recommend a clause known by lawyers as an *in terrorem clause.*** This is a clause that notes that if beneficiaries contest any part of the will with litigation and lose, any provision that leaves them assets will be null and void. Thus, if beneficiaries don't like what is said in the will and resort to fighting it, they risk losing what was left to them."

I interjected, "Steve, I too have seen this time and again. There was the famous Haft case in which the kids fought tooth and nail over the will of the dad, or there have been cases in which the dad dies and leaves a large bequest to some new 'floozy' wife, which enrages the kids to bring expensive litigation. You were so right when you said that parents really need to communicate with their kids about the will and about their property."

Steve nodded in agreement.

Looking a bit puzzled, Matt asked, "Steve, why do single people need wills especially if they have no kids and very few assets?"

Steve reasoned soundly, "Single people might want their assets to go to someone other than their parents such as their siblings, nieces and nephews, and significant others. Moreover, as will be discussed, wills are more than just about disposition of property. They involve concepts like providing for needed life support and organ donations.

"In addition," Steve noted, "you should *always* provide for *alternate beneficiaries* in case the beneficiaries don't survive. For example, you might want to leave your estate to all of your children. However, what happens if a child predeceases you? Do you want to leave his or her portion to your grandchildren of that child or to your remaining living children?"

Matt interrupted by saying, "Wow, there are a lot of serious considerations that go into writing a will. I didn't realize that it was so involved."

Steve laughed with a rare hardy chuckle and said, "Oh, yes, you are so correct. This is why people must *not* be cheap and must take their will drafting very seriously. In fact, I am only getting started. There are some other major provisions that we haven't touched on yet."

Steve was on a roll when he continued, "You should also always provide a *survivorship clause* in case of simultaneous death. This can happen with an airline crash or car crash. Otherwise, the state law might presume that another spouse survives and use his or her will. For example, this could be a problem if one of the spouses has kids from another marriage."

I decided to tease Matt a bit by asking, "Steve, what happens if I want to disinherit a child?" while winking at Steve.

Taking the cue from me, Steve responded with a deadpan face, "If you want to disinherit a child, always specifically name the child in the will to show that the disinheritance wasn't accidental. I will never forget reading about a case in law school in which the deceased said in his will, 'To my son Charles, whom I promised not to forget: Hi Charles. Was that enough of a remembrance because you will be getting nothing from my estate.'"

Matt and I both agreed that Charles must have ticked off his dad greatly.

"Also, all wills should name an *executor* to manage the estate, deal with probate issues, manage property, pay any taxes due, and distribute the property. You want an executor who will avoid conflicts. I would normally *not* recommend a bank to be executor unless you know the bank employee well that will perform as executor. Moreover, banks tend to charge a lot of money for these services. You should consider whether the bank's being the executor is worth the money."

"Moreover," Steve continued, "people need to plan for pets. Will provisions leaving property directly for the support of pets aren't enforceable. However, in over 46 states,[2] you can have a trust that will be directed to care for the pets. If your state does not have a provision for a *pet trust*, you need to name a trustworthy person to get the pet.

"Finally," Steve added, "if you move to a different state, your will and trusts should be reviewed. Each state might have some different requirements, not to mention different inheritance tax rules. Thus it is vital to have all of your documents reviewed by an attorney located in your new state of residence."

Steve then paused for everyone to get their bearings and said to Matt, "Matt, just to make sure that you have everything down, please summarize the important points about making a will and some elementary will provisions."

Matt then looked at his notes and summarized the following:

- **Everyone, even single people, should have a will, or there can be lots of problems.**
- **If you don't have a will, the state will draw one up for you and may give your property to people that you wouldn't necessarily want to be given the property.**
- **If you have minor children, always have a guardianship provision. People need to give really careful consideration to naming a guardian.**
- **Although life insurance and IRA monies are not controlled by the will, don't leave these funds directly to minor children but rather to a trust for their benefit.**
- **Avoid family wars. This can be accomplished through communications among family members. In addition, always consider adding an *in terrorem clause* that will prevent family members from receiving their inheritance if they try to contest the will and lose.**
- **Always provide for alternative beneficiaries in case the main beneficiaries don't survive.**
- **Always provide a survivorship clause in case of simultaneous death.**
- **All wills should name an executor to manage the estate.**

- **If there is a pet involved, use a trust to take care of the pet if the state allows this. If the state does not, name a trustworthy person to take care of the pet.**

Matt then slyly asked, "So, Steve, how did I do so far?"

Steve chuckled, "Matt, you're a great student. When you graduate from law school, come see me. I might have a job opening for you," which made Matt smile greatly.

Special Situations

There are many special situations for which documents need to be prepared: partial incapacity, second marriages and blended families, complete incapacity, significant others, and disabled kids and spendthrift family members.

Partial Incapacity

Steve wanted to discuss some special situations and started with incapacity when he said, "Most people think that the typical scenario is for someone in perfect health to simply and suddenly drop dead. This is not usually the case. Many times people become incapacitated as a result of sickness or a major accident or some form of dementia."

Steve turned to Matt and put him on the spot by asking, "Since you have a master's in financial planning and you've also passed the CFP exam, can you explain what documents people should have to take care of these potential problems?" Steve winked at me with that question to show that he was just teasing Matt a bit.

Matt, however, really rose to the occasion and said, "Well, people should have a *durable power of attorney*, which is a special document that takes effect upon incapacity. It will provide that someone, usually a trusted relative, will be able to make financial decisions for the incapacitated people while they are alive. The durable power of attorney applies to gifts, Medicaid elections, and trusts, and it can be used to make changes in insurance, annuities, retirement account beneficiaries, and/or distributions.

"In addition, there are two types of these durable powers of attorney: immediate and springing. *Immediate* comes into play when the people know that they need immediate help. The normal document is the *springing power of attorney* that comes into effect only when documented incapacity takes effect and stops when incapacity no longer applies, which is why it is called a *springing power of attorney:* because it springs into action upon a specified event."

Both Steve and I just sat there with an astonished look. I couldn't believe how proud I was of my son, nor did I realize how mature he had become. When Steve got over his surprise, he said, "I mean it, Matt. Come see me when you want a job after law school."

Second Marriages and Blended Families

"Sadly, the divorce rate in this country is approximately 50 percent, with divorces among second and third marriages being much higher,"[3] Steve noted. "Thus, people should be planning for divorces. In addition, if there is a second marriage, people must update their legal documents for the new family and account for any new kids that came about after the will and/or trust was drafted."

Creating Prenuptial Agreements. "One very important document, especially if there are either children from earlier marriages or if either party has a lot of assets, is a *prenuptial agreement*. It is amazing to me how few people have this with the exception of the really superrich. I consider this an essential document, apart from a will, for everyone who meets either of the two conditions that I just noted."

Continuing on, Steve noted, "What is important about prenuptial agreements is that each party must have it signed by not only the parties but also by a separate attorney representing each spouse. This is important for the courts to legally enforce these agreements.

"Moreover, the will should specify whose assets will pay for long-term care. In addition, there should be provisions that specify what will occur upon the death of a spouse. For example, will each party's kids inherit their respective parent's share, or will all assets be split up among all of the children? These questions need to be addressed with the attorney or planner."

Creating Joint Revocable Trusts. "One possible solution to handle the questions that arise from blended families is to have a *joint revocable trust* until one spouse dies. The key here is to fund the spouse or 'significant other' with property in trust for the kids. The trust would then determine which kids get which property and the amount of assets given to each beneficiary. The trust's assets, as noted below, pass outside of probate and are not controlled by the will provisions."

Updating Legal Documents for Blended Families. Steve then noted, "When there are blended families resulting in remarriages and newly arrived kids, all documents, and not just the will, need to be reviewed and updated to accommodate these changes. This includes possibly changing powers of appointment, as well as other assets that are *not* controlled by the will such as beneficiary changes to your pension plan, IRAs, trust documents, annuities, and life insurance policies. Also all joint account owners should be reviewed because jointly owned property isn't controlled by the will. You may not want your ex-spouse to get your property because he or she was a joint owner of the property."

Complete Incapacity

Steve continued, "The documents needed to prepare for complete incapacity are known as *healthcare proxies*, *living wills*, or *advance healthcare directives*. These are other essential legal documents that many people don't have. They are used for completely incapacitated people, usually in comas. They are documents that name some trusted person to make medical decisions for another person because that person is not capable of making those decisions. This also involves spelling out specific criteria for any organ donations as well as provisions for providing or withholding medical treatment. Thus, if someone is barely being kept alive by feeding tubes and has no brain activity, the person named in the proxy can direct the hospital to cease care. Careful consideration must be given to the provisions in this document including clear instructions to the person who will be making these decisions. It must usually be signed by two adult witnesses.

"You might remember the Terri Schiavo case. It was a heartbreaking case involving Terri Schiavo who had no brain function, was in a vegetative state, and was kept alive by using feeding tubes. Her husband wanted the tubes removed so that she could die of natural causes. Her parents fought the husband in court in order to try to prevent the removal of the tubes. The case involved 14 costly appeals including a decision by the Florida Supreme Court. Had a valid healthcare proxy been in place, none of these costs would have been incurred."

> **Bottom line: Always have a healthcare proxy noting your organ donation decision and making specific provisions regarding medical care and continuation of treatment should you become highly incapacitated.**

Significant Others

"Sadly, unless you are deemed married under the laws in the state of your partner's death, most states don't protect surviving partners in the same manner as spouses. In most cases, an estate of a person who dies intestate (without a will) would have to pay between one-third and one-half of the estate to the surviving spouse. Unmarried, significant others are not protected unless they are deemed *registered partners* (which only a few states have) or they are deemed married. Thus, most people in this situation might want to expressly provide for their unmarried partner in the will, trust, and healthcare proxy. Moreover, you need to check beneficiary designations in retirement plans and life insurance policies.

"As noted above, some states allow people of the same sex to marry, such as Massachusetts and New York. Some states, however, have registered partnerships, which are treated similarly to married couples. These states include Oregon, Vermont, California, Hawaii, Maine, New Hampshire, Nevada, New Jersey, and the state of Washington, as well as the District of Columbia."

Disabled Kids and Spendthrift Family Members

Steve grimly noted, "Severely handicapped kids might need protection for the rest of their lives. This is a concept that parents need to understand. Certainly one way to provide enough assets for the kids' support and maintenance would be to be very rich, in which case the parents could set up the necessary funds in trust or they could set up a life insurance trust. Using joint ownership would not be suitable since the kids probably would need some form of management and control of the funds by an independent expert."

Steve then continued, "One very important consideration regarding severely disabled relatives is the planning for their *supplemental security income* (SSI) payments and other state support. If disabled people receive too much income, they might not get supplemental security income. The key here is to set up a *special needs trust*, which should avoid the income limits for supplemental security income. The key planning point here is that the beneficiary can't be able to do the following things."

- Control the amount and frequency of trust payments
- Revoke and use the trust principal

The bottom line is that the beneficiary of the special needs trust can't have any control over the payments. This control has to be within the sole discretion of the trustee. Thus, you need a very good reliable trustee such as an older sibling, aunt, uncle, or trusted friend.

Steve then paused to look at some notes when he said, "Spendthrift family members are a whole other case. They may not look or seem disabled, and usually they can work. However, they do have a form of disability that prevents them from controlling their spending. They might buy a huge amount of shoes regardless of need. One lady that I know spent tens of thousands of dollars on special dolls and even a huge amount on some alleged moon rocks, if you can believe it. Spendthrift people really can't control their spending."

Matt couldn't help making the bad quip, "The lady was full of moon rocks," to which I couldn't help but chuckle.

Even Steve sniggered at this comment and said, "Yes, it is a real problem. It is a disease. These people just can't control their spending."

As we were talking about this, I wondered if my wife really needed as many shoes as she has, not to mention all of the clothing.

"The key to planning for relatives that have this spending problem is to have what is known as a spendthrift trust that has a lot of safeguards against impulsive spending. This type of trust would not make payments upon divorce and would pay only for food, clothing, transportation, medical care, and other necessary support. It is a critical trust that must have some very tightly designed wording so that the impulsive beneficiary can't get at the money. People should rely on a professional who really understands how to draft up this type of trust."

Avoiding Probate

Steve wanted to shift gears and start discussing methods used to reduce probate costs before he got into his discussion about estate and inheritance tax reductions. He started off by questioning Matt, "Matt, do you know what the word *probate* means?"

Matt responded with that clever gleam in his eye, "Yes. *Probate* means to prove. Thus when we probate a will, we prove to the court that the will is valid."

Steve looked appreciative of Matt's knowledge and said, "Yes, that is exactly correct. The will controls what passes to heirs through the estate. Generally anything in your name is controlled by the will. This includes your investments, real estate, cash, cars, jewelry, and even the value of your business and/or annuities. If you have no will, the state's rules for intestacy will control who gets the property.

"The main problem with probate," Steve added, "is that it can be very expensive. When we refer to probate costs, we are basically talking about fees incurred by the state to process assets that are controlled by the will. They involve filing fees and all legal fees. In these cases, lawyers don't charge their normal hourly fees, which can be very high to begin with. Instead, they usually charge between 2 to 4 percent of the probate estate. Thus, if you have a net worth of $3 million, the probate charges could be as high as $120,000, and this is in addition to any estate or inheritance taxes, which are not considered probate cost. Even worse, out-of-state real estate has its own separate probate. Thus, you would need a lawyer in each state in which you own some real estate in addition to having a separate probate in your state of domicile or your home state. Thus, if you have a main home in New York but have some rental property in Connecticut and a second home in Florida, you could have three separate probates and probably three separate legal and filing fees."

Since I lived in Maryland and owned some rental property in Virginia, I was paying particular attention to this topic.

"The good news," said Steve, "is that probate costs can be almost completely eliminated with proper planning. The key is to transfer title in such a way as to not have the property included in the probate estate."

I then prodded Steve by asking, "Can you outline the ways we can restructure title to any property so that there are no probate charges?"

Steve then quickly responded, "Yes, here is a list of strategies that I have personally recommended to clients. I will also outline any downsides to these strategies as well. I want to mention at the outset that these strategies will primarily be used to avoid probate. They will not in most cases reduce any estate taxes or state inheritance taxes."

Joint Ownership

"*Joint ownership* has been called 'the poor man's will' because jointly owned property passes outside of probate. A joint owner gets the property upon the death of the other joint owner. The problem is that this type of ownership doesn't avoid estate taxes, which will be discussed below. Also, if you don't want the other joint owner to own the property upon your death, it shouldn't be placed in joint ownership.

"Remember the story of my limo driver's grandmother who put all of her bank accounts in joint name with one granddaughter?"

Both Matt and I nodded.

"This can result in a major problem. The granddaughter got the bank accounts, even though it was contrary to the grandmother's wishes in the will, because wills don't control what happens with jointly held property."

Revocable Trusts

"A *revocable trust*, also known as a *living trust*, is the second way to avoid probate. You would set up a trust while you are alive that can be revoked at any time or that can be supplemented with additional contributions at any time. Thus, as an example, Sandy, your assets would be titled 'Sandy Botkin revocable trust,' *not* just 'Sandy Botkin.' These assets would be exempt from probate, which is why many people recommend it. The trust determines who the beneficiaries are and the circumstances in which they can get the income or principal of the trust. It is great for controlling funds for the kids so that they don't blow through them as quickly as possible, as some kids are prone to do."

Matt quickly added, "Hey, I am *not* one of those types of kids. I believe in saving money."

Steve and I both laughed at Matt's need for a sudden defense. "Matt, I don't think that Steve was referring to you with that comment."

Steve then reiterated:

Using a living trust is one of my favorite strategies for avoiding probate because of its flexibility. Moreover, it is great for owning real estate. If you place your out-of-state property and even your home in this trust, you completely avoid probate on these properties in both the state that the properties are located and your state of domicile (which means your home state)!

"This one tip can save your readers tens of thousands of dollars."

Matt then asked a very wise question, "Steve, some states, such as Florida, allow for a *homestead exemption* that precludes the home from being taken for most debts and has lower property taxes. If you put your main home in a living trust, will this preclude the use of the homestead exemption?"

Steve, being quite impressed with Matt's sage question noted, "Living trusts will *not* preclude the homestead exemption. Thus, you will still get the exemption while the home is in trust."

(See also Appendix G, "State Rules Providing Homestead Protection for Your Home," for additional information.)

Steve chuckled and added, "I do want to mention two drawbacks in the use of a revocable trust."

First, you need a lawyer to draft it up, which makes it somewhat costly. Second, and more important, it is a myth that revocable trusts are exempt from estate taxes. Revocable trust funds are *included* in the estate for estate and inheritance taxes. They may work to save probate costs but not estate taxes!

Pension Plans

Steve then added, "Pension plans and IRAs are transferred outside of the probate estate and are not controlled by the will unless they are payable to the estate, which shouldn't be the case. It is the plan documents and elections made by the owner of the plan that determine who will get the pension funds. Thus, when you remarry or have more kids or if you have a newly merged family, carefully reviewing the beneficiaries of these plans is essential to make sure that your fund will be distributed to the correct people."

Life Insurance and Annuities

"Finally," Steve said, "insurance products such as life insurance and annuities also pass outside of probate and are not controlled by the will *unless* they are payable to the estate, which is rarely, ever recommended. If there is a merged family, a new spouse, or new kids, the beneficiaries of these plans must be reviewed."

Pay-on-Death Accounts

Steve chuckled and said, "I bet neither of you have ever heard of *pay-on-death accounts*," to which Matt and I both looked at each other in surprise because we had not. "These are accounts designed primarily to apply to stocks and brokerage accounts, and they operate similarly to joint ownership accounts. However, they avoid the problems associated with joint ownership in that the beneficiary is specifically named in the pay-on-death accounts. In 44 states, these can even be used for mutual fund shares, and a few states (Kansas, Connecticut, Missouri, California, and Ohio) allow this type of account to be used for automobiles. In fact, some states even allow these accounts to be used for boats too."

Steve then grimly added, "Do you remember my story about the limo driver whose sister got all of the grandmother's bank funds that were put in joint names in order for the sister to pay the grandmother's expenses?"

Both Matt and I nodded that we remembered the story.

Steve then said, "If pay-on-death accounts had been used instead of the property's being owned jointly, the grandmother could have accomplished exactly the same goals that she wanted without the drawbacks. She could have had her granddaughter pay her expenses, but the fund would have gone to the grandmother's child upon the grandmother's death. Sadly, this wasn't done correctly."

Yearly Gifts

"A final way to reduce the probate estate," Steve added, "is to make gifts to family members. You can give each year up to $13,000 per recipient if you are single and up to $26,000 per year to each recipient if you are married, using a *split gift election on the gift tax return.*

"Thus, if you have two married kids and three grandkids, and you are married, you can give $26,000 each year to each of your two kids, to each of their spouses, and to each of your grandkids without incurring any gift tax.

In this example, you can give away annual gifts totaling $182,000 worth of property without incurring any gift tax. Moreover, if needed, you can give away up to $5 million during your lifetime above these annual exclusions, which will reduce your estate tax exemption in the future. Thus, you can give away a lot of gifts in order to reduce probate."

Avoiding Estate Taxes

We took a quick refreshment break because my son, Matt, was hungry (for a thin guy, he surely can eat a lot). Once Matt got to have lunch, Steve was eager to finish up the discussion with estate tax planning. He said, "If you had come to me five years ago, I would have devoted much of our discussion to estate tax planning." Steve then turned to Matt and asked, "Matt, do you remember what the estate tax exemption was five or more years ago?"

While munching on some cookies, Matt responded, "Yes, it was $1 million with a top estate tax rate of 55 percent."

Steve nodded and said, "Yes, that is correct. To put things in perspective, your readers need to understand how the estate tax works. Most people, even at that time, felt that a $1 million exemption was more than enough to not worry about the estate tax, and to the detriment of their family, relatively few people planned for it.

"In calculating the estate tax, the IRS would combine all of your assets at their fair market value. Thus, the IRS would combine all of the investments you owned, including stocks and bonds and cash; all of your real estate holdings at their fair market value, including your home; the value of your goods such as jewelry and cars; and even the value of your pensions and IRAs and the value of jointly owned property (less any contribution made by the other joint owners).

"If this weren't bad enough, the IRS would also add the value of your annuities and life insurance at face value if they weren't owned correctly and the value of any business you owned! To this total number, you would be subject to liabilities and a $1 million exemption, and you would then pay a tax at the whopping 55 percent rate that was in force at that time. (However, you could get, and still can get, some time to pay off the taxes, especially if much of the estate was a family farm or constituted a small business.) Even worse, if most of the assets were not liquid, such as real estate holdings, the IRS could force the sale of the property at even lower prices. The estate tax was really a terrible tax that could wipe out the fortune of families."

Both Matt and I agreed.

Steve went on, "Fortunately, the estate tax was recently made less applicable to many people because of two changes that Congress made.

The first was to make the exemption $5 million. The second change was to lower the rate to 35 percent for estates that have net assets (net of liabilities) above the estate tax exemption. This $5 million exemption really has significantly reduced the number of families who need to worry about it."

I then added, "Yes, Steve, I am glad that Congress made that change. It was terrible that people could work all of their life and build up an estate for their family only to have it wiped out with the estate tax."

Steve responded, "Yes, it was a terrible tax that no one thought was fair."

Steve then quickly added, "However, there are still a number of people who have net estates of $5 million or more when you take everything that they own into account, including the face amount of life insurance. Thus, this discussion will be addressing them." Steve also quickly added, "Also, this $5 million exemption from estate tax is scheduled to expire by the end of 2012. If Congress doesn't renew it, it would automatically revert to the $1 million dollar and a top estate tax rate of 55 percent." My son quickly responded with, "Ouch," which made us all chuckle.

Steve took a deep breath and said, "Before I begin our discussion about saving estate taxes, I want to reiterate that many of the probate reduction strategies that we discussed don't work for estate tax savings. Thus, owning property jointly might avoid probate, but generally the value of the jointly held property is included in the estate for estate tax. Likewise, property titled in revocable trusts or pay-on-death accounts is included in the taxable estate. Even gifts, outside of the annual gift tax exclusion that I noted above, made within three years of the death of the deceased are included in the estate.[4] Moreover, although life insurance is usually exempt from probate, unless it is owned correctly, as noted below, the face value of the life insurance and not just the cash value is included in the taxable estate for estate tax computation. Thus, what do you do?"

Steve turned to Matt and decided to test his knowledge by asking him, "Okay, Matt, here is your time to shine. Name some of the top estate planning techniques that will reduce or even eliminate estate taxes."

Make an Irrevocable Life Insurance Trust the Owner of All Life Insurance

Matt noted a number of strategies, but Steve stopped him at each one. "One strategy that most people should do, if they are subject to possible estate taxes, is to set up an *irrevocable life insurance trust* that will receive the proceeds and own the policy."

Steve smiled appreciably at that answer and asked, "Why should an insurance trust be set up? What is the problem?"

Matt was quite prepared and responded, "The problem is that if decedents can change the beneficiaries or cancel the policy, they will be deemed to have the *incidents of ownership*. This simply means that the face value of the life insurance will be included in their estate for estate tax purposes. However, if an irrevocable insurance trust is set up to own the policy and make those ownership decisions, the policy is *not* part of the estate as long as the proceeds are payable to a beneficiary or the trust and not the estate. It is an easy way to reduce the taxable estate that many people aren't doing."

After giving Matt an obviously appreciative look, Steve inquired, "If this is so easy to do, why would you think that many people don't do this?"

Matt thought for a minute and said, "There are several reasons. First, the insurance agents may not be that knowledgeable about this. Second, agents are so happy to get the sale that they don't want to throw a monkey wrench into the works by suggesting a trust, which would complicate things and may even kill the sale. Finally, people, in my experience, are very cheap. They don't want to pay for planning. If they can get a cheap will, they will generally do that." I looked at Matt and with a wink at Steve I said, "Well, your only experience is with starving students who will have to be cheap," which made all of us laugh.

Steve was very taken aback by this mature response from a 26-year-old and said, "I couldn't have put I better myself, Matt. When you open up your own financial planning practice, I think you will be very successful," which made both Matt and me smile. I was really proud of Matt.

Steve then added, "Insurance has long been used for estate planning for tax purposes. Many times, families don't have the liquidity to pay the taxes. With insurance, cash is immediately provided. It is a lot cheaper to pay 1 to 2 percent of the estate taxes that would have been due each year, which is what the insurance premiums would cost, than to pay 100 percent of the estate taxes when they are due. Essentially, with insurance, you pay the taxes with pennies on the dollar. Moreover, the premiums used for the insurance are also out of the estate.

"One bit of caution is needed, however," Steve noted. "It is vital to set up the insurance and the trust more than three years prior to the death of the decedent, or the insurance can be pulled back into the estate. In addition, no insurance company will issue a policy for people who are deemed terminally ill anyway."

Make Yearly Gifts Under the Annual Gift Tax Exclusion

Matt then noted the second major strategy that is used to reduce estate taxes, which is to make annual gifts under the *annual gift tax exclusion*. He noted, "People can make yearly gifts of under $13,000 per donee (which means recipient of the gift) without those gifts being pulled back into the estate. Thus, a single mom with two kids could give each of them $13,000 per year. If she had grandkids, she could give $13,000 to each grandchild each year with no gift tax and not have the gifts pulled back into the estate. Married people can give away up to $26,000 per year per donee (recipient) since there are two people who are deemed to make the gift."

Steve responded, "Yes, I have been suggesting this strategy to my clients for years."

Use a Credit Shelter Trust

Matt then said, "A very common strategy for married couples is to use a *marital trust*. Here is the problem. The estate tax gives an unlimited exemption to any assets left to a spouse. Thus, if a person has a net worth of $8 million—that is, net of his or her liabilities—the person can leave the whole amount to his or her spouse without an estate tax. The problem is what happens when the spouse dies. At that point, the spouse will get an exemption of only $5 million. The other $3 million worth of assets, plus any appreciation, will be taxed at 35 percent. Thus, the family will have to pay over $1 million in estate taxes alone, plus an inheritance tax that is found in some states."[5]

Matt then quickly added, "The way around this is to use what is called a *credit shelter trust*. Thus, you would leave $5 million to the spouse and the remaining $3 million to the credit shelter trust that can be used for the health, maintenance, support, and education of the surviving spouse. You would leave the remaining assets to the spouse. If this is set up correctly, upon the death of the second spouse, the only assets that would be included in his or her estate would be the $5 million left to him or her plus any appreciation that might result. The assets in this credit shelter trust would *not* be counted as part of the estate. This would potentially eliminate estate taxes up to a total estate of $10 million. It is a great, low-cost way to save a lot of estate taxes."

I looked at Steve and could tell that we both appreciated Matt's knowledge in this area.

Leave a Residual in Your Home to a Charity

Matt added the fourth strategy that isn't known by a lot of people when he said, "Another strategy, which is particularly beneficial for those people who do not have kids, is to *leave a remainder interest in your home to a charity*. Thus, people could take large charitable deductions but continue to live in the home for the rest of their lifetime. Upon their death, the charity would get the home, which is why there would be a current charitable deduction. This is ideal for single people who have no beneficiaries to whom they want to give their home."

I grinned at Matt since I, being a tax lawyer, didn't even know about this.

Set Up a Charitable Trust

Steve was getting very excited, so we realized that something big was about to be discussed. He sat down with a glass of wine and looked at us very intently while saying, "Matt, you left out four of the biggest estate tax reduction strategies that the rich can use."

Steve began his explanation: "The first major strategy for the very rich is to set up *charitable trusts*. Here is the problem. If people sell appreciated stock or real estate, they have to pay tax on the gain. In addition, upon their death, they have to pay a whopping estate tax. Wouldn't it be much better if you could get an income for years off of the property, take a charitable deduction on your taxes, and pay no estate taxes and no current income taxes on the sale of the property? Well, you can! Consider setting up a charitable trust, and contribute these assets to the trust. There would be no capital gains and no estate tax or probate. The trust could then spin off an income for many years or even for life! Seriously, it is almost too good to be true.

"The trust would sell the property and invest the assets in income-producing assets. The trust would need to pay out at least 5 percent or more of the initial market value. Even better, the trust could buy a life insurance policy on you or your spouse payable out of the income from the trust property."

Matt then asked, "Aren't there several types of charitable trusts?"

Steve responded, "Yes, there are two types of trusts. The first, which is called the *charitable remainder trust* (CRT), will pay out at least 5 percent or more of the initial proceeds and earn a charitable deduction on the present value of the remainder after the years of payments to the donor. Thus, after a period of years, the charity gets what is left in the trust.

"The second type of trust is called a *charitable lead trust* (CLT). Here the charity gets the income for many years, and the beneficiaries get the remainder of the property once the term of the trust expires. The donor gets to take a charitable deduction based on the present value of the income flow."

Matt thought about this and said, "Steve, this isn't just for very wealthy folks because these benefits of receiving an income for life or getting the remainder while still getting a big charitable deduction can apply to many people; for example, this almost seems ideal for those who make a lot of money and want a big charitable deduction and/or who want to provide a long-term income flow to a disabled relative."

Steve nodded and said, "Yes, you are right, but it also works on estate taxes too. The only drawback to this is that the income distributed to the donor, if you pick that option, is ordinary income and not a capital gain, which would have occurred if the property had been sold. However, the donor is getting a big charitable deduction to offset this."

Set Up a Foundation

"Another strategy," Steve added, "for really rich people, which means generally estates of $20 million or more, and preferably much more, is to do what Bill Gates did: set up a foundation.

"Foundations are like charitable trusts; however, you would in essence be creating your own charity. You would set this up using a lawyer who knows how to create these entities. When you transferred property to the foundation, you would get a big charitable deduction. Unlike that of the charitable trusts, there is no income flow to either the donor or the charity. However, you can receive a yearly management fee for running the foundation. Also, unlike a charitable trust, upon the death of the donor, the kids can run the foundation and receive a yearly management fee. Thus, you are providing an income flow to your family for potentially many generations.

"I should note that this type of entity isn't cheap. You have to get an expert in this field to set up the foundation, and you have to get an IRS ruling approving it. You also have to distribute most of the income to charities. You just can't drain the foundation by simply paying management fees to the family."

Set Up a Qualified Personal Residence Trust

"There is one technique that we can take from the playbook of the rich and famous. This is to set up a *qualified personal residence trust*, also known as a QPRT."

"Steve," I prodded, "although I have heard of QPRTs, I really would like to know exactly what they are and why they are so advantageous."

Giving us his normal wry smile, he said, "Setting up a QPRT is a very straightforward strategy to ensure minimal lifestyle changes while removing a home's value from both estate tax and probate calculations and from inheritance tax calculations. It applies to a grantor who wants to minimize his or her estate and inheritance taxes while not giving away too much."

I turned to Matt and said, "That is exactly what I want to do," which made Matt chuckle a bit.

Steve added, "An individual would transfer the title to a principal residence, vacation home, apartment, or a summer home to a QPRT. The individual would retain the right to live in the home for a specific length of time, such as 10 or 15 years. During that period, the person would *not* pay rent but would agree to pick up all the other maintenance expenses such as taxes, repairs, insurance, and utilities. Thus, during this 10- or 15-year period, the individual would not notice any change in his or her lifestyle since he or she would still be living in the home and paying the same yearly expenses of maintenance and taxes.

"At the end of the 10- to 15-year term, assuming the individual is still alive, the home would pass to his or her children free of estate and inheritance tax. The individual may remain in the home, if he or she agrees to pay rent to the children at the going rate for such rentals, although the IRS has allowed a 20 percent discount for being a good, reliable tenant."

Matt interrupted Steve and said, "Isn't this a taxable gift subject to a possible gift tax?"

Steve smiled at Matt's sagacious remark and responded, "Yes, it is subject to gift taxes. However, if the individual gets the right to live in the property for 10 to 15 years, the gift is based on the actuarial value of the remainder. This could cut the value of the gift by 50 percent or more. Thus a $1 million house that has the grantor living there for 10 to 15 years would have a gift value of between $450,000 and $550,000. Since there is a current gift tax exemption for gifts up to $5 million, there would be no gift tax and the house would be out of the estate for both estate tax and inheritance tax calculations."

Matt then said, "Wait a minute. I learned that there is a problem if the grantor dies before the 10- to 15-year time frame expires."

Steve said, "Matt, whatever graduate program you went to was worth it. You are really knowledgeable for your age. Yes, if an individual dies before the 10- or 15-year term ends, the entire value of the property will be includable in his or her estate. The grantor would not have accomplished anything, but nothing would have been lost. The amount that was originally allocated to the gift would be restored. For this reason, individuals should choose a term of years that they are likely to survive."

Steve then went on to note, "Moreover, if you are married when you do this, you can transfer one-half of the home's value to the QPRT and one-half to the marital trust and thus transfer even more to the family without a gift tax.

"The bottom line," summarized Steve, "is that a QPRT can be very beneficial to wealthy taxpayers who want to remain in a home with a high fair market value so they won't have to make any lifestyle changes while still minimizing their estate and inheritance taxes. It is a good tool to know about."

Matt and I both nodded and agreed that this could be very beneficial to both me and other fairly wealthy taxpayers who have accumulated a decent estate and have a valuable home.

Set Up a Family Limited Partnership

Steve took a sigh and said, "Here is the final technique that the rich and famous have been using for years. If you have a closely held business or some investment real estate worth $10 million, as an example, when you die, this full amount is included in your estate. With the current $5 million exemption, you would pay an estate tax on the remaining $5 million unless you used a credit shelter trust with your spouse as noted above. How would you like to leave the same $10 million or more of assets to your family but get as much as a 30 percent discount on the value of these assets?"

Matt and I smiled at this question since we knew exactly what Steve was going to say.

Steve also chuckled a bit at our reaction and said, "Yes, you know what I am talking about, which is to set up a *family limited partnership*. This is a device that is used primarily to hold the family business or some investment real estate. The business or real estate is transferred to the family limited partnership where the transferor (donor) manages the partnership as the general partner and gives the kids a limited partnership interest. The kids can have only limited say in management. The owner can remain in charge of the daily operations while providing a future succession plan."

Excitedly Steve added, "The advantage of this is that when the owner, donor, dies, the value of the partnership can be considerably less than the full value of the business or real estate. The reason is that the partnership interests are harder to sell. Thus, the beneficiaries can claim as much as a 25 to 35 percent discount on the value of the underlying assets."

I prodded Steve by saying, "Steve, I don't think our readers may understand the tremendous importance of this device. Can you give a specific example?"

He thought about this and said, "Okay, here is an example. Let's say that a person had a big commercial building whose value was $10 million. If this were kept in the owner's name, the full value of this building would be part of the gross estate for estate tax purposes. However, let's assume that the owner has transferred this building to a family limited partnership and maintains a 5 percent general partnership interest for managing the building and a 45 percent limited partnership interest. The kids would get the remaining 50 percent limited partnership interest.

"Upon the owner's death, you would think that 50 percent of the $10 million worth of real estate, or $5 million, would be included in the estate. This would not be the case because the partnership interests aren't as marketable to a willing buyer as the property itself. There would probably be a 30 percent discount due to this lack of marketability. Thus, the same property that the kids would inherit would be included in the owner's estate at only $3.5 million. Also, the other $5 million worth of equity given the kids and/or the rest of the family as limited partners will be subject to gift taxes but at a 30 percent discount, which is $3.5 million. Not a bad deal considering that a lawyer would only charge a few thousand dollars to set this up correctly."

Matt whistled at this result and said, "Wow, nice result. But aren't there some specific steps that must be taken to help ensure that this will work?"

Steve nodded and said, "Yes, the IRS has tried to attack this technique. Thus, it must be done correctly. This means that everyone must adhere to the following steps."

- **The partnership must be treated as a real partnership.** This means that separate bank accounts should be set up and not commingled with personal accounts. Yearly financial statements should be prepared. In addition, the partnership should hold regular, documented meetings to discuss partnership and management issues.
- **There should be a formal written partnership agreement.** This is self-explanatory.
- **Don't violate the P.I.G. rule.** Don't transfer all of your assets to the partnership. Just do this for business interests or investment property. Don't go too crazy here.
- **Document a nontax business reason for forming this partnership.** A lawyer should issue a letter as to the nontax business reasons for setting up the partnership other than to simply avoid estate taxes. Examples of what a partnership might accomplish would be to establish protection from creditors such as nursing homes and to prevent ethical conflicts. Other reasons might be to provide professional management of the property and avoid probate fees. Get a legal letter noting the nontax reasons for setting this up.

I then prodded Steve, "What are the gift tax implications for giving the kids a limited partnership interest?"

Steve responded, "These transfers are subject to federal gift taxes. However, you can avoid yearly gifts of up to $26,000 to each relative if the donor is married or up to $13,000 to each relative if the donor is single.

Moreover, you get a $5 million gift tax exemption from gift taxes above these annual exemptions in 2012. Finally, the gift of a limited partnership interest also gets a discount due to the lack of marketability of the partnership interests. Thus, as I previously mentioned, the $5 million, which is 50 percent of the property's value, would be reported for gift taxes at only about $3.5 million or even less due to the lack of marketability of the limited partnership interests and the lack of control of the partnership.

"Well, that ends our discussion about estate planning."

Steve turned to Matt and said, "Using your notes, let's summarize what you learned."

A Review of What You Have Learned

- Everyone, even single people, needs estate planning.
- When people die without a will, they are deemed to have died *intestate*. The problem is that if people don't have a will, the state will draft one for them that might not meet their needs.
- The following are important will provisions:
  - Always have well-considered guardians for kids.
  - Don't leave IRA and pension money directly to minor children. Use a trust instead.
  - Pension plans and insurance and annuities are not controlled by the will. Always check to see who the beneficiaries are in case of remarriage or merged families or new kids.
  - Avoid family wars by communicating your intentions clearly.
  - Consider an *in terrorem clause* that will preclude beneficiaries from getting anything if they contest the will and lose.
  - Always provide for alternative beneficiaries in case the primary beneficiaries predecease you.
  - Always provide a survivorship clause between you and spouse should there be a simultaneous death.
  - Always name an executor to manage the estate.
  - Many states allow for special trusts for pets. If you live in a state that doesn't allow for this, leave your pet to a trustworthy person.
- Always have a durable power of attorney drafted in case you are incapacitated.
- If you are getting married and have substantial assets or a business, always consider a prenuptial agreement. And if you do enter into such an agreement, make sure that it is witnessed and signed by lawyers representing each party.
- If there is a blended family, the will should provide for whose assets will pay for long-term care.
- Always have a healthcare proxy that will allow a trusted person to make medical decisions for you should you become incapacitated. This proxy could also list any organ donations that you would like to make.
- Make sure the will provides for your significant other, especially in states that don't allow marriage between those of the same sex or do allow for registered partnerships.

- Set up a special needs trust for disabled people, and use a knowledgeable and trusted trustee. Consider having life insurance to help support these disabled folks in case of your death. It is important to set these documents up properly:
  - The beneficiary of the special needs trust *cannot* revoke the trust.
  - The beneficiary *cannot* have any control over the frequency and amount of trust payments.
- Use a spendthrift trust for beneficiaries who are irresponsible about their spending.
- The costs of probate can be 2 to 4 percent of probate assets. Anything controlled by the will involves probate.
- The following are some ways to avoid probate:
  - Joint ownerships and revocable trusts avoid probate.
  - Pension plans payable to beneficiaries or trusts avoid probate.
  - Insurance policies and annuities payable to beneficiaries or trusts avoid probate costs.
  - Pay-on-death accounts and jointly owned properties avoid probate.
  - Trusts avoid probate, even revocable trusts.
  - Gifts can avoid probate if they do not exceed the annual exclusions.
- The following are some ways to avoid estate taxes:
  - Set up an irrevocable life insurance trust (ILIT).
  - Make yearly gifts under the annual gift tax exclusion limits.
  - If you are married and the value of your estate is more than $5 million, net of your liabilities, use a credit shelter trust with your spouse.
  - Leave a residual interest in your home to a charity.
  - Set up a charitable trust.
  - Set up a foundation.
  - Set up a qualified personal residence trust (QPRT).
  - Set up a family limited partnership for closely held businesses and for investment real estate and for commercial buildings.

Notes

1. The community property states are Arizona, California, Idaho, Louisiana, Nevada, New Mexico, Texas, Washington, and Wisconsin.
2. Forty-six states and the District of Columbia allow for pet trusts. The four states that do not allow for pet trusts as of February 12, 2012, are Kentucky, Louisiana, Minnesota, and Mississippi. See http://www.aspca.org/pet-care/pet-care-tips/pet-trusts-laws.aspx.
3. www.divorcerate.org.
4. As will be discussed, annual gifts that are less than the annual exclusions are exempt from being pulled back into the estate. For single donors, the annual exclusion is $13,000 per recipient. For married couples who elect to split the gift, the annual exclusion is $26,000.
5. States that have a separate inheritance tax are Alabama, Florida, Indiana, Kentucky, Maryland, Nebraska, New Jersey, Ohio, and Tennessee.

15

Retirement Planning

Money can't buy happiness, but it can make you awfully comfortable while you are miserable.

—Claire Booth Luce

What You Will Learn
- Three sources of retirement funds
- Killers of retirement plans
- Estimating retirement financial needs
- Ways to bolster retirement income
- Three rules for retirement financial planning
- Pension maximization

For this subject, I decided to interview my friend Marc because I felt that a financial planner would know a lot about retirement planning.

It was summer. The geese were out by the lake where Marc lives. Our summer day today was swelteringly hot. In fact, I cannot remember having a summer that had as many days of 100 degrees or more. It thus felt good to be in Marc's air-conditioned house. Marc ushered us into his home office, and he must have read my mind since he had a cold pitcher of water with chilled glasses for each of us. No wonder he is so successful.

"Marc," I said, "I want today's discussion to be about retirement planning. It is such a crucial area, and most folks seem ill prepared for it."

Marc nodded thoughtfully and responded, "It is more crucial than I think even you might know. Did you know that studies have shown that only 4 percent of those who reach 65 will be able to retire with the same standard of living that they had before retirement? Many will either have to continue working, live with their kids, or reduce their standard of living."

Matt decided to tease me and said, "Well, Dad, I guess the odds are that you will be living with me," which made Marc and me chuckle.

"Here is another interesting statistic," added Marc. "Twelve percent of the elderly live in poverty. Moreover, 74 percent of these are women!

"Even worse," Marc noted, "is that generation Xers, who were born between 1965 and 1980, are in worse shape than the baby boomers, who are in bad shape already. The reason is that many are overburdened with debt, and they are less likely to get both a pension and social security. In fact, fewer people are being covered by a pension than ever before. On top of that, with the horrendous federal debt that we have now and the rising annual deficits, taxes will significantly eat into the earnings of the younger generation unless Congress starts to take action immediately."

I asked Matt, "Doesn't this worry you a lot?"

His answer was definitely vintage Matt: "Dad, I want to become a partner in a financial planning firm. These problems will mean that people will need someone like me more than ever. I see this as a great opportunity."

Both Marc and I couldn't help but smile at Matt's sagacious response.

Three Sources of Retirement Funds

Marc then continued, "There are only three sources of retirement income, not counting the unlikely chance of winning the lottery or getting a huge inheritance. They are the following."

- Savings and investments
- Company pensions
- Social security benefits

Killers of Retirement Plans

"Before we get into our retirement planning discussion, I do want to discuss the major killers of retirement and show people how to estimate how much they may need for retirement."

We completely agreed with Marc about starting this topic first.

"There are three main killers of retirement plans, and the first is this: **People are living longer.**"

I teased Marc and said, "I *really* want to have this problem," to which Marc smirked.

Marc then went on and added, "You would think so, Sandy. However, if you live too long without proper planning, your longevity will exceed your ability to support yourself. With advances in medical care, people are living longer than ever. Thus, we need to plan so that we will have assets even past age 90!

"The second killer is this: **Many people end up spending more than they had planned**. Many times I hear clients say that they can live on much less since their kids are out of college and their mortgage is fully paid off. However, this assumes that they will stay in a rocking chair and not do anything.

"In reality, there are many expenses that occur during retirement. For example, as people get older, they have increased medical and dental expenses. In addition, people like to travel, which isn't cheap. Also, many people take up hobbies such as golf. Hobbies can be quite expensive. Moreover, many parents want to help their kids with new businesses, subsidizing their new home purchase, and so on. Kids also get divorced and lose their jobs. It is quite common for kids to come back home. Believe me, there are plenty of expenses that occur after retirement."

Upon hearing this, I had to admit that I had a sick feeling in my gut about all these new upcoming expenses.

"The third killer is this: **People do not allow adequately for the negative effects of inflation on the value of their savings.** If you don't plan for inflation, your savings will quickly dwindle."

Estimating Retirement Financial Needs

I then asked Marc, "How can we estimate our retirement needs?"

His answer was very interesting. "I assume a 3 percent return on investments. Actually, most people can do much better than 3 percent. However, they have to plan for taxes and for some reinvestment for inflation. Thus, if people have $1 million of investable assets, I calculate that they will net (assuming that they save the difference for inflation) about $30,000. With $2 million, this figure would increase to $60,000 per year."

"Marc," I inquired, "having a million or two of net investable income is nice, but it is probably beyond the reach of most people. Thus, how do they survive?"

Rolling his eyes at this question, he said, "Sandy, people don't just live on their investments. They get social security, which can be as high as $2,513 per month[1] as of 2012. In addition, their spouse will get social security. Finally, many people will be getting some sort of pension. Thus, depending on your other sources of income, you may not need $2 million or more. The bottom line is to ask how much you need to live on now. Project your yearly social security and pension. If there is a difference, you divide the difference by 0.03. This will give you the amount of investable assets that you will need. Let me give you an example.

"Let's assume that you are living on $75,000 a year of family income now. If you get social security of $2,300 per month times 12 months, you would be generating $27,600 per year. Assuming that your spouse didn't work and gets half of your benefit, you would have social security benefits of $40,400 in total per year. This will leave you a shortfall of $34,600. If you get a pension to equal this, you don't need to have investable assets. If you have no pension, then you will need $34,600/0.03, or $1,153,333, of additional investable assets to equal what you are making now and to cover inflation. Do you understand that?"

Matt nodded that he understood that fully, but I had to look at this example for a while until I too understood the math. To make sure I understood it, I reinforced this discussion by saying, "So the formula for figuring out how much in investable assets we need in order to have the same lifestyle that we have while working is as follows."

> **Retirement income needed = (today's income from work – social security to be received – pension to be received)/0.03.**

Marc agreed that this formula is a reasonable approximation of what will be needed.

Ways to Bolster Retirement Income

Matt then inquired, "Marc, what happens if, based on the formula, people still don't have enough to have a reasonable standard of living?"

Marc gave that some thought and answered, "They have a number of options. They can continue working. In addition, here are some other options that could give them some extra tax-free income."

- They can accumulate and use airline frequent flyer miles, which are tax free.
- They can work at a job for which they receive a commuter tax benefit of $230 a month for their parking and mass transit costs.
- They can work part time and get some tax-free fringe benefits.
- They can cozy up with some rich relatives. Gifts and inheritances are tax free.
- They can rent out their residence for extra income. Also, if they rent out a property for no more than two weeks a year, the entire rent is tax free. If they are willing to pay the taxes, they can rent out rooms in their house for the whole year.

- They can reduce their expenses by house sitting for people, which is tax free and cost free.
- They can learn about fixing plumbing and electrical work, which will cut their repair costs.

"As you can see," Marc added, "there are a number of options.

"Also, most retirees feel that they should own only bonds or certificates of deposit. The problem with these investments is that they don't offer much protection to investors against inflation. In fact, some of these investments are paying no more than 1 percent. All investors at any age should own some investments that go up with inflation. These can be stocks, gold mining shares, and real estate or real estate investment trusts (REITs). Generally the older you are, the fewer of these investments you should have in your portfolio, but they should always be included to some extent. Here is a great example of someone who didn't own any inflation-oriented assets and stuck with CDs.

"A woman I knew had $2 million in CDs. She was earning at that time 2.5 percent. This produced $50,000 a year in income for her, and she received her social security, which sounds good. However, she had to pay taxes on all this, which was around 33 percent. Thus, she was left with $33,333 a year. If inflation were 4 percent, she would be what I call 'going broke slowly.' It is vital that all retirees plan for inflation."

Three Rules for Retirement Financial Planning

Marc gave us the following three general rules that should guide people in their financial planning for their retirement savings.

Always Start Saving as Early in Life as Possible

"Although you may have mentioned this in Chapters 4 and 5 on saving money, Sandy, I still want to point out a key element about retirement, which is this: **Always invest as early as possible in life for retirement.** Retirement savings become greater with time. Here is an example of what happens when someone puts away $6,000 a year for 25, 30, and 40 years in a typical mutual fund. I have used conservative projections at 6 percent."

Savings of $6,000 per Year after 25, 30, and 40 Years

25 years of savings: $346,631
30 years of savings: $501,893
40 years of savings: $1,000,724

"If the contribution doubles, so does the amount at retirement, which is why people should maximize their 401(k) investments, which allows for up to $17,000 per year. In fact, if you reach age 55 while working, you get to add an additional $5,500 in catch-up contributions. Thus, you can put away up to $22,500 on a tax-deferred basis."

Marc then added, "These figures assume a rate of return of 6 percent, but mutual funds have actually had a long-term rate of return of 9 percent. Thus, I am being very conservative. In fact, you can get stocks such as some utilities—Verizon and others—that pay 5 percent or more. Also, older people, who have less time, can achieve the same results by adding more money each year."

Time Your Retirement Account Investments to Your Best Advantage

Marc then noted, "The second key rule about savings and retirement is this: **Invest your money in your retirement account as early in the year as possible.** The reason is that the earlier in the year that you invest the money, the greater the balance at retirement. In other words, it is much better to invest your money in a retirement plan at the beginning of each year than to wait until the end of the year.

"Here is a startling example. As we noted above, if you save $6,000 per year for 40 years, you will have approximately $1 million at retirement in your 401(k). However, this figure assumes that you invested the $6,000 at the end of the year. If, however, you invested the same $6,000 for the same 40 years but you did so at the beginning of each year, you would have a retirement nest egg of $1,068,645. This is roughly an extra $68,000 more at retirement on the same contributions!"

"Marc, I have some great calculators on my sandybotkin.com website in the Tools section. There are also a number of other sites such as Bankrate.com that have some financial tools too."

"Yes, I like your site. It is easy to navigate, and it doesn't have a huge number of calculators that can confuse people."

For Tax-Advantaged Retirement Plans, Use Investments That Produce Ordinary Income

Marc then noted the third general rule for retirement planning. "For tax-advantaged retirement plans such as annuities, pensions, and IRAs, use investments that aren't tax advantaged and that produce ordinary income anyway. This way, you are not converting capital gains to ordinary income. In other words: **for tax-advantaged plans such as IRAs,**

annuities, and other pension plans, use investments that produce ordinary income.

"Thus, the best investment for pension plans and IRAs would be bonds, mortgages such as Federal National Mortgage Association (FNMA) mortgages, REITs, and other investments that produce ordinary income. Stocks can be okay, but you are better off owning them outside of a pension plan because they produce capital gains, which are taxed at much lower rates."

Although I had never thought about this, Marc's reasoning seemed sound to me.

Pension Maximization

After taking a brief snack break, since Matt was getting hungry again, we started in with a vital topic.

"I now want to cover one of the most important retirement planning topics in the country and probably in the world as well. This is the concept of *pension maximization*." Marc clearly had my attention with this opening.

"Here is the problem. Many private sector employees and many federal and state employees are given an option at retirement. They can receive their full pension, or they can take a significantly reduced pension with payments made to their spouses for their lifetimes if the employees die."

I interrupted Marc to say, "Yes, my dad, who was an elementary school principal, was offered this option."

Marc responded with, "Yes, and I will bet that he took the *survivorship option* for your mom," which he did. "Most people do take the survivorship option. Sadly, if they are in good health, this is the *wrong choice*."

I swallowed a bit when I said, "Yes, it certainly was for my dad because my mom died, and he got stuck with the reduced pension forever."

Marc stared at me a bit sadly and said, "Yes, that is clearly the problem. If an employee's spouse dies prematurely, in many cases the employee is stuck with the reduced option forever. This isn't always true for all workers, particularly federal and military workers. Thus, some investigation must be conducted by employees to find out if their employer allows them to change the election in case of premature death of the spouse. However, this is the general rule for most people.

"So," Marc asked, "which is the better approach? Most employees certainly don't want their spouses and families to be destitute.

"The correct approach, which most people don't think about, is to take the full pension! They should also take out a life insurance policy that will produce enough income to make up for the lost pension plus account for inflation. This means that the amount that the spouse would have gotten had she or he survived is divided by 0.03, which should equal the amount of life insurance needed. Thus, if the normal pension is $60,000 per year but by taking a survivorship option, it is reduced to $40,000, which is reduced for the survivorship of the spouse, you would take the $40,000 and divide it by 0.03, giving a needed life insurance policy payout of about $1,333,333.

"Thus the advantages of using this approach are the following."

- The retirement income is higher due to the pension's being written for a single life expectancy.
- There is greater protection of the surviving spouse due to there being a life insurance policy on the retiring member.
- The income is higher in the event that the worker's spouse dies first. In addition, the family can get a nice tax-free lump sum from the insurance policy, or the family can get the cash value of the policy.
- The worker has the flexibility to name new beneficiaries if the spouse predeceases the worker.
- The political uncertainties surrounding state and local government pension obligations are eliminated.

Matt quickly interrupted with an important question, "Marc, this isn't ideal for everyone, right? If so, who is the ideal person for this?"

Problems with Pension Maximization

Marc responded, "Yes, you are right. Not everyone can do this. For example, if someone is uninsurable, he or she can't use this technique. Moreover, sometimes the insurance is a lot more than the decrease in the pension. Thus, it is ideal to take out a policy on the worker's life about three to five years before retirement. The ideal time to apply for a policy is when the worker becomes age 50 or 55. This timing would provide cost-effective premiums that would probably be less than the decrease in the pension should the survivorship option be elected. This would also be an ideal age since the worker will probably be in good health and therefore insurable."

Matt then inquired, "Marc, what type of insurance would you recommend: term with a side investment or permanent?"

Marc quickly responded, "I would recommend some form of permanent insurance such as whole life because this is clearly a permanent need. Using term insurance at an older age can be very expensive too.

"Also, as I mentioned above, some employers, especially the military, allow workers to cancel their survivorship benefits and get the higher amount. Pension maximization won't be as necessary for them. **Thus, it is** vital that people check out what policy the employer has toward canceling survivorship benefits in case of the death of the spouse."

Taxable or Tax-Free IRAs and 401(k)s

Matt sat with a puzzled look and asked this question: "Marc, people have two choices: they can put away money into a 401(k) or IRA and get a deduction. Or they can put away money into a Roth IRA or a new Roth 401(k) and not get a deduction but get that money tax free forever. Which do you think is better?"

Because I am a tax lawyer, I decided to chirp in here with the answer. "Matt, for years I was telling people to use a deductible 401(k) and/or a deductible IRA. After all, they would get a deduction. This advice also assumed that people would be in a lower tax bracket after they retired than they were in when they were working. However, with a $15 trillion federal debt that is still rising, I have changed my mind. I am now recommending using either a Roth 401(k) or Roth IRA. My main reason is that when the money comes out, it will be tax free forever!"

I continued, "Also, with regular IRAs and 401(k)s, you must start taking out the money (otherwise known as a *required minimum distribution*) either over your life expectancy or once you hit age 70. This is not true, however, for Roth IRAs and Roth 401(k)s that have no minimum distribution requirements.

"I should note that you can take money out of a deductible IRA without penalty, although you will pay taxes on the withdrawal, once you hit age 59½. Moreover, and this surprises many people, if you meet certain limited exceptions, you can take money out of an IRA without penalties even before age 59½. Some examples are the following circumstances."

- You can take out $10,000 to purchase a home if you will be a first-time homeowner.
- You can take out money to pay medical expenses that exceed 7.5 percent of your adjusted gross income (AGI). (That amount is going up to 10 percent with the Affordable Healthcare Act becoming effective in the year 2013.)
- You can take out the money over your life expectancy.
- You can take out money if you become disabled.
- You can take out money to pay for medical insurance.

Matt then inquired, "Dad, aren't there income limits that prevent people from setting these up?"

I smiled at Matt's knowledge and said, "There are no income limits for a Roth 401(k). In fact, you can invest the same amount of money that you can invest in a regular 401(k), which is $17,000 as of today and an extra yearly $5,500 catch-up contribution once you hit age 55. This is determined as of December of the year.

"As for the Roth IRA, the limit is $5,000 per year, although you can make an extra $1,000 catch-up contribution if you are age 55 or older as of December of the year. However, what Congress gives it sometimes takes away: you can't contribute to the Roth IRA if you earn over a certain income amount. Married people will see a phaseout of the Roth IRA at between $166,000 and $176,000 or more of adjusted gross income (AGI). For single people the phaseout is between $105,000 and $120,000. For married people filing separately, the phaseout is between 0 and $10,000. I guess Congress didn't like folks who are married filing separately.

"Here is a comparison chart that I think everyone will find useful."

Comparison Chart for Types of Retirement Accounts		
Type of Retirement Account	**Contribution Limit**	**Mandatory Withdrawal Rules**
Regular IRA	$5,000 with $1,000 catch-up	Age 70½
Regular 401(k)	$17,000 with $5,500 catch-up	Age 70½
Roth IRA	Same as regular IRA but not tax deductible; no minimum required	Tax-free distributions if left for at least 5 years and no mandatory withdrawals.
Roth 401(k)	Same as regular 401(k) and same catch-up	Same as Roth IRA; contribution not tax deductible, but distributions tax free. Moreover, no mandatory withdrawals.

I also added, "Matt, I have a way around the income limits for Roth IRAs. As I have said before, where there is a way . . . there is a lawyer. Here is what people can do. Contribute to a regular IRA. Next year, convert this regular IRA to a Roth IRA by directly transferring the money to the Roth trustee. You will have to pay taxes on the conversion as if you received all the money, but you can then fund your annual Roth IRA without worrying about the income limits.

"Did you agree with all this, Marc?"

Marc smiled and said, "If you ever want to become 'of counsel' to my firm, Sandy, I would love to have you."

Marc then reiterated, "I have some final comments. First, IRAs and 401(k)s and other pension plans are not governed by a will or subject to probate as long as they are payable to a beneficiary other than the estate. If you get remarried or have more kids, you should review the beneficiary designation found in these plans.

"Second, *always* maximize your contributions to a 401(k) *especially* if the employer makes some matching contributions. To ignore free money is particularly idiotic.

"Third, *never, ever* put all of your 401(k) monies into your employer-company's stock. If the company goes bankrupt or does badly and fires you, you have a double whammy of being unemployed and also owning stock that has declined in value. This is what happened to Enron employees to their regret.

"Fourth, *never* borrow money from your 401(k). Yes, you can do it, but you are limited to one-half the balance up to $50,000. There are many reasons why borrowing from a 401(k) is a bad idea such as these."

- You will not be saving money for retirement. Many plans prevent future contributions until the loans are repaid. Also, even if the plan doesn't have this requirement, if you have to repay the loan plus accrued interest, you might not have enough money to make your additional yearly contributions.
- You will lose the long-term growth opportunity because there will be less money in the 401(k) to earn income. In addition, you will lose appreciation that would have occurred on the additional contributions that you may not be making.
- You will become somewhat trapped in that the loan must usually be repaid if you quit your job.
- You will have less flexibility in life. If your financial situation deteriorates—for example, if you lose your job—you may not be able to repay the loan. This could be a disaster because the current loan balance may be treated as a withdrawal subject to both income tax and a 10 percent early withdrawal penalty if you are under age 59½.
- You will lose your cushion that you will need for retirement.
- Borrowing from retirement plans goes against two of the rules (secrets) in Chapter 4 for building up your savings: pay yourself first and never borrow in order to save money.

"Finally, invest your IRA and 401(k) monies in a diversified way. Using balanced and global mutual funds is a good bet."

I thought this was a great discussion, and I thanked Marc for sharing his wealth of knowledge; in addition, Matt was starting to get hungry for dinner. He is such a chow hound!

A Review of What You Have Learned

Here is a review of the notes I took.

- Proper planning for retirement is crucial. Retirement comes faster than many people realize. Failing to plan will leave many people either poor or having to work till they die or having to live on some form of charity.
- There are three ways to save for retirement:
  - Savings and investments
  - Company pension
  - Social security, which usually covers only about 25 percent of retirement needs
- There are three killers of retirement plans:
  - People live a longer life than they had planned for.
  - People end up spending at retirement more than they had planned to.
  - People do not take into account adequately the effects of inflation on their savings.
- The formula for figuring out how much in savings you need for retirement is as follows: Retirement income needed = (today's income from work − social security to be received − pension to be received)/0.03.
- There are a number of ways to supplement retirement income and cut costs if you can't save what is projected by the above-noted formula.
- *Always* start saving as early in life as possible.
- Always contribute to your pension plan as early in the year as possible.
- Retirement plans are great for assets that produce ordinary income such as bonds, mortgages, and REITs.
- Pension maximization: It is rarely a good idea to take a survivorship option with a company pension because your spouse can predecease you. However, some companies allow for cancellation of the survivorship option (such as federal employees). Be sure to find out which policy your company has.) Instead of taking the survivorship option, consider taking the following steps:
  - Take the full pension and also take out a life insurance policy to produce enough assets to cover the survivor's pension that would be lost.
  - Take out insurance at age 50 or 55 and/or at least five years before retirement. This will make the premiums cheap enough to be less than what you would have lost by taking the survivorship option.
- Generally, we recommend contributing to Roth 401(k)s and Roth IRAs over traditional 401(k)s and IRAs. We feel that tax rates will be going up, and getting the distributions tax free forever outweighs the deduction.
- If you make more than the income limits allowed by a Roth IRA, consider contributing to a regular IRA or 401(k) and then rolling them over each year into a Roth IRA. You will pay taxes on the rollover, but future distributions will be tax free forever.
- *Always* maximize your 401(k) contributions. And maximizing your contributions is especially important if your employer makes matching contributions.

- Never put all or even most of your 401(k) money in your employer's stock.
- Invest your IRA and 401(k) monies in a diversified manner. Using balanced and global funds is ideal. Also, investing in assets that produce ordinary income for your pension plans is ideal. Thus, bonds, notes, REITs, and even CDs would be good investments for your pension plans.

Notes

1. http://ssa-custhelp.ssa.gov/app/answers/detail/a_id/5/~/maximum-social-security-retirement-benefit.

16

Asset Protection

Lawsuit abuse is a major contributor to the increased costs of healthcare, goods, and services to consumers.
—Charles W. Pickering

What You Will Learn
- Get insurance
- Use common sense in your life
- Get a prenuptial agreement before you get married
- Own property as tenants by the entirety
- Take advantage of your state's homestead exemption protection
- Set up trusts
- Use corporations and limited liability corporations
- Make some investments in assets that are protected by law
- Establish family limited partnerships

With lawsuits being filed every four seconds in this country, not to mention new law schools being churned out every few years, we decided that we needed a chapter devoted to asset protection. I felt that the best person to discuss this information would be a friend who is both a litigator and a specialist in collection. Thus, I contacted my friend Howard. Howard is a great guy. He is outgoing, fun, and very smart. He has built up a great practice, and he was kindly willing to meet Matt and me in order to share his knowledge.

When we got to his house, I couldn't believe what I saw. This was a mini-mansion. It had to have at least 10,000 to 12,000 square feet. It had beautifully manicured lawns, which I would bet that Howard had hired someone to take care of. It was also surrounded by stone, and not just brick. My first reaction was to tell Matt, "This is the lifestyle of a successful litigator. You should really consider this when you get out of law school."

Matt simply shrugged his shoulders and said, "Maybe, but this is not what I want. I don't want the stress that comes with litigation. Everyone is mad at you and at each other."

Howard greeted us at the door and ushered us into his home office. What struck me was all of the cool toys and games that he had as decoration. He had a striking Monopoly set and a Scrabble set, which had gold-plated letter tiles and was manufactured by the Franklin Mint. He had trains on his wall and a very cool large puzzle map of the world. He even had an antique slot machine, which I declined to use. As I said, Howard is an interesting guy.

"Okay, Howard, we are here to discuss asset protection. We want strategies that work and are simple to use. And it would be even better if they would give a collection attorney like you a headache in order to be able to collect on judgments."

Howard smiled at my attempt at humor.

Get Insurance

Howard surprised me by saying, "We really have a problem in this country. It is literally raining lawsuits. There is 33 percent chance that your readers will be involved in a lawsuit in their lifetime.[1] If they have a business, it is even more probable. The worst part though is that even if you win, you are stuck with paying huge legal costs."

Howard then continued, "Many people, even those with incorporated businesses, are sitting on a personal liability time bomb. The problem is that although they think that their corporation will protect them from liability, in many cases, it won't for several reasons. First, most people don't keep up with the corporate formalities of having yearly stockholder meetings and resolutions. This could subject them to personal liability.

"Think about this. Most people have dreams. They want a good education for their kids, and they have saved up for it with some planning. They want some decent vacations, and they want to retire with some dignity and with a good standard of living. One bad lawsuit can wipe out those dreams and kill the education funding, kill the retirement planning, and wipe out the ability to take vacations. In fact, in many states, even the family home could be at risk!"

Matt and I both got a bad chill down our backs about this.

Howard grimly continued, "I am being very harsh and unrelenting about this because asset protection is a *big* deal. People really need to take it as seriously as a heart attack. Therefore, I want your readers to really read over what we will be discussing today and to take the information to heart. In addition, they should meet with an attorney about what is presented here and discuss the best ways to diffuse these legal time bombs."

After completely bumming us out about the hazards of lawsuits, Howard became a bit more cheery since he knew that there were ways for most people to easily protect themselves with some planning.

Accordingly, Howard's first recommendation was this: "There is no question. The best liability protection is to have insurance and a good umbrella policy. Insurance not only covers the risks but it also provides legal representation in order to avoid the frivolous suits that seem to permeate this country. I can't say that strongly enough. A huge number of cases have been settled out of court because it frankly didn't pay the defendant or the insurance company to fight about it."

"Howard," I said, "you just reminded me of an unpleasant experience that I had with my company. There was a lady who snuck into one of my seminars. At some point, she fell over some of the cords that I used in the seminar. At that time, I was using a slide projector in my seminars. Subsequently, she sued me for the loss of sexual function and her inability to play golf," which made both Howard and Matt laugh. "We hired a detective who got pictures of her playing golf afterward. Despite all this, my insurance carrier, State Farm, settled with her for $10,000. When I complained about this, the company responded that it was cheaper to settle the case than to go to trial. Since they were paying all the bills, they made the decision to settle."

Howard nodded and said, "Yes, lawsuits are in many cases being used as extortion. We really do need some form of tort reform where the loser of a lawsuit will pay the winner's legal fees."

Matt interrupted and said, "We were told by someone else to get at least $3 million of liability umbrella insurance and maybe even $5 million worth of umbrella insurance. Do you agree with this?"

Howard responded, "Yes, that should cover at least 98 percent of the damage suits that people would face. However, there are some exceptions. If you have a lot of assets, you might want to insure even more since you will be a target. Let's face it, you have more to lose. Also, liability umbrella insurance has the following limitations that everyone should know about."

1. It doesn't cover any sort of malpractice. You might need separate insurance for malpractice lawsuit protection.
2. It doesn't cover damage from floods. You might need separate insurance for these events. You should get flood insurance if you live in a flood zone.

3. It doesn't cover any damages or liabilities arising from conducting a business. Therefore, these require separate insurance policies.
4. It doesn't cover uninsured motorists who are at fault. This is why people have uninsured motorist coverage on car insurance.
5. It doesn't cover high-risk activities with your car such as drag racing.
6. It doesn't cover damage to your own car or property.
7. If you commit a crime and are forced to pay restitution, it isn't covered by your umbrella policy.

Howard then went on to add, "In order to decrease their liability exposure, people need to know what activities increase their exposure. Some examples of these items that increase your risk of a lawsuit are the following."

- Owning a business, especially if there are employees. Employees are walking lawsuits.
- Having a long commute to work if you drive, which is why insurance carriers charge more based on the normal mileage that people drive to work.
- Driving during rush hour when most accidents occur.
- Owning a swimming pool in your home.
- Owning a dog.
- Having frequent guests at your home.
- Owning rental property, which usually has significant liability exposure.
- Being on a board of directors, which usually requires special "Board of Director's insurance."
- Owning any investment real estate that you rent out.

"As you can see," Howard added, "there are many risks that the average person incurs that can cause lawsuits. This leads us to the next part of our discussion."

Use Common Sense in Your Life

"Always use common sense in life. With a few minor lifestyle changes, you can significantly cut your risk of a lawsuit. Here are some examples."

- Never, ever take your eyes off the road when you are driving. If you feel that your driving ability is impaired due to old age or a disability, take a taxi or get a friend to drive you. I know someone who was getting older and had significantly diminished vision and reflexes who plowed his car into a number of kids waiting for the school bus. This was a disaster for everyone.

- Don't use a cell phone while driving unless it is on speaker mode only and you have an external Bluetooth system for both speakers and for the microphone.
- If you have a business, always have a strongly worded employee manual showing what employees can and cannot do. Using a good lawyer here can be very beneficial.
- Always fence in your swimming pool, and put locks on the pool entrances.
- *Never, ever* sign a major contract, especially if you are in business, without having a good business lawyer read over the contract.
- Get good insurance on all rental properties. Also, use a strongly worded lease that notes what types of liabilities are assumed by the tenants. Again, use a lawyer here.
- Form a separate *limited liability corporation* (LLC) for each rental property that has tenants. Rental properties, to the surprise of many people, are liability magnets.
- If you have some dangerous objects or conditions in your house or your business's meeting rooms, make sure to mention these items to your guests.
- As the old saying goes, "If you can't say something nice about a person, don't say anything." Don't slander or libel someone unless you can prove every bit of your statement. Even then, avoid demeaning anyone.

"The bottom line," Howard concluded, "is to use common sense in all of your dealings."

Get a Prenuptial Agreement Before You Get Married

"First, I want to note that the divorce rate in this country is about 50 percent for first time marriages and well over 50 percent for subsequent marriages— and rising! Even worse, if you get divorced, many courts will award the spouse 50 percent of what you have *plus* child support *and* probably alimony. If you have significant assets or you have a business, you should always try to get a prenuptial agreement signed by your perspective spouse."

I chuckled at this and said, "C'mon, Howard, how many people are going to say right before 'I do,' 'Honey, I need you to sign away your rights in case of a divorce.' This will put a chill on all marriages, not to mention that it might prevent the marriage." Matt also chirped in, "It will also put a big chill on the honeymoon!," which made all of us laugh.

Howard nodded and said, "I do know that it can be a tough conversation, but the consequences of a divorce can be catastrophic without it. I know a successful hair stylist who had to sell his business in order to split the proceeds pursuant to a divorce.

"The key is that you must do the prenuptial agreement correctly or the courts won't uphold it. This means that you must do the following four things in particular."

1. You must make full disclosure of your personal and business assets and income.
2. Each spouse must be represented by his or her own attorney when signing the prenuptial agreement. Many courts have thrown out the prenuptial agreement if the spouse wasn't represented by his or her own separate attorney.
3. Don't be cheap. Don't use LegalZoom.com or some online legal form service. Get a good divorce attorney to draft the agreement.
4. If you don't want to give half of your pension to your spouse upon divorce, get a separate pension waiver before marriage.

Own Property as Tenants by the Entirety

Howard was on a roll and added, "In many states if property is owned jointly with a spouse, the couple is deemed to own the property as *tenants by the entirety*. This means that if a lawsuit judgment occurs against one spouse, the creditor can't foreclose on the jointly owned property until one spouse dies or the couple gets divorced. This is a built-in asset protection for states that have allowed tenants by the entirety. Here is a list of states that have these types of statutes. Notice that some states allow this only for real estate."

Alaska
Arkansas
Delaware
Florida
Hawaii
Maryland
Massachusetts
Mississippi
Missouri
New Jersey
Oklahoma
Pennsylvania
Rhode Island

Tennessee
Vermont
Virginia
Wyoming

Washington, DC, also offers this type of asset protection.

The states that allow tenancy by entirety for real estate only are these:

Illinois
Indiana
Kentucky
Michigan
New York
North Carolina

Matt then eagerly asked, "Since we live in Maryland, if I get married and put everything in joint name with my spouse, would this mean that I would be fully protected against court judgments for these assets?"

I turned to Matt and teasingly asked, "Matt, did you get secretly married and not tell us about it?" Everyone chuckled at that.

Getting back to the subject, Howard responded, "Yes, those properties in Maryland that are owned jointly between a husband and wife are exempt from creditors. However, remember that if you get divorced or if one of you dies, then the creditors can foreclose on the property since it is no longer owned as tenants by the entirety. Also, if you have mortgaged the property owned specifically as tenants by the entirety, the bank or financial institution can foreclose on that property even if it is owned jointly by husband and wife. Frankly, this isn't a big deal since most banks require both spouses to jointly sign on any mortgages given."

Howard then added, "Certainly, I wouldn't want to depend on using tenants by the entirety ownership for protection because of its vulnerability to death or divorce of the tenants. Thus, using the other strategies mentioned here is vital."

Take Advantage of Your State's Homestead Exemption Protection

After taking a bit of a break to eat lunch, Howard resumed our discussion by turning his attention to the homestead exemption.

"Many states have an exemption for your principal residence that protects the home from creditors. This is designed so that the kids and spouse aren't evicted. Each state has different rules. For example, Florida provides that the full value of the house is protected under their homestead rules. Massachusetts has a $300,000 exemption. Similarly, each state has different rules. However, under all rules a home can be foreclosed on by a bank if there is a signed mortgage by the owners. I have a list of state rules that I downloaded from Legalforms.com that you can use in your book." (We've reproduced the list in Appendix G.)

Set Up Trusts

I then asked Howard about trusts. "Howard, I have heard many asset protection attorneys recommend trusts, especially foreign trusts such as trusts located in the Isle of Man or the Cayman Islands because these jurisdictions have special rules about not enforcing foreign judgments. Moreover, it is supposedly much harder to find property and enforce judgments in certain foreign jurisdictions."

Howard disdainfully said, "Yes, a number of asset protection attorneys highly recommend setting up foreign trusts as a major form of protection. They charge enormous fees for this advice too. Here is the general rule: **if you can get to your money, so can your creditors**. Thus, revocable trusts won't work in any jurisdiction. Irrevocable trusts can work, but there is a real problem with foreign trusts that aren't mentioned by these attorneys. When funds are put abroad in the areas that most of these attorneys use, you, the transferor, have no control over what really happens. If someone steals your money, you are basically out of luck."

"Wait a minute, Howard," I said. "How often does this happen?"

Howard grimaced and said, "Sadly, it happens enough times to be a major worry. I personally know of two major foreign trustees that were used by a wide variety of asset protection lawyers who embezzled all of the proceeds. It is a very serious problem. This is why I am against using foreign trusts.

"Also, a number of attorneys are misrepresenting the use of these foreign jurisdictions by saying that 'these assets aren't reported to the government, and thus taxes can be avoided on the income earned.'

"Sadly again, nothing could be further from the truth. U.S. citizens and Canadians are taxed on their worldwide income! Thus, any income earned in these jurisdictions must be reported as earned and taxes have to be paid.

"Domestic irrevocable trusts in some states such as Nevada can be used for asset protection and can protect people almost as well as foreign trusts, and they provide a lot more protection against embezzlement. However, you can't have unlimited access to your money. There have to be some very strict limitations."

Use Corporations and Limited Liability Corporations

"Both corporations and limited liability corporations or companies (LLCs) can protect the owners personally against most lawsuits *except* those arising from malpractice and those initiated by the government. They also don't usually protect against lawsuits for fraud or lawsuits arising from criminal actions of the defendant. Thus, there are some limitations to the protections these entities offer.

"Of course, any assets owned by these entities can be gotten by creditors who have a judgment against the entity, which is why I recommend that real estate and other valuable assets are not owned by the corporation or LLC that is doing business. The better way is the following."

> **Have a separate entity (usually an LLC) own the assets, such as the real estate or expensive cars and equipment, and lease those assets to the corporation or entity actually conducting the business.**

"The problem with using corporations is that you usually must keep on top of them every year. This means that you should have annual board of directors' meetings and stockholder meetings, and you must keep corporate board meeting minutes. Fortunately, many states have small-corporation laws that allow for the elimination of these administrative hassles if there are very few stockholders and the corporation does limited amounts of gross income. You need to check with your attorney about this.

"In fact," Howard added, "it is so common for incorporated people to not comply with their corporate formalities that I have been recommending services that help them accomplish this yearly. There are a number of them among which is the firm Scott Barnett at barnettandassociates.com. Here are two other companies: Laughlin Associates, which can be found at Laughlinusa.com, and the Nevada Corporate Planners, which can be found at nvinc.com.

"I do want to elaborate on a concept that I mentioned above. There are some states that are particularly good for incorporating or setting up LLCs because of their protective statutes that prevent piercing the corporate veil. Nevada and Wyoming are particularly friendly for protecting owners from creditors who are trying to pierce the corporation and go after the owners personally.

"In those states, it is very rare for this to happen. California and New York, on the other hand, are particularly unfriendly to defendants when it comes to lawsuits. They allow lawsuits for almost anything, and they will allow piercing the corporate veil if people don't rigorously adhere to the corporate formalities. At least with LLCs, there are many fewer formalities, which is why I personally like them."

Howard summarized by saying, "Thus, by setting up a corporation in Nevada or Wyoming or some other jurisdictions, you get the best of both worlds: you get the benefit of entity protection and the benefit of being located in a jurisdiction that is unfriendly to plaintiffs bringing lawsuits."

Make Some Investments in Assets That Are Protected by Law

"I do want to mention that there are some assets that have an intrinsic protection against judgments as long as these assets aren't pledged to the judgment creditor. For example, this type of protected asset includes life insurance policies and life insurance cash values as well as all other insurance products such as annuities, although the protection is somewhat limited for annuities.

"A lot of lawyers have been recommending funding large single-premium cash value insurance policies or modified endowment policies exactly because of the protection that life insurance provides. Sadly, you can't get this kind of protection from buying life insurance policies once you are being sued or before a judgment is executed. Remember, judges are lawyers and so are most legislators. They love to protect us lawyers. Thus, there are *fraudulent conveyance laws* that prevent transfers of property in order to prevent collection of a judgment. If the insurance policies were bought before the lawsuit began, there will be no problem. If they were bought upon losing the lawsuit, the transfer to the insurance policy will probably be set aside by the court. Anywhere in between these times will be a question of fact for the judge."

I then added, "In Chapter 14, 'Estate Planning,' I recommend that all life insurance be owned by a trust. This should increase the protection from creditors, right?"

Howard nodded and said, "Yes, I completely agree with you."

Howard then continued, "The second type of assets that are protected from creditors are known as Employment Retirement Income Security Act plans, which are generally pension and profit sharing plans and 401(k) plans. As we saw in the O. J. Simpson trial, assets that Simpson had in his various pension plans were protected from the parents of Ronald Goldman. Also, his home was also protected from creditors because Florida provides a homestead exemption for the full value of the house."

Matt had a puzzled look on his face and asked, "How about IRAs? These aren't protected plans, right?"

Howard smiled at Matt's knowledge and said, "The problem with IRAs and Simplified Employee Pensions (SEPs) is that they aren't considered qualified plans that benefit from asset protection.[2] Creditors can get at them. I should note though, that if a person is in bankruptcy, SEPs are protected from bankruptcy creditors and IRAs have a $1 million protection from bankruptcy creditors. You need to be in bankruptcy to obtain these protections.[3] However, some states have statutes that protect IRA and SEP monies from creditors. States that I know offer full protection are Texas, Florida, Arizona, and Washington. It is vital that you check with an attorney in your state to see whether your state has protections for IRAs against creditors. Most states don't offer much in this regard."

Establish Family Limited Partnerships

"The final aspect of asset protection that I want to discuss is the establishment of family limited partnerships. In this type of limited partnership, the main wage earner and his or her spouse are the general partners, and the kids are the limited partners. The parents transfer their business and other assets into the partnership. The parents continue to make all decisions regarding the assets that were transferred since they are the managing general partners.

"There are two advantages to this setup. The first is that if there is a judgment against the parents, all the creditors can get is a *charging order*. This means that the creditors will be taxed on their share of the income without receiving any money. They can't foreclose on the partnership property or get any of the property. Second, for estate taxes, the general partnership interest has a much lower value than if it were owned directly. This will significantly reduce the value for estate tax purposes of all of the assets that were transferred to the partnership. It is a win-win for the whole family.

"Obviously, this is a sophisticated technique that requires the services of a good lawyer who understands how to properly set this up."

"Okay, Howard, I think this concludes our discussion. Are there any final remarks that you want to pass on to our readers?"

Immediately Howard said, "Folks can spend a fortune setting up all kinds of entities. However, in my opinion, the best liability protection involves taking the following actions."

- Get general liability insurance, a big umbrella policy of at least $3 million to $5 million, as well as business insurance (if you have a business) and malpractice insurance. No single strategy beats this.
- Use common sense in everyday life. Simple lifestyle changes can significantly reduce any liability exposure.
- If you do have significant liability exposure due to owning rental property or having a business, consider setting up an LLC or a corporation for each business or property.

"Just undertaking those three simple steps will probably reduce most personal liability exposure by at least 98 percent or more."

Matt and I thanked Howard for his time. He certainly gave us a lot of good information.

A Review of What You Have Learned

Here is a summary of the notes we took on asset protection.

- Lawsuits are very common, and they are one of the greatest killers of wealth. Thus, most people should understand this and plan to protect their assets. This is particularly true for people who own rental property or have a business with employees.
- The best way to protect against lawsuits is to have good insurance. This involves general liability insurance, a $3 million to $5 million liability umbrella policy, business insurance (if you have a business), and possibly malpractice insurance.
- Use common sense in life such as never taking your eyes off the road, getting a taxi to drive you if your driving ability is impaired, and watching what you say about people.
- If you have either a business or significant assets, get a prenuptial agreement in which there is full disclosure of assets and income. Make sure it is signed by a separate attorney representing each party.
- In some states, owning property jointly with a husband and wife qualifies as tenants by the entirety. If you live in such a state, this type of ownership will protect your assets as long as you stay together and one of the joint tenants doesn't die.
- Some states, particularly Florida and Texas, have a homestead exemption that exempts part or all of your entire home from creditors. This doesn't work for banks that have a mortgage on your home. (Check Appendix G to see what the rules are for each state.)
- Irrevocable trusts can be good for asset protection. However, if you can get the money out of the trust, so can creditors.
- Watch out for foreign trusts. They can be great for asset protection, but there is a substantial risk that the out-of-country trustee will embezzle the funds.

- If you have any significant liability such as owning real estate or have a business with employees, consider setting up either a corporation or a limited liability company for each entity or property owned.
- Both life insurance cash values and qualified pension and profit-sharing plans are exempt from creditors. This includes 401(k)s, profit sharing plans, and money purchase pension plans. However, IRAs and SEPs may not be exempt from creditors unless the debtor is in bankruptcy. Even then, IRAs only get a maximum protection of $1 million. For other creditors outside of bankruptcy, it depends on state law as to whether your IRA or SEP is protected from creditors. Check with an attorney in your state about this.
- Consider a family limited partnership to help make your assets "judgment proof" and to save on estate taxes. Use a knowledgeable lawyer to set this up.

Notes

1. http://www.ermunro.com/2011/11/your-chances-of-getting-sued/.
2. http://www.ecrllc.com/safequalifiedplans.asp. See also http://www.wmww.com/articles/76-protecting-your-retirement-assets. See also https://www.chase.com/index.jsp?pg_name=ccpmapp/smallbusiness/retiring_investing/page/bb_sep_ira.
3. http://files.ali-aba.org/thumbs/datastorage/lacidoirep/articles/PTXL0802-Altier-Naegele_thumb.pdf.

17

Alternative Housing for the Elderly

Someone has said that the best nursing
home is the U.S. Senate.
> —**Ernest F. Hollings**

Be nice to your kids. They will choose
your nursing home.
> —**Anonymous**

What You Will Learn
- Types of retirement communities
- Questions used to evaluate senior retirement communities and independent-living facilities
- Questions used to evaluate assisted-living facilities and nursing homes

Lori's and my parents are aging, so we thought we would investigate alternative housing for them. Bernie specializes in making housing recommendations for the elderly, and he also provides support services and testing. He is a friendly guy who had impressed Lori with his understanding of the needs of the elderly. We thought he would be the perfect person to interview.

We met in his office in Fort Lauderdale, Florida, for this conference—after all, what better place to find out about housing for the elderly than Florida.

Types of Retirement Communities

After some preliminary chitchat and after introducing Bernie to my wife, Lori, and my son, Matt, Bernie began: "This whole area of housing for the elderly has really taken off in the past 20 years. With people living longer and the huge number of baby boomers who have elderly parents, this information is becoming really crucial.

"There are four basic types of alternative housing situations for the elderly: senior retirement communities, independent-living facilities, assisted-living facilities, and nursing homes."

Senior Retirement Communities

"A *senior retirement community* is the type of alternative housing situation that your dad lives in, Sandy. This type of housing is akin to a country club for seniors. Residents have tennis courts, a clubhouse, and many clubs, all of which offer diverse social and athletic activities. People can eat out anywhere they want, or they can eat in the restaurant located on the premises of the community. The community even takes care of the outside of the residents' home, including their lawn.

"Although you normally need to be at least age 55 to buy a home in these communities, your lifestyle is very similar to what it would be if you were living in your own private home."

I interjected, "Yes, my dad has a fabulous lifestyle that I truly envy. I told him that I want to move there when I retire. Even better, at the older ages, women outnumber guys by at least 2 to 1.[1] My dad is chased by all the ladies," which made Bernie and Matt smile but made my wife frown a bit.

Bernie went on, "However, the first drawback in this type of housing situation is that there are few, if any, support services. This housing is designed for retirees who can live a fully independent life without aid.

"The second drawback is that these clubs and events, as well as all of the maintenance services, aren't cheap. They will run about $900 per month, which will be billed to the residents as *homeowners dues*."

Matt then asked me if he could have my house. He loves my current home and wants to live in it.

I just grumbled a bit and said, "Well, if you can cut a deal with your two siblings and pay me off, I am sure some arrangement can be made if and when I move away."

Independent-Living Facilities

After we all laughed about this, Bernie then said, "The second type of alternative housing situation is known as an *independent-living facility*. Here people rent apartments in buildings. The apartments are very nice. These facilities are made up of mostly apartments that can have one, two, and even three bedrooms, and they might even include utilities as part of the maintenance fee.

"These facilities usually provide at least two to three meals a day for the occupants of the building, so the residents don't have to cook or drive somewhere to eat out. The facilities also usually have a maid clean the apartment once per week, and they have laundry services available for an extra fee."

I teased Bernie, "Another example of everything is free for a small fee," which made everyone chuckle.

"They also usually have nurses on the premises and doctors who are on call. In addition, they usually provide some transportation arrangements for shopping, theater, doctors' appointments, and other similar needs. They have many social events akin to the other types of retirement communities; however, these events are usually fewer in number.

"As you can see, being a resident in an independent-living facility is a lot like living in his or her own home except that there are more support services for those who might need them. In addition, many facilities have monitors in the apartments so that if, for example, the residents do not open their doors at least once by some set time, the facility will check up on them. Thus, if a resident falls or is incapacitated, the facility will send someone to check on the resident so that he or she won't be lying helplessly like a dog on the floor for days.

"The problem with independent-living facilities is that they are not as regulated by either the states or federal government as nursing homes are. Thus, you really need to check these out for yourself."

Lori interrupted by saying, "Yes, my parents are in this type of facility. They love it. Moreover, the total charge is only $2,800 a month, which includes all meals. In fact, I ate there and found the meals to be quite good. They can also have as much as they want to eat."

Since Bernie had found this facility for Lori's parents, he was well aware of it. He thus added, "They also have an assisted-living facility as part of the building for residents who need that much attention, which brings us to our discussion of these facilities."

Assisted-Living Facilities

"*Assisted-living facilities* provide more intensive services than do independent-living facilities. They also provide all meals and laundry services.

"Many of these facilities have an optional lockdown feature for those residents who need it, which prevents the residents from leaving on their own. This is important for those residents with dementia. These facilities also provide around-the-clock nursing assistance, although not as focused as one would expect in a hospital.

"These facilities, as do the independent-living facilities, provide some set doctors' hours, which residents can use for a fee.

"A key difference between these facilities and nursing homes is that most residents in assisted-living facilities are ambulatory. They can walk, and they are usually not bedridden."

Nursing Homes

"The final type of facility is a *nursing home,* of which there are basically two types. In a *skilled nursing care facility,* residents are under the 24-hour care of licensed or registered nursing staff. In an *intermediate nursing care facility,* residents are under the 24-hour care of certified nursing assistants (CNAs).

"Some examples of the reasons that seniors might need 24-hour nursing care are if they were bedbound, if they needed a respirator, or if they had wounds that were not healing and required daily care. Nursing home residents require even more intensive care than do assisted-living facility residents, who are usually ambulatory."

Questions Used to Evaluate Senior Retirement Communities, Independent-Living Facilities, and Assisted-Living Facilities

I then inquired, "Bernie, how does one check out these senior retirement communities, independent-living facilities, and assisted-living facilities?"

Bernie quickly responded, "Sandy, that is the $64,000 question.

"Here are some of things you should ask and/or check in order to evaluate these alternative housing situations for the elderly. Also, you might want to ask many of the questions in the list that follows this one, which is geared to nursing home comparisons, as well. And, conversely, some of the questions below would be helpful to ask in evaluating nursing homes too."[2]

- Does the facility have set hours for nurses' and doctors' visits?
- Does the facility work with a hospice organization in case residents need more intensive care?
- Can prospective residents try it for a while and check out the apartments and food?
- Is there any affiliation with a known company or religion? What is the full extent of the affiliation? The facility might be using only the name.

- Can prospective residents review the financial statements of the facility to see if it has adequate funding? This review could be made by an accountant or an eldercare expert.
- Is cancellation an option, and are refunds available for unused services?
- Under what conditions can fees be increased, and by how much? What notification of increases is given yearly?
- Does the facility ask prospective residents to waive their liability rights? Residents should *never* waive their liability rights.
- What are the policies for transfer to nursing homes or other care facilities?
- What are the rights of the residents in voting for changes in the facility or changes in the rules?
- What types of meals are provided?
- What is the emergency response time for ambulances?
- What type of housekeeping is available?
- What types of recreational activities and events are available? Prospective residents should check out the facility's monthly social calendar.
- Is transportation provided for community activities?
- Are pets allowed?
- Is there a specific religious orientation? If so, are services held on the facility's premises?
- Can the facility cater to special dietary needs for medical conditions such as diabetes? Can the facility accommodate religious or cultural preferences such as for kosher or vegetarian diets?
- Who are counted as staff for purposes of establishing the patient-to-staff ratio? Are gardeners and accountants counted as staff?
- What kind of improvement goals is the facility working on?
- What kind of progress is the facility making on meeting these goals?
- What social activities occur at the facility such as bingo?
- What procedures are in place to avoid theft of residents' belongings?
- Is there any form of monitoring to alert the facility staff if a resident becomes incapacitated?
- What are the smoking policies?
- Can prospective residents obtain copies of any fee schedules?
- What is your first impression of the facility?
- What is the condition of the facility's exterior paint, gutters, and trim?
- Are the grounds well-kept?

- Do you like the view from the residents' rooms?
- Is there an appropriate area for physical therapy and occupational therapy?
- Are beauty and barber shop facilities available?
- Is there a well-ventilated room for smokers?
- Does the administration know the residents by name?
- Do staff and residents communicate with cheerful attitudes?
- How good is the facility's record for employee retention?
- What method is used to select roommates?
- What is a typical day like?
- Can residents choose what time to go to bed and wake up?
- What is the level of participation in activities?
- Are meaningful activities available that are appropriate for residents?
- Does the facility provide transportation for community outings and activities?
- Is a van or bus with wheelchair access available?
- Do residents on Medicaid get mental health services as well as occupational, speech, or physical therapies if needed?
- Does each resident have the same nursing assistant most of the time?
- How does a resident with problems voice complaints?
- What is your impression of the general cleanliness and grooming of residents?
- Are meals appetizing and served promptly?
- Are snacks available between meals?
- How convenient is the facility's location to family members?
- Are there areas other than the resident's room where family members can visit?
- Does the facility have safe, well-lighted convenient parking?
- Are there suitable area restaurants nearby for family members to take residents out for meals?

Bernie summarized, "These are questions that I would ask and check out before signing any independent-living contract."

Questions Used to Evaluate Nursing Homes

"With regard to nursing homes, Medicare actually rates these and gives other great information about them. You can access these ratings at Medicare's website Nursing Home Compare (www.medicare.gov/nhcompare). You should always check out what Medicare says about any facility you are considering. You should also check the evaluations made and reported by the Joint Commission (www.jointcommission.org), formerly the Joint Commission on Accreditation of Hospitals (JCAH).

"Here are some questions that I would recommend asking when you investigate nursing homes; many of these would apply to assisted-living facilities as well. Some of these questions came right from Medicare's website too."

- Can prospective residents talk to some family members of current residents? There are usually people who are visiting at any given time.
- Can the residents decorate their own rooms?
- Can the residents choose what time to get up, go to sleep, and bathe?
- Can the residents get food and drinks anytime? What if they don't like the food?
- Can residents have visitors anytime?
- Is there enough staff for the residents to get the care that they need?
- How is the staff-to-bed ratio given to Medicare computed? For example, are gardeners and accountants included as staff for this computation?
- Can residents use their own doctors? Are doctors regularly on call for the nursing home?
- Is the facility Medicare certified?
- What is the Medicare rating?
- Does the nursing home report show any quality care problems? You should always check out the report written by Medicare.
- What does Medicare say about this facility? See www.medicare.gov/nhcompare.
- What kind of improvement goals is the nursing home working on?
- What kind of progress is the nursing home making on these goals?
- Is the nursing home close to family and friends so they can visit often?
- What does the Joint Commission (www.jointcommission.org), formerly the Joint Commission on Accreditation of Hospitals (JCAH), evaluation say about the nursing home in terms of its quality of care?
- When will a bed be available?
- Will the same staff members take care of a resident most of the time, or do they change from day to day? What is the staff turnover rate?

- Do the *certified nursing assistants* (CNAs) work on shifts of reasonable lengths of time, or are the shifts too long? Are the CNAs available day and night and during meals?
- Is there a social worker or eldercare expert available? If so, can prospective residents meet them?
- What social activities, such as bingo, occur at the nursing home?
- Does the nursing home offer the applicable religious and cultural support that residents might need?
- Does the nursing home cater to any special dietary needs?
- Is the prospective resident's primary language spoken at the nursing home? If not, how will the staff understand the resident?
- Does the nursing home provide a safe environment?
- Is there a guard at the door at all times?
- Is the nursing home locked at night?
- What procedures are in place to avoid theft of the residents' belongings and clothing?
- Are personal monitoring devices available in case the resident becomes confused?
- What are the smoking policies?
- Can prospective residents obtain a copy of the fee schedule? Are there any extra charges not listed?
- What is your first impression of the nursing home?
- What is the condition of the nursing home's exterior paint, gutters, and trim?
- Are the grounds well-kept?
- Do you like the view from the residents' rooms?
- Is there an appropriate area for physical therapy and occupational therapy?
- Are beauty and barber shop facilities available?
- Is there a well-ventilated room for smokers?
- Does the administration know the residents by name?
- Do staff and residents communicate with cheerful attitudes?
- How good is the nursing home record for employee retention?
- What method is used to select roommates?
- What is a typical day like?
- Can residents choose what time to go to bed and wake up?
- What is the level of participation in activities?
- Are meaningful activities available that are appropriate for residents?
- Does the home provide transportation for community outings and activities?

- Is a van or bus with wheelchair access available?
- Do residents on Medicaid get mental health services as well as occupational, speech, or physical therapies if needed?
- Does each resident have the same nursing assistant most of the time?
- How does a resident with problems voice complaints?
- What is your impression of the general cleanliness and grooming of residents?
- Are meals appetizing and served promptly?
- Are snacks available between meals?
- How convenient is the nursing home's location to family members?
- Are there areas other than the resident's room where family members can visit?
- Does the facility have safe, well-lighted convenient parking?
- Are there suitable area restaurants nearby for family members to take residents out for meals?

Bernie ended with, "These are the questions that I use to evaluate various eldercare facilities. I think that if your readers use these as checklists, it will be much easier for them to compare alternative housing situations for elderly people. In addition, there will be many more happy residents."

We thanked Bernie for his wonderful reference material. It will certainly be helpful to us and helpful to you, our wonderful readers.

A Review of What You Have Learned

Here is a summary of our notes.

- The need to know about eldercare facilities is growing as the population gets older. We are living longer, which means that there will be more demand for these facilities.
- There are four major types of eldercare facilities:
  - **Senior retirement communities:** These are similar to living at home, and there are lots of social events. They provide a small number of support services.
  - **Independent-living facilities:** These are much like senior retirement communities, but they usually have fewer events. They also provide meals and laundry services.
  - **Assisted-living facilities:** Depending on the extent of need, these facilities provide around-the-clock care, some social events, and access to doctors and nurses. Many have optional lockdown capabilities to prevent residents with dementia from leaving.
  - **Nursing homes:** These facilities normally provide a relatively high level of skilled nursing care. Many of their residents are mostly bedridden.

- If you are looking at senior retirement communities, independent-living facilities, and assisted-living facilities, use the questions provided in this chapter to evaluate and compare them. Remember, some of these facilities aren't well regulated.
- If you are looking at assisted-living facilities and nursing homes, look into what Medicare says about them because Medicare actually rates these facilities, and it can give you other great information about them too. You can access these ratings at Medicare's website Nursing Home Compare (www.medicare.gov/nhcompare). You should also check the evaluations made and reported by the Joint Commission (www.jointcommission.org), formerly the Joint Commission on Accreditation of Hospitals (JCAH). Also, use the questions provided in this chapter to evaluate and compare them.

Notes

1. http://www.census.gov/prod/cen2010/briefs/c2010br-03.pdf.
2. http://www.medicare.gov/nursing/checklist.asp. See also http://www.ourparents.com/articles/nursing_home_visit_check_list and http://www.nawrockilaw.com/CM/Custom/NursingHomeEvaluationForm.pdf.

18

Evaluating a Financial Planner

The quickest way to double your money is to hold it up in front of a mirror.

—Anonymous

> **What You Will Learn**
> - Types of designations found among financial services professionals
> - Questions used to evaluate a financial planning firm

There are lots of financial planners in the United States. Moreover, most of them aren't very well regulated. In fact, anyone can call himself or herself a financial planner. Thus, Matt and I wanted to give our readers some criteria that they can use to evaluate planners and separate the "wheat from the chaff." We decided to go back to Steve, who is our elder law expert. If anyone could give an independent opinion about this, he would be the one.

We took Steve up on his kind offer to help us, and we met him back in his office. This time, he had a tray of cookies and some fresh Starbucks coffee ready. Who said southern hospitality is dead!

I started in by telling Steve, "As I told you on the phone, we are looking for criteria that our readers can use to evaluate financial planners because anyone can give himself or herself that designation."

Types of Designations Found Among Financial Services Professionals

Steve chuckled a bit and said, "Sandy, you are partially right about this. However, there are some regulations financial services professionals must comply with. First, many of these people are licensed in securities and insurance and other disciplines. This provides some regulation and comfort for clients. Moreover, there is a large number of designations that supposedly provide some standards of competence.

"However, the sad fact is that not all earned designations are equal in terms of indicating the extent of a person's knowledge. Thus, I want to discuss the various designations that some planners have obtained and their relevance to their clients."

"Yes, Steve, I like your idea. Let's do that."

At that point, Steve gave me the following chart that he had prepared before we arrived:

- **Certified Financial Planner (CFP):** This is probably the gold standard in the field. Planners have to take a very tough exam on over 75 topics. It shows a broad familiarity with the financial planning field. It also requires three years of relevant work experience.[1] There are strict ethical requirements that accompany this designation, which are similar to the requirements for CPAs.
- **Chartered Financial Consultant (ChFC):** The requirements for this certification are to take eight courses and have three years of work experience and to pass a test. It is designed primarily for insurance agents. It isn't a bad designation, but it isn't as highly regarded as the CFP. Sadly, I believe that there is no complaint or disciplinary process for people who have this certification.
- **Certified Public Accountant (CPA):** This is the hardest designation to get among all those noted. However, the test doesn't cover many things relevant to financial planning with the exception of taxation. However, as mentioned below, planners who have a CPA background in addition to other certifications are usually well qualified.
- **Personal Financial Specialist (PFS):** This is a special designation that only active CPAs can get. It requires a CPA license and 80 hours of specific financial planning training and a test unless you already passed the CFP or ChFC exams.[2] These advisors also are required to take a lot of continuing education as part of maintaining their CPA license. It is certainly not a bad designation.
- **Chartered Life Underwriter (CLU):** This is a designation that insurance agents can get that shows that they have studied certain

insurance-related topics in depth. They take eight courses, and they must pass a final exam in each one.[3] It probably is the gold standard for insurance agent training. This certification is particularly important because agents are usually given very little financial and insurance training. This certification ensures that they do have a comprehensive knowledge of the field; however, there is no complaint or disciplinary process for people who have this designation.

- **Accredited Estate Planner (AEP):** Generally this is available only to attorneys, CPAs, ChFCs, CLUs, and CTFAs (Certified Trust and Financial Advisor).[4] Accredited estate planners have to be professionally engaged in estate planning, they must have five years of relevant experience, and they must commit to upholding the ethical standards promulgated by the National Association of Estate Planners and Counsels. In addition, AEPs must take a few courses or have at least five years of experience in estate planning. They can waive out of the educational requirements if they have 15 years of experience in one of the professional disciplines shown above.

- **Chartered Financial Analyst (CFA):** This designation requires the person to pass three exams and normally takes between 18 months to four years to complete the program.[5] It is designed for folks who specialize in investment and portfolio analysis. This designation will be common among hedge fund and mutual fund managers.

"Wow," I said, "I didn't realize that there were so many designations that can be earned by financial planners. My questions then are which of these do you feel are the best, and what would you look for in a planner? Those are the $64,000 questions."

Questions Used to Evaluate a Financial Planning Firm

Steve paused a bit to give this a thoughtful answer. "Most financial planners come from four fields before they become planners. These fields are insurance, accounting, stocks and bonds, and law. The designations that they have will give a clue as to their original field. For example, a CLU or ChFC was probably an insurance agent. A CFA might have been a stockbroker.

"I am going to make a comment that stereotypes people, and it's a comment that usually gets me into trouble," Steve said. "However, I have found that many planners whose original fields were either insurance or stocks and bonds brokerage tend to be sales oriented. Some of them focus on commissions more than other types of planners do."

Steve continued, "Accordingly, I would recommend a planner who is either a CPA or an attorney who also has other designations such as a CFP. Attorneys and CPAs tend to be more fee oriented and less commission driven than stockbrokers and insurance agents."

I then inquired, "Steve, you would therefore recommend an attorney or CPA who has a CFP as being the best qualified to help people with their financial planning?"

Steve quickly responded, "I wouldn't be that limiting. To me, the more training, the better, which might be evidenced by multiple designations. I do recommend, however, that as far as designations go, I want to see at least an attorney and/or CPA and a CFP. If an advisor also has a PFS or even a CLU designation too, that would be even better.

"However, the designations alone aren't the only characteristics that are important. There are other questions that I would ask potential financial planners, as follows."

- What experience do you have? (*The answer should include the years of practice and the number of companies associated with.*)
- What type of work experience have you had in the past?
- What are your qualifications? (*Again, you want a CPA-CFP or CPA-PFS or CPA-ChFC or CPA-CLU or attorney-CFP. The reason is that you want a planner with experience and training in several fields such as insurance, taxes, and estate planning. There is no question that planners who only deal with one area primarily shouldn't be called financial planners. The more areas that they know well, the better the service they can provide their clients.*)
- What is your approach to financial planning? (*For example, ask what type of clients that the planner works with. Make sure that the planner's viewpoint isn't too conservative or aggressive for you. Some planners also require that their clients have a certain net worth. You might as well find out now if they will take you as a client.*)
- What services do you offer? (*For example, does the planner offer tax planning assistance, estate planning, or both?*)
- Are your charges primarily fee based, commission based, or both?
- Will you be the only person working with me? (*If not, you may want to meet the other people who will be working with you.*)
- Do you work with outside professionals? (*If so, get their names.*)
- Do you have a written agreement as to how I will pay for your services?
- Are your fees based on a flat rate, or are they based on a percentage of the commissions paid by third parties from products you sell to me, or are they based on a combination of fees and commissions? (*I don't*

object to commissions since many products, such as insurance, are commission based. However, I want a planner whose practice is mostly fee based and who recommends products that have low commissions.)

- How much do you typically charge for a full financial plan and other services? *(The planner should provide an estimate of the hourly charges and hours needed to prepare the plan. Also an estimate of the commissions the planner will receive would be nice, although that might be hard to estimate because the commissions depend on the types of investments the client makes.)*

- Have you ever been publically disciplined for any unlawful or unethical behavior in your professional career? Are you under current investigation for unethical actions? *(The state insurance commission, the Certified Financial Planner Board of Standards [CFP Board], and the Financial Industry Regulatory Authority [FINRA] all have records on the disciplinary history of member planners.)*

- Do you have written agreements that detail the services that will be rendered? *(Be sure to obtain this agreement and store it with your permanent files.)*

- Do you give yearly financial statements, and do you give assistance with tax return preparation?

- Have you written any books or professional articles? *(Ask to see copies of these items.)*

"Finally, although I do recommend that only one planner keep tabs on all investments so that the planner can make sure that the client's portfolio is diversified, I would avoid the Bernie Madoff problems. This means that clients should *not* put more than 10 percent of their investable assets or $500,000, whichever is greater, with any one custodian, especially if that custodian is under the control or direction of the planner."

"Steve, both Matt and I want to thank you for your wonderful, incisive suggestions. I would bet that much of this information wouldn't occur to most people. This really does give people a track to use for finding a good planner."

Steve then suggested, "Okay, let's review what we have learned."

A Review of What You Have Learned
- Anyone can call themselves financial planners. Having the right designations can be very beneficial.

- The gold standard for financial planners would be the CFP exam. Ideally you want someone with a combination of credentials such as CPA-ChFC, CPA-CLU, or attorney-CFP.
- Generally, financial planners come from one of four fields: accounting, stock brokerage, insurance sales, or law. Those who come from either an accounting background or legal background tend to be more fee oriented and less commission oriented. Those who come out of stock brokerage or insurance sales backgrounds tend to be more commission oriented. However, both of these situations aren't always the case. The key, regardless of the planner's initial background, is that they have acquired a lot of knowledge of all aspects of the financial planning fields, which include knowledge of insurance, investment planning, and securities, and they can provide rudimentary accounting services such as yearly financial statements. If they also do tax returns, even better.
- You should always ask the planner the questions recommended in this chapter about their experience, qualifications, services provided, and fees as well as whether they have ever been disciplined by any organization or are under any current investigation that they are aware of.
- Don't forget the anti-Madoff rule: don't put more than the greater of $500,000 or 10 percent of your portfolio with anyone custodian or investment manager.

Notes

1. http://www.cfp.net/downloads/CFPBoard_Principal_Topics.pdf and http://www.cfp.net/become/experience.asp#standards.
2. http://www.aicpa.org/InterestAreas/PersonalFinancialPlanning/Membership/Pages/Personal%20Financial%20Specialist%20Application.aspx.
3. http://www.theamericancollege.edu/insurance-education/clu-insurance-specialty.
4. http://www.naepc.org/AEP_qualifications2.pdf.
5. http://www.cfainstitute.org/cfaprogram/process/enter/Pages/completing_the_cfa_program.aspx.

Appendix A

Comparison Chart for College Savings Plans

Highlights	Prepaid Tuition Plan	529 Savings Plan
Overview	Guaranteed to pay tuition	State-sponsored fund
Offered by	States	Financial institutions
Contribution limits	Depends on plan and state	$100,000–$300,000
Tax free for	Qualified tuition	Qualified expenses (tuition, fees, room and board, computer, and Internet)
Tax deductibility	Some states allow to be fully or partly deductible for state taxes	Some states allow to be fully or partly deductible for state taxes
Investment flexibility	None; account controlled by the state	Professional management
Use of tax credits	Tax credits can be used as long as they are not on the same expenses also covered by any qualified tuition plan	Tax credits can be used as long as they are not on the same expenses also covered by any qualified tuition plan

Highlights	Prepaid Tuition Plan	529 Savings Plan
Effect on financial aid	Student's resources	Based on owner's resources
Assignability	Immediate family, cousins, ancestors, descendants, step-relatives, and in-laws	Immediate family, cousins, ancestors, descendants, step-relatives, and in-laws
Penalties for qualified withdrawals	10%	10%

Appendix B

Getting In-State Tuition Rates for Out-of-State Students

Here is a report that I wrote for my newsletter and Taxbot subscribers.

Pssst. Pass it on. There are a number of ways that you can get in-state tuition rates for your out-of-state kid. Many colleges don't want you to know this because they can charge from double to four times what a resident student pays. With today's high state deficits, this information is, therefore, kept very quiet until now!

Interestingly, there are several ways to accomplish this. All you need to do is to meet any of these special circumstances, and you can substantially reduce your tuition for that out-of-state, state university.

Academic Common Markets

One of the best ways to obtain in-state rates for nonresident students is through what is known as the *academic common market* (ACM). Most states quietly offer in-state tuition to students from their regional ACM member states who attend certain universities *if* the major that the students want is not available in their home state. Thus, if a student wants to study, say, animation or digital arts or some other specialized major, and this major isn't provided at one of the universities located in the home state, the student can attend a state university located in another state with a reciprocity agreement and receive in-state tuition rates. Thus, the ACM is a form of reciprocity agreement among states.

The student would have to first be accepted at the school before he or she could apply for reduced tuition rates.

There are four regional programs in which students can participate:

- **New England Board of Higher Education (NEBHE):** This includes Connecticut, Maine, Massachusetts, New Hampshire, Rhode Island, and Vermont. The board can be reached by calling 617-357-9620.
- **Midwestern Higher Education Compact (MHEC):** This includes Kansas, Michigan, Minnesota, Missouri, Nebraska, and North Dakota. The compact can be reached by calling 612-626-1602.
- **Western Interstate Commission for Higher Education (WICHE):** This includes most of the western states: Alaska, Arizona, California, Colorado, Idaho, Montana, Nevada, New Mexico, North Dakota, Oregon, South Dakota, Utah, Washington, and Wyoming. (Yes, North Dakota belongs to two associations, and it is the only state that does.) It also includes Hawaii. The commission can be reached by calling 303.541.0200.
- **Southern Regional Education Board (SREB) Academic Common Market:** This includes Alabama, Arkansas, Delaware, Florida, Georgia, Kentucky, Louisiana, Maryland, Mississippi, North Carolina, Oklahoma, South Carolina, Tennessee, Texas, Virginia, and West Virginia. The board can be reached by calling 404-875-9211.

Friendly Neighbor Policies

Many states have reciprocity agreements with neighboring states that give residents of a bordering state the right to obtain in-state tuition for their state. For example, students who live in northern Kentucky near Ohio can obtain in-state tuition rates at the University of Cincinnati. However, there are sometimes limitations. Many times students have to either live in certain counties or live within 150 miles of the schools that they want to attend.

Becoming a Resident Before Attending the School

Many states will allow in-state tuition rates if the student becomes a state resident at least one year before starting the school or if he or she lives with a spouse, parent, or guardian who is already a state resident for at least one year before the student starts school.

Example 1. Mary, a Maryland resident, wants to attend school in Nevada where her grandparents have lived for many years. If Mary moves in with her grandparents and she claims that they are her temporary guardians, Mary should be able to obtain in-state tuition rates.

Example 2. Kenny moves to California and obtains a job for one year. He establishes California residency by transferring both his voter registration and driver's license to California, and he files California tax returns. If he subsequently applies to a state university in California, he will be considered a state resident for tuition purposes.

Sandy's elaboration. If your parent, spouse, or guardian relocates to the state that you are now a student in, you may be able to claim residency status immediately. Check with your school to see if it has this rule in place. Moreover, having a child or parent moving to the state and establishing residency before actually applying to the school can save between $10,000 and $20,000 per year based on the difference between in-state and out-of-state tuition rates. This is like earning an extra salary of $17,000 to $28,000 per year!

Military Personnel

If you are in the military or have a parent in the military, there are two major benefits for you besides receiving educational benefits as a veteran.

First, you can declare any state to be your state of domicile and get in-state rates for either you or your dependents.

Second, if you are a veteran who was honorably discharged after 9/11/2001 and you have received either a purple heart or a combat badge, which indicates that you were in combat at some time during your tour, some state universities will give you in-state tuition rates even if you were previously domiciled elsewhere.

You will need to call the school to see if it honors this policy.

Independent Status

Once students have been at a college for one year, they can usually apply for a change in resident status. To obtain this, however, they will need to show that they are *independent of their parents*. Thus, they will need to change their voter registration and driver's license, and they will need to file their tax returns for the state in which they attend school.

In addition, they will have to show that all of the expenses for tuition and room and board were paid by the students themselves out of the students' own funds! Students can accomplish this either by working or with proper planning, by having sufficient assets in their own names. They can also borrow all the funds necessary and then pay all of their expenses out of their own accounts.

Finally, the parents will have to stop taking the students as dependents on the parents' tax returns.

Example 3. Chris had $50,000 of funds that had been placed in his name over the past 10 years by his grandparents to pay for his college education. If his parents don't claim him as a dependent during the first year of college and Chris pays for all of his tuition, rent, food, and books out of his own account with his own money, and he also establishes other indicia of his being a state resident (such as changing his voter registration and driver's license and filing state tax returns for the school's state), he can probably establish his independent status and state residency to obtain the in-state tuition rate.

For independent status, the money would need to be in the students' accounts for at least four months before they enrolled in the schools. The schools will ask for bank records in order to check on this. The schools will also want canceled checks and other proof that the students paid all of their own expenses throughout the year.

Students can also establish independent status using funds obtained from financial aid and working. Thus, if possible, students should have any aid paid to them given to them personally. Students would then deposit those funds in their own accounts, and then they would write their own checks to the college for the tuition and fees. (Working can also provide funds to cover any gaps between the financial aid and the costs of attending the college.)

Sandy's elaboration. Putting money in a kid's name can have some undesirable consequences. For financial aid purposes, any funds or investments in the kid's name (other than assets located in insurance products such as cash value insurance and annuities) are counted more heavily than those same assets owned by the parents. Thus, if you are considering a private school for your kid's college education, keeping assets in your own name would be the better choice. However, if it is probable that your kid will attend an out-of-state university, the technique of establishing independent status can work very well.

In Short

There are a number of ways you can obtain in-state tuition rates for an out-of-state student. You will need to become familiar with the state's rules regarding this, and you will need proper advanced planning. However, with proper planning, you can save a bundle and make your life much less taxing.

Always remember, $1 saved is akin to almost $2 earned because you don't pay taxes on the dollars saved!

Appendix C

Comparison Chart for Term Versus Permanent Insurance

Term	Permanent
Insurance and not investment	Forced savings because folks won't save
Can buy more insurance when you need it and less when you are older. If annual renewable term, premium goes up each year.	Expensive but locks in premium for life
Pay forever until canceled	At some time, cash value can pay premium
Commissions lower than for permanent insurance	Usually very high commissions and cost

Appendix D

Normal Retirement Ages

Year of Birth	Retirement Age for Receiving Full Benefits
Before 1938	65 years
1938	65 years and 2 months
1939	65 years and 4 months
1940	65 years and 6 months
1941	65 years and 8 months
1942	65 years and 10 months
1943–1954	66 years
1955	66 years 2 months
1956	66 years 4 months
1957	66 and 6 months
1958	66 and 8 months
1959	66 and 10 months
1960 or later	67 years

Appendix E

Benefit Reductions When Beneficiaries Retire Before Their Full Retirement Age and Take Benefits at Earliest Age Possible

Year of Birth	Percentage of Benefits Reduction
1938	20.8
1939	21.7
1940	22.5
1941	23.3
1942	24.2
1943–1954	25.0
1955	25.8
1956	26.7
1957	27.5
1958	28.3
1959	29.2
1960 or later	30.0

Appendix F

Yearly Benefit Rate Increases When Beneficiaries Retire After Their Full Retirement Age up to Age 70

Year of Birth	Yearly Percentage Rate of Increase
1933–1934	5.5
1935–1936	6.0
1937–1938	6.5
1939–1940	7.0
1941–1942	7.5
1943 or later	8.0

Appendix G

State Rules Providing Homestead Exemption Protection for Your Home

The laws cited below are for your general information only. You should check the state codes for the most current versions. All amounts are stated in general terms; again, you should check with the state's codes to verify the exact amounts and variations.

Alabama: Up to $5,000 in value, or up to 160 acres in area. Code of Alabama, §6-10-2.

Alaska: Up to $64,800 in value, and no area limitation. Alaska Statutes, §09.39.010.

Arizona: Up to $100,000 in value, and no area limitation. Arizona Revised Statutes, §33-1101.

Arkansas: Up to $2,500 in value, or at least one-quarter acre for city homesteads or 80 acres for rural homesteads. Arkansas Code, §§16- 66-210, and 218; Arkansas Constitution Article 9.

California: Up to $50,000 in value. California Code, Annotated, §704.730.

Colorado: Up to $45,000 in value, and no area limitation. Colorado Revised Statutes, Annotated, §38-41-201.

Connecticut: Under the Connecticut exemption system, homeowners may exempt up to $75,000 of their home or other property covered by the homestead exemption. Married people who own property jointly get a $150,000 homestead exemption. In addition, the homestead exemption is

$125,000 if you are trying to protect your home against a money judgment from a hospital bill. Connecticut General Statutes, Annotated, §52-352b.

Delaware: None provided. Delaware Code, Annotated, §4901-3.

District of Columbia: Provides an exemption equal to owner's aggregate interest in real property. No monetary or area limitations. District of Columbia Code §15-501. The District of Columbia does not call this a "homestead exemption."

Florida: Exemption equal to value of property as assessed for tax purposes. No monetary limitations. Area limitations of one-half acre urban land or 160 acres rural land. Florida Constitution, Article 10, §4.

Georgia: Up to $5,000 in value, and no area limitation. Code of Georgia, Annotated, §§44-13-1 and 44-13-100.

Hawaii: Up to $20,000 in value, but the head of a family and persons 65 years of age or older are allowed up to $30,000 in value, and no area limitation. Hawaii Revised Statutes, §§651-91, 92.

Idaho: Up to $50,000 in value, and no area limitation. Idaho Code, §55-1003.

Illinois: Up to $7,500 in value, and no area limitation. Where there are multiple owners, the value can be increased to $15,000. Illinois Compiled Statutes, Annotated, §734-5/12-901.

Indiana: Up to $7,500 in value for residence, up to $4,000 in value for additional property, and no area limitation. Co-owner, if also a joint debtor, may claim additional $7,500 in value. Indiana Code, Annotated, §34-55-10-2.

Iowa: No monetary limitation, but a minimum value of $500 in value, and area limitations of one-half acre urban land or 40 acres rural land. Iowa Code, Annotated, §§561.2 and 561.16.

Kansas: No monetary limitation. Area limitations of 1 acre urban land or 160 acres rural land. Kansas Constitution, Article 15, §9, and Kansas Statutes, Annotated, §60-2301.

Kentucky: Up to $5,000 in value, and no area limitation. Kentucky Revised Statutes, §427.060.

Louisiana: Up to $25,000 in value, but may include entirety of property in cases of catastrophic or terminal illness or injury. Area limitations of 5 acres urban land or 200 acres rural land. Louisiana Statutes, Annotated, §20:1.

Maine: Up to $25,000 in value, but may be up to $60,000 in value under certain circumstances, and no area limitation. Maine Revised Statutes, Annotated, §4422.

Maryland: Up to $3,000 in value, but in Title XI bankruptcy proceedings, up to $2,500 in value, and no area limitation. Code of Maryland, Annotated, §11-504.

Massachusetts: Up to $300,000 in value, and no area limitation. Laws of Massachusetts, Annotated, §188-1.

Michigan: Up to $3,500 in value, and area limitations of 1 acre urban land or 40 acres rural land. Michigan Compiled Laws, §600.6023.

Minnesota: Up to $200,000 in value, but up to $500,000 in value if used primarily for agricultural purposes. Area limitations of one-half acre urban land or 160 acres rural land. Minnesota Statutes, Annotated, §510.02.

Mississippi: Up to $75,000 in value, and area limitation of 160 acres. Mississippi Code, Annotated, §85-3-21.

Missouri: Up to $8,000 in value, and no area limitation. Missouri Statutes, Annotated, §513.475.

Montana: Up to $100,000 in value, and no area limitation. Montana Code, Annotated, §§70-32-101, 70-32-104, and 70-32-201.

Nebraska: Up to $12,500 in value, and area limitation of 2 lots of urban land or 160 acres of rural land. Revised Statutes of Nebraska, §40-101.

Nevada: Up to $125,000 in equity, and no area limitation. Nevada Revised Statutes, §§115-010.

New Hampshire: Up to $50,000 in value, and no area limitation. New Hampshire Revised Statutes, Annotated, §480:1.

New Jersey: No homestead exemption is provided, but an exemption for personal property of up to $1,000 in value is allowed. New Jersey Statutes, Annotated, §§2A: 17-1 and 2A: 17-17.

New Mexico: Up to $30,000 in value, and no area limitation. New Mexico Statutes, Annotated, §2-10-9.

New York: Up to $10,000 above liens and encumbrances in value, and no area limitation. Consolidated Laws of New York, Annotated, CPLR §5206.

North Carolina: Up to $10,000 in value, and no area limitation. General Statutes of North Carolina, Annotated, §1C-1601, and North Carolina Constitution, Article X.

North Dakota: Up to $80,000 in value, and no area limitation. North Dakota Century Code, Annotated, §47-18-01.

Ohio: Up to $5,000 in value, and no area limitation. Ohio Revised Code, §2329.66.

Oklahoma: Unlimited in value. Area limitations of 1 acre urban land or 160 acres rural land. However, where more than 25 percent of the property is being used for business purpose, the value drops to $5,000. Oklahoma Statutes, Annotated, §§1 and 2.

Oregon: Up to $25,000 in value. Area limitations of one city block if within a city or 160 acres rural land. Oregon Revised Statutes, §23.240.

Pennsylvania: No homestead exemption provided, but a general monetary exemption of $300 exists. Pennsylvania Consolidated Statutes, Annotated, §§8121, et seq.

Rhode Island: Up to $150,000 in value, and no area limitation. General Laws of Rhode Island, §9-26-4.1.

South Carolina: Although no homestead exemption is provided, an exemption for personal and real property of up to $10,000 in value may include property claimed as a residence. Code of Laws of South Carolina, §15-41-30.

South Dakota: No monetary limitation. Area limitation of one dwelling house and contiguous lots used in good faith. South Dakota Codified Laws, §§43-31-1 and 43-31-4.

Tennessee: Up to $5,000 in value, but may be up to $7,500 in value if claimed by two people as a homestead, and no area limitation. Tennessee Code, Annotated, §26-2-301.

Texas: No monetary limitation. Area limitation of 10 acres urban land or 100 acres of rural land if claimed by a single person. A family may claim 200 acres of rural land. Texas Property Code, Annotated, §§41.001 and 41.002, and Texas Constitution, Article 16, §51.

Utah: Up to $20,000 in value, but only $5,000 in value if the property is not the primary residence. Area limitation of one acre. Utah Code, §78-23-3.

Vermont: Up to $75,000 in value, and no area limitation. Vermont Statutes, Annotated, Title 27, §101.

Virginia: Up to $5,000 in value, but may be increased by $500 for each dependant residing on property, no area limitation. Code of Virginia, §34-4.

Washington: Generally, up to $40,000 in value, but may be unlimited if used against income taxes on retirement plan benefits. No area limitation. Revised Code of Washington, Annotated, §6.13.030.

West Virginia: Up to $5,000 in value, but an additional $7,500 may be available in cases of "catastrophic illness or injury." No area limitation. West Virginia Code, Annotated, §§38-9-1 and 38-10-4.

Wisconsin: Up to $40,000 in value, and no area limitation. Wisconsin Statutes, Annotated, §815.20.

Wyoming: Up to $10,000 in value. Each co-owner is entitled to a homestead exemption. Wyoming Statutes, §1-20-101.

Appendix H

Additional Helpful Websites and Other Resources

Websites

www.sandybotkin.com: This website provides lots of financial tools and articles and tax-saving products.

www.taxbot.com: This great website has applications for using Droids and iPhones for tax-related record keeping and vehicle mileage tracking. It also has articles I've written and videos I've produced that provide useful financial information.

www.burnettandassociates.com: Access to this website can be had for the measly price of $124 a year, and for that low price, it makes sure that your corporation minutes and resolutions are up to date. These steps will help you protect your assets. The tools available on this website make it a particularly good, inexpensive deal.

www.laughlinusa.com: Like Barnett and Associates, Laughlin Associates form entities for both corporations and LLCs in all states. It also gives entity and asset protection and estate planning consultation as well.

www.nvinc.com: This is the site for Nevada Corporate Planners. It also forms entities in all states and gives entity consultation for both LLCs and corporations and has a variety of services to help ensure that corporations will be in full compliance.

www.IRS.gov: This is a great website for obtaining IRS publications, forms, and general information.

www.taxsites.com: This website provides links to other tax and accounting sites.

www.ftc.gov: This is a very good website for checking whether there are any fraud investigations being conducted against a particular firm or if there have been investigations conducted in the past. This is also a good website for registering a complaint against a firm.

www.fraud.org: This interesting website lists various types of frauds currently being perpetrated on the public.

www.socialsecurity.gov: This is a great website for getting all types of information related to the social security program.

www.naela.org: This is the website for the National Association of Elder Law Attorneys. It is also useful for finding eldercare experts.

www.bankrate.com: This website has lots of excellent financial tools and articles.

www.Kiplinger.com: This website has a lot of general articles related to many aspects of your financial life.

http://fisher.osu.edu/fin/cern/cernpop.htm: This is a good website maintained by Ohio State University, and it lists a number of other good financial websites.

www.Stockmaster.com: This website has many tools related to investing in stocks.

Books

Edelman, Ric, *The Truth About Money*, 4th ed., New York: Harper Collins, 2010. This an easy reading, although a bit fluffy, treatise on family financial issues.

Lerner, Joel, *Financial Planning for the Utterly Confused*, 6th ed., New York: McGraw-Hill, 2008. This is a good basic treatise on family financial issues.

Weisman, Steve, *Boomer or Bust: Your Financial Guide to Retirement, Health Care, Medicare, and Long-Term Care*, Englewood Cliffs, NJ: Prentice Hall, 2007. This is a good, practical treatise on eldercare issues.

Index

About the Authors

Sandy Botkin is a former IRS attorney and CPA. During the past 10 years, through his Tax Reduction Institute based in the Washington, DC, area, Mr. Botkin has taught hundreds of thousands of taxpayers how to save millions in taxes with his seminars and information from his bestselling book *Lower Your Taxes—Big Time!*

Matthew Botkin is a CPA with a master's degree in financial planning. He has passed the Certified Financial Planning exam and is currently in law school.

DEC   2012